GLOBAL TRENDS 2005

An Owner's Manual for the Next Decade

Michael J. Mazarr

St. Martin's Press
New York

Tables 15.2, "U.S. Crime Rates, 1974-1992," and 18.1, "Stress Levels," are reprinted from *American Demographics* magazine, August 1995 and June 1996, respectively. Copyright 1995 and 1996. Courtesy of Intertec Publishing Corporation, Stamford, CT. All rights reserved.

The quotes from the *Tao Te Ching* are from the version translated by Victor A Mair, translation copyright © 1990 by Victor A. Mair. Used by permission of Bantam Books, a division of Random House, Inc.

Figure I.1 © 1996 The Economist Newspaper Group, Inc. Reprinted with permission. Further reproduction prohibited.

The graph in Figure 12.3, "Declining International Telephone Costs," is reproduced from *Wired* 5.09, copyright © 1999 Conde Nast Publications. All rights reserved. Reprinted by permission.

Chapter 20, "The Pessimism Syndrome," previously appeared in somewhat different form in *The Washington Quarterly* 21, no. 3 (Summer 1998). The author expresses his thanks to MIT Press Journals for the right to reprint the material.

Library of Congress Cataloging-in-Publication Data

Mazarr, Michael J., 1965-
    Global trends 2005 : an owner's manual for the next decade
    Michael J. Mazarr.
            p. cm.
    Includes bibliographical references and index.
    ISBN 0-312-21899-0
    1. Twenty-first century—Forecasts. 2. Social change—Forecasting.I. Title.
CB161.M3871999
    303.49—DC21   98-48336
                                                                  CIP

Book design by Acme Art, Inc.

First edition: June 1999
10 9 8 7 6 5 4 3 2 1

TABLE OF CONTENTS

Acknowledgments v

**INTRODUCTION:
A TRANSFORMATION OF
HUMAN SOCIETY** 1

**TREND ONE:
THE FOUNDATIONS** 25

1. A Story of Two Worlds 29

2. A Price Spike Economy 49

3. A Foundation of Human Perception: Culture 65

**TREND TWO:
THE ENGINES OF HISTORY** 71

4. The Engines: Science and Technology 73

5. The Engines: Social and Psychological 85

6. Chaos and Complexity Theory 93

7. Where Are They Taking Us? 99

**TREND THREE:
A HUMAN RESOURCES ECONOMY** 115

8. A New Kind of Economy 117

9. The Reorganization of Work 123

10. Other Aspects of the New Economy 133

11. Conflict in the Knowledge Era 151

TREND FOUR:
AN ERA OF GLOBAL TRIBES 157

12. The Process of Globalization 159

13. Tribalism, Fragmentation, and Pluralism 175

14. Tribalism within Globalism 187

TREND FIVE:
A TRANSFORMATION OF AUTHORITY ... 195

15. Phase One: The Decline of
    Hierarchical Authorities 197

16. Implications: Social Instability and a
    Political Crisis 213

17. Phase Two: The Rise of New Authorities 217

TREND SIX:
A TEST OF HUMAN PSYCHOLOGY 237

18. "In Over Our Heads":
    Postmodern Life and Human Psychology 239

19. A Habit of Alienation 249

20. The "Pessimism Syndrome" 261

CONCLUSION
TOWARD A NEW SOCIETY 279

21. A New Kind of Society 283

22. The Authors of Our Own Destiny 295

Notes 297

Index 323

ACKNOWLEDGMENTS

The author gratefully acknowledges the contributions of the Global Trends 2005 Core Study Group during the initial phases of writing and thinking on the project, whose advice and suggestions made a major contribution to this effort. They were a delight to work with. I imposed upon the time of countless experts in dozens of fields and nearly always met with kind cooperation and insightful suggestions; to all of you, many thanks.

CSIS wishes to thank the donors whose financial support made the project possible: The McCormick-Tribune Foundation, The Korea Foundation, and The BP-AMOCO Foundation. Of course, the contents of this book are my responsibility, and do not reflect the views of the donor organizations or CSIS as a whole.

On a more personal note, I'd like to thank Michael Flamini, my editor at St. Martin's, for having faith in the project when many others didn't. Alan Bradshaw, Mara Nelson, and the staff at St. Martin's guided the manuscript along with expert hands, and were so friendly in the process that you'd never have guessed I must have been driving them crazy. The idea for looking at the future at CSIS came from the former president of CSIS, David Abshire, who served as mentor, guide, and advocate during the preparation of this book; without him, this volume would not have happened. Tony Smith helped to keep the project alive with timely financial support and was an unflagging advocate for it— and a good friend besides—at CSIS. The staff at EEI Communications in Alexandria, Virginia furnished a superb editorial assistance and prepared a dynamite index. Joseph Rende at the Young Presidents' Organization in Dallas gave me a dozen fine ideas, brought my work to a new audience, and became an intellectual soulmate.

And I'd like to thank my beautiful wife Jen and my gorgeous son Alexander for—well, being fabulous. I'm sure Jen must have tired of my little anecdotes and flights of philosophical fancy, but she never showed it; and Alex, born in the middle of my research for the book, gave me renewed reason to care about the trends that will shape the world in which he'll live. With a family like mine, you can't help being optimistic about the future.

A Transformation of Human Society

Foreknowledge is but the blossomy ornament of the Way,
and the source of ignorance.

Tao Te Ching

"Every few hundred years in Western history there occurs a sharp transformation. Within a few short decades, society rearranges itself—its worldview; its basic values; its social and political structure; its arts; its key institutions. Fifty years later, there is a new world."[1] So wrote the eminent social theorist Peter Drucker in 1993. As he went on to explain, the nations and peoples of the West—and, I would add, most of the rest of the world—are living through precisely such a transformation today. It is recasting the character of human life the world over, generating profound new challenges as it opens up unprecedented vistas of promise.

This book is about that transformation. It is an effort to understand the historical passage now shaking the foundations of human society and to explain it in terms that anyone interested in the changing world can understand. It is about the trends shaping the next decade and the implications of those trends for our everyday lives. It is both a primer for the twenty-first century—an "owner's manual for the next decade," as the subtitle puts it—and a handbook for understanding the evening news.

My basic argument in the coming pages is that rapid and accelerating advances in science and technology—and the social, political, and psychological changes that follow and complement them—are transfiguring society, economy, politics, and warfare in profound ways. In its simplest and most fundamental sense, this transformation is a shift from an industrial age to a knowledge era. This new phase of human history promises to empower human beings, to bring democracy to the globe and the workplace, and to create a sustainable relationship between humankind and its natural environment.

But as the philosopher Alfred North Whitehead emphasized, all major social transformations cause instability and exact a price. "The major advances in civilization," he wrote, "are processes that all but wreck the societies in which they occur."[2] The rise of the industrial era kindled social and economic infernos, from the awful conditions faced by millions of factory workers to devastating social movements such as fascism and socialism. We tend to forget, when we consider the problems of modern society, that we are undergoing precisely such a transformation in the 1990s, and that we should expect turbulent social and psychological dislocations in the bargain. Because of this larger context, there is now little question that the early twenty-first century will be a time of social upheaval, of reactions to the processes of globalization, democratization, and other aspects of our new age. Whitehead's concise warning establishes one of my recurring themes: Historical transitions can exact a severe human toll.

This volume identifies six fundamental trends reshaping the United States and the world as we approach a new millennium. Most of the events we confront in the daily newspaper, from rising or falling crime to welfare reform to improved economic growth, can be viewed partly as a subset of one of these six essential phenomena. Each of the following six trend analyses examines one of these subjects at length; each is divided into several short chapters, one or more of which can be read and digested in a single sitting. This introduction offers a few thoughts and themes to keep in mind as you plunge into the trends.

A KNOWLEDGE ERA

Virtually all social commentators agree that we live in an "information age," that the search for and the use of information—or, in the more

FIGURE I.1

Paper vs. Electronic Transactions, 1980—2010

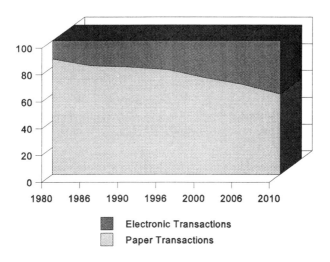

Source: "Technology in Finance," *The Economist*, October 26, 1996, p. 4, citing The Tower Group.

encompassing term I will use, knowledge—represents the fundamental social activity of our time. Futurist Alvin Toffler says that information "is the basic raw material" of the period (the "third wave" of human society, as he calls it).[3] Famed sociologist Daniel Bell argues that, whereas industrial society involved "the coordination of machines and men for the production of goods," postindustrial society will be "organized around knowledge, for the purpose of social control and the directing of innovation and change."[4]

Industrial-era society was primarily about *building* things—churning out vast numbers of tangible products. The knowledge era is about *manipulating information,* both for its own sake and to improve the efficiency of manufacturing. Neither activity excludes the other; industrial-era businesses used plenty of information, and knowledge-era societies will require an unprecedented array of products. But the focus of economic and social activity is changing.

The practical, everyday ramifications of this new era are obvious, so much so that we tend to take them for granted. Computers, mass distribution of information and entertainment, instant worldwide communications—these and other hallmarks of a knowledge era have become commonplace. Many readers will no doubt react with surprise to the claim that we are moving "into" the knowledge era. Aren't we there yet?

To employ a durable cliché, if you think we already in the midst of a knowledge era, "you ain't seen nothin' yet." We have seen the hints of how a knowledge society works—the first seeds of virtual corporations, for example—but those hints have yet to fully weave themselves into the fabric of human society. As figure I.1 suggests, something like three-quarters of all business, academic, and other social transactions still take place on paper: The performance evaluations you get at the office, the bills you receive in the mail, the grades posted outside the professor's classroom. About 90 percent of all information already stored remains on paper; one estimate I've seen suggests that only 5 percent of companies have made the transition to modern information technologies. And that's just the story for the developed world: Forty percent—almost half—of the world's workers remain in the agricultural sector, the vast majority of them in developing nations.[5] (In most modern economies, the equivalent figure is well under 10 percent.) Half the world's people may have yet to place a telephone call. Taken together, the trends that make up the shift to a knowledge era will rewrite the rules of economics, environmental policy, sociology, and political and military science. And they leave us with a profound sense of living amid change. As the novelist and Czech president Vaclav Havel puts it, "Today, many things indicate that we are going through a transitional period, when it seems that something is on the way out and something else is painfully being born. It is as if something were crumbling, decaying, and exhausting itself, while something else, still indistinct, were arising from the rubble."[6]

A leading aspect of this process of decay and rebirth is a partial retreat from the basic principles of the so-called Age of Reason. Newtonian science, with its emphasis on natural processes that are orderly and linear in their movements; classical economics, with its assumption of a rational consumer possessing perfect information; and perfection-seeking social science theories such as Marxism, with their bent toward social engineering—these and other heirs of the Western rationalistic tradition will be more and more circumscribed in the

ISSUE FEATURE: THE NEW SCIENCE

Throughout the book, I will refer to the insights of such "new" sciences as complexity theory and quantum mechanics. It is important to have a sense of what we mean by these concepts from the beginning, and one of the best and most eloquent guides to these subjects is the business management expert Margaret Wheatley.

In her book *Leadership and the New Science,* Wheatley explains that "Each of us lives and works in organizations designed from Newtonian images of the universe. We manage by separating things into parts, we believe that influence occurs as a direct result of force exerted from one person to another, [and] we engage in complex planning for a world that we keep expecting to be predictable."[7] As the hard sciences move away from that clocklike model, social organizations, business management, and human perception will follow them.

> "The participatory nature of reality has focused scientific attention on relationships."
> —Margaret Wheatley

In place of an orderly, predictable, linear universe capable of being understood in pieces, complexity theory and quantum mechanics substitute a very different kind of world.

- "In new science," Wheatley writes, "the underlying currents are a movement toward holism, toward understanding the system as a system and giving primary value to the relationships that exist among seemingly discrete parts."
- As a result, our view of a universe of discrete bits and pieces must be revised. It is in the *relationships* among the parts that reality truly emerges.
- A renewed focus on relationships of all kinds puts an emphasis on the normative aspects of human interactions—community, trust, dignity, ethical values.
- Living systems have a strong tendency toward self-renewal and self-organization. Organizations that make these tendencies work for them can reap substantial rewards.
- Given the unpredictability of large-scale systems and the creativity unleashed through freedom, attempting to exert ironclad control is a losing strategy.
- Nature is *participatory,* and nations and organizations should maximize the talents and abilities of all their members.

coming decade, as the Issue Feature on "the new science" suggests. (Issue Features provide more in-depth analysis of a particular topic.)

Two characteristics of this particular look at the trends reshaping the future make it somewhat different from the many other examples of the genre. One is its *interdisciplinary perspective*. Many recent trend analyses, departing from the tradition established by early authors in the field (such as Alvin Toffler), have focused on a single arena—economics, for example, or technology, or sociology, or military affairs. This volume takes insights from a host of disciplines—economics, sociology, political science, and scientific fields such as biology and physics, environmental science, and others—and molds them into a comprehensive view of the forces shaping the future. Such an approach is especially important today, because, as we shall see, the knowledge era tends to break down boundaries between disciplines, industries, and countries.

This study also differs from similar efforts in its *time frame*. Most other works in this field tend to take a very long-term perspective, attempting to forecast out 40 or 50 years, sometimes even a century or more. In one outstanding case, the historian of civilizations Arnold Toynbee had the wonderful temerity to look *2,000* years into the human future. My scope is much more limited: I am interested in the coming decade, roughly spanning the years 2000 to 2010, a more modest analytical telescope that sidesteps the inevitable risks of peering out decades into the future. The book's title refers to the midpoint of the decade, when the trends described here will be in full flower.

THE DANGERS OF FORECASTING

My predictive ambitions of this work are very modest. I do not make detailed numerical forecasts in the various trends I outline, nor do I speculate on particular consumer products or social fads that might emerge. I don't try to foretell the precise nature of future wars or revolutions.

But any thinking about the future demands some degree of forecasting, at least of a broader sort. I hope to identify the basic trends that will unfold over the next decade, the broad social processes that will help to explain many of the events we read about in the daily newspaper or see on the evening news. And, while I am aware of the dangers of prediction as well as the paradoxical nature of the knowledge era (a theme I will discuss in a moment), I have made some definite choices between two or more alternatives. Thus, for example, I suggest that, at least during the next decade, information technologies will undermine traditional authorities and make dictatorship less feasible rather than opening the way to an Orwellian, knowledge-era totalitarianism. I contend that the nation–state–in–decline thesis is exaggerated, that the next decade will not be a period of natural resource shortages for most of the world, and that globalization is indeed creating a more uniform world.

My respect for the bombshells of fate, however, has led me to a specific methodological tool in the chapters that follow, devices I call *surprise scenarios*. Each one investigates the impact of a potential discontinuity, an unexpected lurch off into a new economic, social, or political direction. The surprise scenarios are not predictions; I do not necessarily *expect* them to happen. But I have chosen the specific scenarios I use not merely as thought exercises to get the reader thinking about inevitable quirks of historical fate but also because they represent perhaps the most likely surprises that we might face through 2005 or 2010.[8]

My thinking about the nonlinear and discontinuous flow of history is also informed by the new sciences of chaos and complexity, which direct our attention toward surprises—the unexpected new turns of the flock or the swarm of events. Surprise scenarios represent part of my effort to keep firmly in mind that the next decade will not turn out exactly as we foresee it today—that surprise, large and small, important and trivial—is inevitable. Merely because discontinuities exist, however, does not rule out the possibility of underlying patterns in world affairs, patterns such as the growth of economic and political freedom. And even in an apparently chaotic world, human beings do have influence; our actions can move events in one direction or another, for good or ill.

A CAUTIOUS OPTIMISM

Often when people pick up a new volume that purports to address the future, the first thing they want to know is whether the book is optimistic or pessimistic. Does it forecast a brilliant and prosperous

SURPRISE SCENARIO: GLOBAL ECONOMIC MELTDOWN

A severe worldwide economic downturn is the most basic surprise scenario for the simple reason that so many of the trends in the pages that follow depend on continued economic growth. Global economic progress can be slow or rapid, smooth and even, or rough and patchy, but it must continue over the next decade if trends like free-market reform, democracy, globalization, and the death of distance are to remain strong. A sudden economic collapse—on the order of a worldwide depression, much more severe even than the Asian financial crisis of 1998—would be the one event to at least temporarily render moot much of the analyses that follow.

This scenario envisions several avenues to a global economic collapse, including a massive deflationary spiral leading to unemployment, ruined personal savings, and collapsing wages; a worldwide collapse of stock markets; or a sudden shortage of capital that would ratchet up interest rates and choke off growth. Any set of developments that would ravage the global economy would have ripple effects throughout the range of social, technological, political, psychological, and other issues I will take up in subsequent trends. A number of the specific economic effects, and some of their most directly associated implications, would include the following.

- Massive unemployment in the developed and developing worlds alike, creating a social and economic pressure cooker that could produce mass violence in some areas.
- Destruction of personal savings and collapsing wages, reversing years of growth and creating as much as a decade-long hiatus in world economic and social progress.
- Intense protectionist pressures leading to major damage to the world trading system and, perhaps, geopolitical tensions—and wars—in the bargain.
- Burgeoning political and military tensions among the major trading powers as trade disputes suddenly take on a more sinister character.
- Plummeting social investments in a host of areas, from welfare programs to new technologies, such as renewable energy.
- Exploding poverty in the developing world.

future for humankind or a disastrous one? Does it view the next decade as a stable and peaceful time or an unstable and violent one?

Much of the existing forecasting literature on the future tends too much toward the extremes. Claims from groups such as the 1970s' Club of Rome that the world was headed toward a nightmare of overpopulation and resource scarcities were countered by volumes suggesting that all human affairs would become sweetness and light under the soothing influence of the knowledge era. Pessimism confronted optimism, and the resulting debate of extremes often left out the more complex middle ground—sophisticated analyses of competing hopes and dangers.

Thus another rationale for this study is to provide a partial antidote to the habit of futurist extremism and offer neither an inherently pessimistic nor an inherently optimistic view, but one that is as objective as I can make it regarding the trends we will face over the next decade. I am not suggesting that this is the first analysis to make use of this middle ground; far from it. But the proportion of the literature that falls into this category needs fortifying—especially at a time when, as I will contend in Trend Six, the media emphasizes the negative and pessimistic side of events and therefore creates perceptual crises of faith where no real crisis exists.

Within this context, the general view I take of the next decade and beyond is one of *cautious optimism.* I choose optimism, because the fundamental thrust of many of the trends of the knowledge era runs in the direction of freedom, prosperity, empowerment, and ecological health. Yet I remain cautious because all of these trends generate powerful reactions and countertrends that, if not adequately met, could send world politics as a whole or individual societies in particular spinning off into disorder and warfare. To put it another way: I am optimistic because the trends of the knowledge era furnish human beings and human societies with an unprecedented ability to create a free, prosperous, and empowering future; I am cautious because I cannot yet be certain if humanity will use that power effectively and wisely. I am at least hopeful enough to reject the surprisingly popular views that history is a determined engine of malevolence, that human beings are thoroughly corrupt and prone to aggression, and that rational progress is a terrible myth.

THEMES OF THE ANALYSIS

Several themes weave through all the trends I outline in the coming sections. These themes, not counting as trends themselves because they are too general and amorphous, nonetheless provide important clues to the character of the knowledge era and the particular challenge posed by its trends. None of them is an independent phenomenon; all represent elements of a complex, integrated whole that is the knowledge era. I introduce each theme with a relevant quote from the *Tao Te Ching*, a volume of Asian moral wisdom whose focus on self-awareness, paradox, and the holistic interconnection of life have important resonances in our age.

Theme One: Paradox

True words seem contradictory.

Tao Te Ching

Although it is difficult to nominate one theme above others as the most important of our age, the single overriding aspect of the social transformation under way today might be its paradoxical and contradictory nature.

The British business expert Charles Handy, one of the most insightful and eloquent chroniclers of the knowledge era, titled one of his recent books *The Age of Paradox*. "Paradox has almost become the cliché of our times," he writes. It is "inevitable, endemic, and perpetual. The more turbulent the times, the more complex the world, the more paradoxes there are."[9] In part this is true because our society is not the opposite of previous societies but their successor, representing an evolution from rather than a reversal of their basic character. The notion, for example, of "postmodernism" does not represent the reverse of modernism but a further articulation of it; one writer refers to postmodernity as "fully developed modernity."[10] That it combines modern and postmodern elements helps to account for the fact that the knowledge era turns out to be a time of inconsistency, of paradox, and of ambiguity. It embodies decentralization within globalism, fragmentation within mass culture, expanded individualism within stronger community, and absolutism within relativism. Such paradoxes make it difficult to identify uncomplicated trends; because the era is so ambivalent, every trend carries with it a mirror, an opposite—a phenomenon probably common to all transformational periods.

The prevalence of paradox may help account for the growing relevance of spiritual beliefs like Zen Buddhism and Taoism—approaches that emphasize dealing with ambiguity, seeing the world in shades of gray—in the knowledge era. "We're turning into a society that's got far more ambiguity," management expert and Montreal Zen Centre director Albert Low told *Fast Company* magazine. Today's business manager "needs to be totally at home in uncertain, yes-no-maybe situations."[11]

Thus, while the rest of this book outlines the basic trends in current society—trends such as diversity, the crisis of authority, and alienation—each also makes clear that every trend or concept has an antithesis. Society is not merely diverse, it is diverse in the context of a global mass culture. Its crisis of authority involves not only the decline of old authorities but the rise of new, more participatory and less coercive ones.

Yet the reality of paradox, like the reality of chaos and complexity in human affairs, is not a barrier to careful thinking and action. Handy writes that "Paradoxes are like the weather, something to be lived with, not solved, the worst aspects mitigated, the best enjoyed and used as clues to the way forward. Paradox has to be *accepted,* coped with, and made sense of, in life, work, in the community, and among nations."[12] By describing and discussing some of these paradoxes, this book tries to meet that challenge.

Theme Two: A Blurring of Boundaries

> *How nebulous / then as the ocean;*
> *How blurred / then as though without boundary.*
> Tao Te Ching

The knowledge era is also a time when boundaries—between disciplines, industries, and social enterprises—tend to break down. Things we are accustomed to seeing as highly distinct endeavors, such as "military" and "civilian" technology development, become if not one and the same, at least much more alike than they have been. Put simply, the knowledge era is an *interdisciplinary* time.[13]

Boundaries between industries, says the latest management thinking, are fading; successful businesspeople do not think about what industry they are in but about what core competencies they have to offer—and what industries they *could* enter. In an age when the technologies used by military forces, such as computers, are most advanced in the civilian sector, the dividing line between military and civilian research and development—and therefore between war and peace—is less and less meaningful. In an era of empowered consumers able to custom-design their own products and empowered workers running their own businesses, the distinction between consumer and producer is disappearing.

The new sciences of complexity remind us that boundaries between problems and disciplines are less important than the threads that connect them. "The majority of real-world problems," explain science writers Peter Coveney and Roger Highfield, "do not fit into neat compartments. To solve them, people must be able to communicate across traditional boundaries, to approach issues in a collaborative, integrated way." Complexity theory thus points us in the direction of interdisciplinary research, Coveney and Highfield write, "in the Renaissance style."[14]

The collapse of boundaries also has significance for the supposedly victorious economic and social ideology of our time: capitalism. I will argue later in the book that some variant of capitalism will remain the dominant organizing principle for human society in the next century. But it will be a capitalism of a new form, a capitalism that reflects the interests of a wider number of people, elements of the natural environment, and animal life. The progress of history is more dialectical than linear: Whereas today we can say that capitalism has triumphed over socialism, 100 years from now we might say that capitalism *absorbed* the most important lessons of its competitor and that the best ideas of both fused into a new social ideology.

One obvious implication of an interdisciplinary era is that it demands interdisciplinary research. This fact, as I mentioned, encouraged the holistic view I have taken in this study, but it also points to the need for fundamental changes in the way we conduct education. Twenty-first-century students will need to know at least as much about the interrelationships among biology, physics, philosophy, sociology, and political science, to name a few major disciplines, as they do about each of those separate fields of inquiry, but high school– and university–level education remains singularly ill-equipped to provide such holistic thinking. There are precious few, if any, courses in American universities, for example, on "The Knowledge Era," but precisely this kind of broad-based, systemic thinking offers one of the best antidotes to a creeping pessimism that results from the fragmented news of a hundred perilous social trends.

Theme Three: Networks, Systems, and Holistic Thinking

> *The sage holds on to unity*
> *and serves as the shepherd of all under heaven.*
>
> Tao Te Ching

An interdisciplinary age is obviously one in which our ways of understanding phenomena that cross boundaries—such as networks and systems—become critical to an appreciation of daily events and long-term trends. As boundaries between disciplines fade, the lines *connecting* those diverse fields, the threads of our interdisciplinary reality, become crucial. And we understand many of those threads as networks and systems.

Such facts led the sociologist Manuel Castells to title his recent book *The Rise of the Network Society* and to conclude in it that "dominant functions and processes in the information age are increasingly organized around networks. Networks constitute the new social morphology of our societies."[15] Networks are everywhere: They are the organizing principle of computer systems; of increasingly virtual corporations coming together, amoebalike, in temporary partnerships and alliances; of information technologies linking societies closer together; of highly advanced military forces increasingly taught to act like bees swarming against an enemy rather than like lemmings marching into it. Networks are the hard-wiring of an age that is increasingly interrelated, interdisciplinary, and interlinked.

Ours is therefore also a time that is increasingly *interdependent,* with interdependence as much a subtheme of network logic as it is of blurring boundaries. Businesses, governments, and individuals are losing the capacity for independent action, coming more and more to rely on the contributions of others in society to achieve their goals.

Virtual corporations are constellations of groups that are interdependent for at least the duration of a given project. Governments are losing their unquestioned dominance as social actors and seek to form partnerships with other organizations, such as nonprofit groups. In an age of global economics and ecology, the fate of sovereign nation-states is tied together more closely than ever before.

"The turn of the twentieth century," writes educator Stephanie Pace Marshall, showed the limits of a linear, mechanistic worldview "and heralded the conception of an ecological universe—a holistic, dynamic, and inextricably connected system in which everything seems to affect everything else."[16]

The lesson here is that the kinds of social agents or historical processes produced by a networked era cannot be understood as individual enterprises or singular processes. They must be thought of as *systems,* as interactive sets of enterprises that move forward in a coevolutionary pattern with one another. Often the ways these various processes interact and influence each other, rather than their unique momentum or characteristics, comprise the most important bits of knowledge of our time.

Theme Four: Process Not Product; Becoming Not Being; Experience Not Thing

> *The great vessel is never completed.*
> Tao Te Ching

Partly through its encouragement of a shift from manufactured products to forms of knowledge as the basic good of economic life, the knowledge era reduces the emphasis on tangible things and increases the emphasis on *abstraction;* it is an age dominated by ideas, concepts, and knowledge. "Matter," former Citicorp chairman Walter Wriston has argued, "has become the enemy of wealth, not its source."[17]

The growing dominance of process and experience manifests itself in a number of ways. One is the distinction between product and process: Services, for example, are a form of process rather than a specific product. We think of haircuts or financial advice as products only because of a confusion in our use of terms. Education has become a lifelong process rather than a one-time event. Even manufactured goods issued by knowledge-era industries, such as computer chips, now advance so quickly that they acquire the character of a continuing process. Management theorists from W. Edwards Deming to Margaret Wheatley have emphasized that the overall quality of an organization can often be deduced from the quality of its processes—the interactions of its employees with and among themselves. And all of this matches nicely with the insights of complexity and quantum sciences, which stress the importance of relationships, systems, and interactions as opposed to particles or atoms or individual things of any kind.

In an era of rapid change, moreover, we find more emphasis on the idea of "becoming"—constantly improving and advancing, never reaching a permanent level of stasis—rather than on "being." Static, industrial-era companies and governments could simply attain their power, influence, education, or market share and spend the rest of their personal or institutional lives either living off of or defending what they had acquired. Today, as Trends Three and Five will make abundantly clear, the imperative is something closer to the reverse—we must adjust our mind-sets for an era of constant change and inexorable innovation. From rapid product turnover in business to the wave of economic and political freedom washing over the globe to perpetual grassroots experimentation as a model for public policy, society has never been as thoroughly engaged in becoming rather than being, in advancing and developing rather than remaining in place.[18]

Yet paradox reigns here as well, because in another sense, the timeless notion of "being" has growing resonance. When conceived of as an emphasis on the present moment, as an effort to become grounded in the reality that surrounds and pervades us, a thirst for "being" accords not only with such age-old philosophies as Buddhism but also with the new sciences of complexity and quantum physics as well as with the knowledge era's disdain for boundaries and love for systems and relationships. Perhaps the best way to say it is this: The new era values being *and* becoming, and the creative tension between them, more than ever before.

This theme also suggests the growing importance of experiences over possessions. "Mature consumers," business consultant Ken Dychtwald writes of aging Baby Boomers in the United States, "are more

ISSUE FEATURE: THE "CULTURAL CREATIVES"

Many of the themes outlined in this introduction are reflected in the values of a rapidly growing segment of the American population: what Paul Ray of the San Francisco company American LIVES calls "Cultural Creatives."[19] He suggests that Americans can now be divided—by values, attitudes, and behavior—into three basic groups. *Traditionalists,* 29 percent of the population (56 million adults), have conservative religious beliefs, tend to live in or idolize small towns, and place scant emphasis on feminism and civil rights. Nearly half of Americans—88 million adults—are *Modernists,* and hold values associated with the Baby Boom: They prize personal success, consumerist materialism, and technological progress.

> "A major change has been growing in American culture. It is a comprehensive shift in values, world views, and ways of life."
> —Paul Ray

But Ray identified a third segment of Americans, by the mid-1990s already 24 percent of the total (44 million adults), one that represents many of the values of the knowledge era and is growing impressively: the *Cultural Creatives.* This group is altruistic, environmentally aware, community-oriented, and spiritual. Their values parallel the themes in this section:

- *Cultural creatives favor process over product, experience over things.* They are disenchanted with "owning more stuff" and instead are the "prototypical consumers" of "intense, enlightening, enlivening experiences rather than things."
- *They have an integrative, holistic vision.* Cultural creatives are "powerfully attuned to global issues and whole systems." Ray says this group symbolizes an "integral culture" and uses the phrase "holistic everything" to describe their approach.
- *They reflect a strong spiritual sense and awareness of moral values.* They are characterized by "altruism, self-actualization, and spirituality."
- *They are empowered citizens of the knowledge era.* "It's a paradox, but Creatives are likely to be information junkies," Ray explains, following news and reading while watching less TV than average. But "while they take in a lot of information from a variety of sources, Creatives are good at synthesizing it into a 'big picture.'"

interested in purchasing 'experiences' than things,"[20] a phenomenon also reflected in the Cultural Creatives described in the last issue feature. In an age of infotainment and virtual reality, the experience will be the thing, and purchasing the equipment that enables one to have it will be secondary. Two business consultants have predicted the rise of an "experience economy," arguing that experiences represent the next logical progression in economic value.[21]

Theme Five: The S-Curve

> *Act before there is a problem;*
> *Bring order before there is disorder.*
>
> Tao Te Ching

The basic model of social advance in the knowledge era, as much or more than it has been in the past, is the sigmoid, or S-curve, represented in figure I.2. This simple curved line conveys one of the fundamental challenges of our time: to recognize the inevitable downslope that accompanies any progress and to prepare for it, to look "ahead of the curve" and get a new upswing going before the last one falls into decay. History is littered with the remains of empires, companies, and individuals that failed to recognize the inevitability of the S-curve and paid the price. And with the acceleration of history compressing S-curves in time, it becomes more urgent than ever for organizations to pursue the creativity and innovation that can jump-start a new cycle.[22]

Perhaps the best example is in business, where, as Trends Three and Five will show, new theories of corporate strategy point to the importance of recognizing compressed product or process life cycles and preparing for the next advance even as the current one is succeeding. In part, too, the S-curve represents chaos theory applied to history: Complex adaptive systems often behave like S-curves, and comprehending this discontinuous process of social advance requires the sort of complex, nonlinear thinking I will examine in Trend Two.

Unless the downturn is so severe that it ceases to exist, any complex adaptive system will represent not one S-curve but a series of them, either overlapping or laid end to end. The most critical moments occur

FIGURE I.2

The Sigmoid Curve

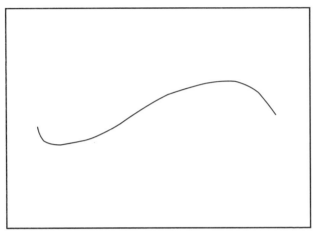

at the points of overlap—the periods when one S-curve begins ramping up, even as the previous one continues to peak. Business futurists Stan Davis and Bill Davidson refer to this as a "life-cycle curve" of gestation, growth, maturity, and aging; ideally for any company or individual, the oncoming cycle's gestation should be under way during the current cycle's maturity phase.[23]

"A good life," Handy remarks, "is probably a succession of second curves, started before the first curve fades."[24] Consider the implications of that profound notion: Now more than ever before, people, companies, and other organizations must constantly ask themselves about their place on their current sigmoid curve. What phase are we in? Have we begun to decline? Is it time to begin a new phase—through a change in careers, in product line, in function?

The sigmoid curve powerfully corroborates the Whitehead thesis on the transitional instabilities that attend the arrival of any new era. According to Handy, many institutions, individuals, and even whole societies are in that crossover period between S-curves—between eras— right now. "It is a time of great confusion, uncertainty, and fear. People do not understand why things that have worked so well up to now no longer do the trick. That first curve is peaking everywhere."[25]

Theme Six: Values and Responsibility

The Way gives birth to them and integrity nurtures them.

Tao Te Ching

In an era of rapid change, the importance of a clear and effective set of social values becomes more obvious than ever. Existing value systems are questioned at the same time as the social authorities that promote values, from the church to the family, are in a period of relative decline. The result can be a stark amorality as individuals and groups seek selfish rewards unbalanced by a consideration for the health of the society as a whole or of its less fortunate members. The other side of the knowledge era's coin of empowerment is responsibility, and a more profound sense of individual and group norms and values will be critical over the next decade.[26]

The kinds of values we will need over the next decade are not those either of the "left" or the "right" but a new combination of both. Liberal social movements and ideologies have much to teach us about compassion, social equity, charity, and the well-being of the natural environment. Conservative philosophies, parties, and movements can instruct us on the limits and fallibility of human nature, the importance of personal responsibility, and the role of religion and spirituality in life. The moral value system we need over the next decade embraces all these ideas, and more, in a new and holistic approach to responsibility that transcends party line or ideology. The first signs of a movement in this direction are already apparent, as we'll discover.

Theme Seven: Perception Increasingly Equals Reality

The more clever devices people have,
the more confused the state and ruling house.

Tao Te Ching

In an era characterized by interactions at the level of ideas and thoughts rather than concrete reality, it is no surprise that how people perceive issues becomes at least as important as the objective facts about those issues. In the knowledge era, this phenomenon becomes pervasive—so much so that we risk losing touch, on some issues and at some moments, with reality itself.

In one critical economic sense, for example, the rise of financial markets has emphasized the role of perception in addition, and sometimes as opposed, to hard economic facts—economic "reality," however conceived. How the markets perceive a country or corporation's prospects becomes as important as any "objective" economic measures. Some observers worry that an economy run increasingly on perception can whipsaw back and forth more radically, and dangerously, than in the past—a trend on display throughout Asia during the region's recent financial and political crises.

Trend Six discusses some particularly disturbing implications of this theme at length, including the fact that, because of the sensationalistic canon of today's news media, most of our perceptual realities run in a negative direction, a phenomenon we term the "pessimism syndrome." One result is that the citizens of many developed and developing nations acquire a skewed vision of their own social situation, frequently assuming that their economies and societies are far worse off than is actually the case. Taken to an extreme, such negative perceptions can be dangerous, prompting calls for radical, and counterproductive, social change.

Theme Eight: Change Is Costly

Reversal is the movement of the Way.
Tao Te Ching

Theme Eight reinforces the lesson of the Alfred North Whitehead quote I employed earlier—that major social transformations are immensely disruptive for the societies in which they occur. The creative destruction of history does its work crudely and blindly, without an eye to the social stresses and psychological strains it is creating. The trends that follow brim with references to the reactions to and unintended (and sometimes dangerous) by-products of the shift to a knowledge era. These could take a number of forms, from protest movements to terrorism to the clash of civilizations that political scientist Samuel Huntington expects. They represent some of the discontinuities against which complexity theory teaches us to be on guard, and they can become forces bending the sigmoid curves of history from progression down to decay.

Such costs of change will create an urgent need for social values. Without a strong sense of responsibility to our fellow human beings and to the future, we may not be able to beat back these reactions to change. This fact reinforces the importance of reforming what we know as "capitalism" to help ensure that it leaves in the wake of its creative destruction only the hulks of outmoded practices rather than masses of dispossessed people and a ruined natural environment. To be clear: I am not predicting an "end" to capitalism; rather, I expect capitalist practice to evolve in new directions that represent a revolution in capitalist economic theory—a blurring of the boundaries between capitalism and its rivals and greater sharing of authority among a diverse array of social actors rather than just governments.

Theme Nine: An Age of Empowerment

The unyielding and the mighty shall be brought low;
The soft, supple, and delicate will be set above.

Tao Te Ching

The final and most fundamental theme of this work is that the knowledge era is a time of empowerment, for individuals and groups alike. It empowers people and their civic associations against large institutions, such as governments and corporations; it empowers small towns and poor developing countries; it empowers women and minority groups throughout the world. It does this by leveling the playing field. In an economy and society that runs on ideas and information, and in a situation where anyone can have an idea and anyone can gain access to most of the information needed to make it work, power and authority become radically decentralized.

This is not to say that impoverished or oppressed people will suddenly be freed from their chains in the next ten years. In this area as in others, the knowledge era does its work slowly, fitfully, with pauses and reversals along the way. Individual empowerment will not emerge

ISSUE FEATURE: TELLING A STORY

To a notable extent, the successful people and organizations of the next decade and beyond will be storytellers.

Human beings have long preferred stories to numbers or declarative statements. Stories come alive, they humanize the points they're meant to illustrate, and they entertain. As the management guru Tom Peters has written, "People live, reason, and are moved by symbols and stories."[27] That's why the best nonfiction writers don't just make a point, they tell a story (of a person, a town, a country) in order to make it. That's why the most successful writers and moviemakers of our time, from Stephen King to Steven Spielberg, are masters of the storytelling art.

In an age when people are going to be drinking information from a fire hose, distinguishing one piece from the rest will be awfully hard. One important way to go about it will be telling a story.

> The knowledge era asks all organizations a key question: "What's your story?"

Take the business world. In order to build trust and empathy with its customers, futurists Watts Wacker and Jim Taylor contend, a knowledge era company needs to tell stories, to draw people into an ongoing narrative.[28] And indeed, storytelling pervades advertising today, from multi-episode commercials to companies like Saturn automobiles and Gateway computers that tell their own stories.

Storytelling is just as important inside a company. Tom Peters says management is about symbols as much as anything else, and that "The best leaders, especially in chaotic conditions . . . almost without exception and at every level, are master users of stories and symbols."[29] Idealab founder Bill Gross (the Idealab story will be told in more detail in Trend Three) gives all his employees equity in their companies, partly because, as he writes, "it involves a story. There's a protagonist (the company) and an antagonist (the competition); a struggle; and a victory and a hero. Equity means drama. Annuity, by contrast, is boring because you already know the ending. It's a dull story."[30]

More and more in the knowledge era, whether you work in a company or in government or for a nonprofit organization, you are going to have to answer a basic question: What's your story?

on its own; it must be molded from the clay of the knowledge era by human choice. In the analysis that follows, I have tried to sketch out a few examples of the kinds of choices that would move us in this direction over the next decade.

THE CHALLENGE OF SOCIAL TRANSFORMATION

"We are in a phase when one age is succeeding another, when everything is possible." Vaclav Havel's words capture the limitless potential of our age—a potential that, as we shall stress repeatedly, bears equal measures of opportunity and peril. It is in reflection of this basic contrast that I concluded my list of themes with two that represent each of its elements: Together, the risks of social change and its potential for empowerment point yet again to a stance of cautious optimism—cautious because of the price of change, optimistic because of the empowerment it promises.

Human social progress is a real phenomenon. Our societies do evolve and advance, and we have the power to mold this evolution to the good. The question for the next decade is not whether we will have the chance to fashion a better world but whether we have the individual and collective responsibility to seize the astonishing opportunity for beneficial progress that is already in the process of taking shape. Without that response, the trends of the knowledge era, left to their own thoughtless and undirected advance, could manufacture an ill-omened future. The choice is ours to make; and in order to make it effectively, we will need something that has been in short supply in recent years: a clear and compelling *vision* of the future we want to create. "There is absolutely no inevitability," Marshall McLuhan reminded us 30 years ago, "as long as there is a willingness to contemplate what is happening."[31]

Let's begin thinking about what's happening on the cusp of a new millennium with the story of four crucial global issues and the challenges they'll pose over the next decade: demography, natural resources, the environment, and human culture.

The Foundations

Things may be diminished by being increased,
increased by being diminished.

Tao Te Ching

Let me introduce you to two countries, Country X and Country Y. They represent the split personality of the issues we discuss in this initial trend.

Country X is a rich industrialized nation and it is aging rapidly. Declining birthrates and longer lifespans have doubled its population of individuals over 60 years of age from 8 million in 1950 to 16 million in 1990, and will *more than double it again* by 2025—while the country's working-age population will drop by 10 million. By the year 2015, one in four of its citizens will be 65 or older. Its Health and Welfare Ministry recently pointed out that, if the trend of plunging fertility rates continues, the country's population will shrink to 500 in the year 3000 and to just a single human being in the year 3500. An aging population and a shrinking workforce will do serious damage to Country X's prosperity. Pension and health-care costs will skyrocket and there will be fewer workers to pay taxes to foot the bill.

Country Y faces the opposite problem. Although its fertility rates are slowing, it has experienced massive population growth. From just 50 million people in 1970, its population skyrocketed to 93 million in 1995 and is expected to hit 143 million by 2030. Within a single lifetime, its population will have tripled, and it has an enormous number of young people as a result: In 1995, 57 percent of its population was 24 or younger, 36 percent 14 or younger. Country Y thus faces the flip-side of Country X's challenges: improving child welfare, providing quality education, and finding enough jobs for young people entering the workforce—a million jobs a year at the current pace of new workers.

These two nations also embody divergent global trends in natural resources and the environment. Businesses that deal in knowledge are cleaner, and use fewer resources, than manufacturing ones. Country X reflects this trend toward efficiency and green values in the developed world: per-capita use of wood, cotton, metals, concrete, and even plastic is declining, and air and water pollution per dollar of GDP is down. Country Y, on the other hand, is fast becoming a case study of the dangers inherent in the rapid growth of emerging market countries. It has the highest deforestation rate of any country in the world; nearly a third of its farmland is undergoing severe soil erosion; less than 10 percent of the wastewater flowing out of its capital city is treated; and massive doses of pesticides kill 5,000 agricultural workers a year.

Country X is Japan; Country Y is Mexico; and the challenges they face—similar only in their scope and intensity—furnish some clue to the kinds of demographic, resource, environmental, and cultural factors that together will establish the context in which other trends will unfold over the coming decade. Think of this first Trend as a foundation for the subjects that follow, a glimpse at the tectonic plates that underlie surface trends in economy, politics, society, and conflict. I largely portray these foundational issues as constants over the next decade; apart from surprise scenarios, these trends should remain relatively steady and not produce major global discontinuities, at least during the next ten years. Food availability and oil supplies are not likely to swing radically in one direction or another; prices of other resources, such as minerals, should remain fairly constant; and I expect no global environmental catastrophe in this period.

Nonetheless, while few demographic, environmental, and resource questions will create major crises, the coming years will offer important clues about their ultimate resolution. We will undertake a painfully slow transition to a lower-population, renewable-resource world—a world

ISSUE FEATURE: AIDS IN THE DEVELOPING WORLD

What many Americans don't know is that, while AIDS infection rates and deaths seem to be under control here, the disease is skyrocketing in precisely those places of the world that can least afford its impact: poor areas of Africa and, increasingly, Asia and eastern Europe as well.[1]

In southeastern Africa, countries like South Africa, Botswana, Zimbabwe, Kenya, Uganda and Zambia will see between 10 and 25 percent of their populations die of AIDS during the coming decade. Life expectancies are plummeting: In Botswana, they have dropped from 61 years in 1993 to 47 in the late 1990s, and down to 40 by 2005; in Swaziland and Zimbabwe, from the mid-50s to under 40. These trends give rise to searing tales of human tragedy: A personnel officer in Zimbabwe says he hires three people for every job, anticipating that two will die during training; companies that once offered medical care for sufferers now won't even pay for coffins or funerals.

> "One has to go back to the 16th century and the introduction of smallpox in the Aztec population, . . . and before that to the bubonic plague in Europe," to find a pandemic on the scale of Africa's AIDS crisis.
>
> —Lester Brown

The virus has hit the educated classes—where men have enough money to travel away from their families, use prostitutes, and otherwise place themselves at risk—especially hard. In Rwanda, a 1987 study found, among pregnant women, infection rates to be 9 percent if the husband was a farmer, 22 percent if he was a soldier, 32 percent if a white-collar worker, and 38 percent if a government official. In South Africa, the economic engine of the southern part of the continent, as many as a third of sexually active adults in the country's biggest province, and 15 percent of civil servants, are estimated to be HIV-positive. By decimating Africa's best and brightest, AIDS will destroy untold numbers of new ideas, new companies, new educators, and new leaders.

These sad tales may soon not be unique to Africa. Infection rates seem to be growing rapidly in India and China. The World Bank has pointed to Russia and eastern Europe as another potential hotbed of growth, given the rising rates of sexually transmitted disease in general, of divorce, and of drug use in those countries: one forecast calls for a million Russians infected with HIV by 2000. Clearly, AIDS represents a demographic, environmental, and economic trend of massive proportions and of immense importance over the next decade.

that reflects the paradoxical quote from the Tao Te Ching quoted earlier. "After a very long preparation," scientist Jesse Ausubel points out, "our science and technology are ready to reconcile our economy and the environment."[2] Yet as promising a transition as this is, it poses an immense challenge—the requirement, in essence, to deal with the last, dangerous gasps of the industrial era. Thus a recurring theme of this trend as well as the others is the importance of issues and transitional challenges that, although they will not mature or emerge within the next decade, can be solved only if we begin taking actions within that period.

Apart from the idea of transitional challenges, I develop two other broad themes in this trend. One is the sharp distinction between the demographic and resource situation in the vast majority of the world—developed nations, the rapidly industrializing states of East Asia, and most of Latin America—and an emerging "arc of crisis" that includes Africa, much of the Middle East, and South Asia. The worst effects of global demographic, environmental, and resource pressures will focus on a handful of nations, where the issues surveyed in this trend *will* drive history over the next decade.

A third theme is the potential for surprise—major discontinuities in these trends. Supplies of energy, food, and other resources should be sufficient to meet demand over the next decade. But the world's cushion in many of these areas is declining—smaller oil and food reserves, for example, and less capacity for rapid production increases, as demand more nearly matches production, as corporations shift more and more to "just-in-time" delivery strategies, and as governments reduce their role in maintaining large reserves. Because such markets will be more susceptible to rapid, unpredictable price shifts, I will propose a model not of shortage or plenty but of *recurrent price spikes amid generally sufficient supply* for such resources as energy and food.

A Story of Two Worlds

I turn first to the distinction between developed and developing nations. In two key areas—demography and the environment—trends at work in these two "worlds" diverge sharply.

DEMOGRAPHY: A FIZZLING POPULATION BOMB?

The first and most basic element of the human environment is the size and character of the human population—demography. Overpopulation has been a constant fear since the time of Thomas Malthus, the English clergyman who two centuries ago warned of a coming demographic disaster. So far technological and institutional advances have proven Malthus wrong, but today we face new predictions of doom. What is the truth behind demography?

The sheer numerical advance of humanity over the millennia is certainly astonishing, never more so than today. Most recently, the nations of the world have added 3 billion people to the planet in the space of only three decades. (See figure 1.1.) Additions to world population are occurring at a staggering rate: humankind did not accumulate its first billion people until 18 centuries after the time of Christ—but it added another billion in just a century, and is now adding a billion people to its teeming numbers every decade. That adds up to the equivalent of a new Pittsburgh or Boston every two days, a new Germany every eight months, and a new Mexico every year.[1] As

FIGURE 1.1

World Population Growth and Annual Increments of Growth,
1955–2015

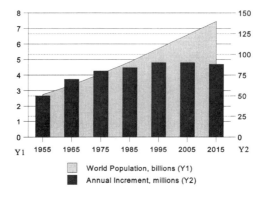

Source: The United Nations, *World Economic and Social Survey 1995* (New York: UN, 1995), p. 146.

demographer Joel Cohen notes, "Within the lifetime of some people now alive, world population has tripled; within the lifetime of everyone over 40 years old, it has doubled."[2]

And yet, because of such global forces as modernization, education, and the expansion of women's rights—all of which tend to suppress fertility—the world's population growth *rate* is declining. The world-wide Total Fertility Rate (the average number of children born per woman) has declined from 4.5 in the mid-1970s to about 3 for the years 1990 to 1995.[3] Today's population growth rate is the lowest since 1945:[4] World population increased 1.73 percent from 1975 to 1990, 1.57 percent annually during the first half of the 1990s, and is projected to grow by only a bit over one-half of 1 percent in the middle of the next century.[5] (See figure 1.2; the same phenomenon is reflected in the declining annual increments of population noted in figure 1.1.) In short, world population growth is not out of control, and in the long run (50-plus years) it is expected to level off between 8 and 12 billion people and, eventually, begin to decline.

While fertility rates are decreasing, however, the average number of people added to the world population will continue to rise—from 80

FIGURE 1.2

World Population Growth Rate

Annual Change, in Percentage, 1950-2035

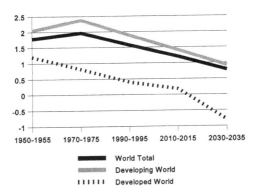

Source: United Nations, *World Economic and Social Survey 1995* (New York: UN, 1995), p. 146.

million people a year in the early 1980s to 90 million a year over the next decade—because record numbers of women are entering childbearing years and because death rates have slowed more rapidly than birth rates.[6] Only after 2020 might annual additions to world population begin to decline. For the period examined in this study, the world's population may grow by as much as a billion people to reach a total of close to 7 billion.[7] But this population growth will not be evenly distributed—its effects will vary dramatically by region, in particular between the rapidly growing developing world and the aging developed world. Demography, in short, embodies not just one trend but many.

A Population Explosion in the Developing World

The Mexican case symbolizes the first important subtrend, *massive population growth in the developing world*—more specifically, in the African–Middle Eastern–South Asian arc of crisis. Ninety-five percent of population growth between 1990 and 1995 occurred in developing

SURPRISE SCENARIO:
INSTABILITY IN THE PERSIAN GULF

The nations of the Persian Gulf will experience some of the most dramatic population growth in the world over the next 10 to 20 years—precisely at a time when many of the region's ruling families face succession crises and when the countries' long-term future of oil revenues begins to look suspect. The first surprise scenario of this trend examines the possibility and potential impacts of serious social instability in oil-producing Persian Gulf nations within the next ten years.

My point is not to predict such instability. Experts differ widely on whether to expect real social upheaval in the Gulf, and trying to forecast the evolution of complex systems such as societies beyond a few years quickly becomes sheer speculation. But as with all the surprise scenarios to come, my idea is not to forecast that this event will happen, but that it could, and therefore that we should endeavor to understand its possible ramifications.

I considered the possibility of unrest in the Gulf led by masses of young unemployed and disaffected youth, fueled by a slightly eroding standard of living and a rising challenge to regional oil-producing states. Results of such instability could include:

- *The influence of religious, and possibly radical, Islamic regimes in the region would grow* as social revolutionaries appealed to faith for both an inspiration to rebel and a justification for rule once the revolution had succeeded.
- *The Arab-Israeli peace process would slow or reverse* as combative fundamentalist regimes ceased the tacit or explicit support lent to the process by current regimes.
- *Oil supplies might not be permanently threatened,* as even fundamentalist regimes would have to sell oil to keep their societies running. But initially, or in a crisis, such regimes would be more likely to impose embargoes than current Gulf governments. They would also be more likely to seek new agreements to boost the price of oil.
- Even if unsuccessful, attempted revolts would spark *growing authoritarianism in the region and perhaps encourage Gulf monarchies to take a hard line in the peace process* as a way of fending off political attacks from fundamentalists.

countries, and that percentage will inch higher in coming decades. (See figure 1.3.) By the year 2045, the United Nations expects growth in the developed world to be negative, so that all of the world's population increase will occur in the developing world.[8]

Even within the developing world, demographic factors show wide disparities. The fertility rate in developing nations as a whole is only 3.4 and falling, a fact that reflects progress in selected countries, including China (a fertility rate of roughly 2), South Korea (under 2), Thailand (2.1), Indonesia (2.8), and Argentina, Brazil, Chile, and Colombia (all well under 3). Yet in many of the poorest countries, the rate remains near 6; in India, only now is it inching under 4.[9] Thus Africa will grow from 650 million people to 1.6 billion by the year 2025; China will grow much more slowly, from 1.13 billion to 1.5 billion; and, without accelerated declines in the fertility rate, India may grow from 850 million to 1.5 billion people.[10] In other words, over the next decade, the vast majority of the growth in world population will take place in a handful of low-income countries.

This disparity in population growth will produce accelerating inequities, both within and among states. As we shall see in later trends, the knowledge era holds opportunities as well as risks for developing countries—opportunities on display, for example, in the hopeful, if uneven, economic performance of "emerging-market" countries such as Indonesia, Chile, and Brazil. And yet countries in the throes of spectacular population explosions, even if they do manage to attract outside investment, may be unable to keep up with economic and environmental pressures.

One result of population growth in the developing world alongside minimal, or even negative, growth in the developed world will be intense new pressures for immigration and migration. The United Nations High Commission on Refugees estimates that worldwide there are now 20 million refugees, eight times the 1974 number—with almost a million refugees a year joining the teeming ranks of the world's homeless.[11] It looks as if the immigration debate in the United States, France, and Germany has just begun, while in developing nations, such as China, population growth and urbanization will produce enormous internal migrations that may overload the ability of cities to cope.

Another result of population growth outstripping natural and institutional support systems—more destitute people will be born in

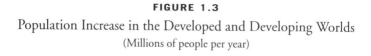

FIGURE 1.3

Population Increase in the Developed and Developing Worlds
(Millions of people per year)

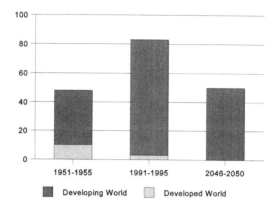

Source: United Nations, *World Economic and Social Survey 1995* (New York: UN, 1995), p. 146.

India alone in the next few decades, for example, than all the poor who suffered through Europe's Dark Ages of roughly A.D. 1000 to 1500[12]— is an accelerating catalogue of humanitarian disasters. "The frequency and scale of humanitarian crises . . . have increased substantially in recent years. The number of people affected by disasters (both natural and political) rose from about 44 million in 1975 to more than 175 million in 1993," and the number of those helped by the United Nations "rose from 1 million in 1970 to 17 million in 1993."[13] This trend will continue—and accelerate—in the years ahead, creating a permanent requirement for humanitarian and peacekeeping operations.

Population growth in the developing world is overwhelmingly urban in character, and the next decade will also witness accelerating urbanization. Worldwide, the size of cities has swelled over the last several decades. The numbers astonish: Urban populations soared from 29 percent of total world population in 1950 to 40 percent in 1980 and 45 percent in 1995. (See figure 1.4.) Taking a longer view, from 1800 through 1995, "the fraction of people who lived in cities surged from perhaps 1 in 50 to nearly 1 in 2," while the "absolute numbers of city dwellers rose from perhaps 18 million to 2.3 billion."[14]

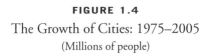

FIGURE 1.4

The Growth of Cities: 1975–2005

(Millions of people)

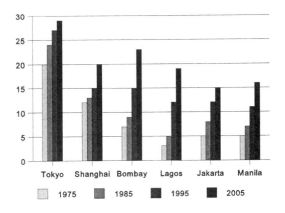

Source: U.S. Department of State, *Population Trends Over the Coming Decade* (August 1994), insert map.

And the trend continues. Today population growth rates in cities are three times higher than in rural areas; urban populations in developing countries have doubled since the mid-1970s.[15] The United Nations estimates that by the year 2025, 61 percent of humanity—more than 5 billion people—will be living in cities.[16]

Because the cities of the developed world have already undergone their growth spurts, today's growth in urban populations is taking place largely in developing nations. Ninety percent of urban growth over the next decades will take place in developing countries—especially in Africa and Asia, which now are only 30 to 35 percent urban. Some 150,000 people join the urban populations of developing countries *every day.* By the year 2005, half a decade hence, there could be 33 "megacities" in the world—vast urban areas with populations over 8 million each—and 27 of them will be in developing countries.[17]

According to the joint United Nations, World Bank, and World Resources Institute publication *World Resources 1996–1997,* "The world is in the midst of a massive urban transition unlike that of any other time in history."[18] But the issue is not merely, or even necessarily, one of hulking new supermetropolises. In some cases, such as Mexico City, the biggest of cities have reached something of a natural limit and, for reasons of cost and convenience, begun to shed population to outlying areas, which have become some of the world's fastest growing "metropolitan" areas.[19] This phenomenon represents something of a paradox: Even as major cities grow, they radiate more and more of their population into nearby urban sprawl, and "cities such as São Paulo, Mexico City, Jakarta, and Bombay are all experiencing increasing *decentralization*" even as they remain vibrant economic units.[20]

The implications of urbanization are not all bad. Because cities are more efficient economic units than rural areas, urbanization helps to produce higher incomes and improved health—and in the knowledge era, cities, with their concentration of knowledge and information technologies, may have a renewed competitive advantage.[21] But these benefits come with a substantial environmental and social price: Already in cities, 220 million people lack access to clean drinking water, 420 million to latrines of any kind. Over 1 billion people live in cities with unhealthful levels of air pollution. Today in developing world cities 20 to 50 percent of municipal waste goes uncollected. With half of the developing world's poor living in cities by the year 2000, urban areas will face an immense challenge of job creation.[22]

In addition to the accelerating growth of cities, the exploding population in the developing world will also magnify an emphasis on youth. By 2010 almost 60 developing countries will experience "youth bulges," with 20 percent or more of their population in the 15- to 24-year-old age group. This includes two dozen states in sub-Saharan Africa and such important Middle Eastern nations as Egypt, Iran, and Iraq.[23]

These youth bulges will make it more difficult to maintain order in a developing world already beset by dozens of social, economic, and ecological challenges. Center for Strategic and International Studies (CSIS) Middle East expert Anthony Cordesman has mapped out some results for those developing world countries hardest hit by population explosions.[24] Examples include:

- In North Africa, Algeria, Egypt, Libya, Morocco, and Tunisia will all experience a population explosion from 1990 to 2005, with citizenries growing by 25 to 40 percent. Instability in these countries will exacerbate Europe's immigration challenge.

- In the Arab-Israeli context, besides Egypt's demographic crisis, Syria's population is expected to grow from 12 million in 1990 to 20 million by 2005, and Jordan will nearly double in population from 3.2 to 5.9 million. Populations in Gaza and the West Bank will nearly double, from a combined total of roughly 1.5 million in 1990 to 2.75 million by 2005. Overcrowding, urbanization, declining living standards, and social instability may create fertile soil for Islamic fundamentalism and complicate the Middle East peace process.

- And in the Persian Gulf, Cordesman argues that "population growth is a critical threat to Iran, Iraq, Saudi Arabia, and Yemen. Oil wealth cannot offset a steady drop in per-capita income." Saudi per-capita income has declined in real terms to half what it was in the mid-1980s; Iranian living standards have slipped back to 1972 levels; Iraqi per-capita income had already declined by 50 percent during the 1980s, *before* the Persian Gulf War and its attendant economic sanctions. Meanwhile the population of all three countries continues to soar—from 15.8 million in 1990 to 25.8 million in 2005 for Saudi Arabia; from 56 million to 85 million in Iran; and from 18 million to 28.4 million in Iraq.

The Demographic Flip Side: An Aging Developed World

As the example of Japan has already suggested, if soaring populations have ominous implications for developing countries, slowing population growth in industrialized nations carries challenges of its own. In brief, the *developed world is growing older.*

Low birth rates and longer life spans, combined with massive post–World War II generations that were followed by much smaller successor groups, mean that the balance of developed world populations is shifting in the direction of more retirees and fewer working-age people. This process underlies the well-known crises of social security and old-age medical systems. Throughout the developed world, the number of people over 65 will rise 60 percent by the year 2025.[25] In the United States, Florida is commonly depicted as a retirement haven; by the year

FIGURE 1.5

Japan's Looming Old-Age Crisis

Working-age population and population 65+, in millions

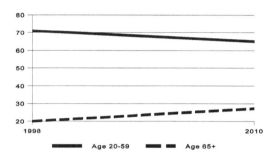

Source: U.S. Census Bureau, "Japan: Demographic Indicators" (1998), at www.census.gov/cgi-bin/ipc

2025, almost 30 American states will mirror Florida's demographic balance.[26]

Elsewhere in the developed world, the picture is either just as bad or far worse. In France, the number of working people ages 25 to 59, which rose by 6 million from 1950 to 1990, will level off through 2025—while the population over 60 grows by 6 million. Italy's predicament is even more dire: From 1990 to 2025 the working-age population, which rose by 7 million since 1950, will decline by the same number, and the population over 60 will rise by 5 million. Japan's population of individuals 60 and over was a mere 8 million in 1950; that number doubled by 1990 and will more than double again by 2025—while the working population plummets by 10 million.[27] (See figure 1.5.)

The aging of the developed world will have dramatic economic implications. With workforces shrinking, how will nations in Europe and Asia maintain economic growth? With retirees drawing down their savings and workers paying higher taxes, will savings rates plummet— and will the world face a currency crunch and rocketing inflation? How will we keep our economy viable and taxes low when the proportion of U.S. GDP spent on health care will more than double? No one knows the answers to these questions.

ISSUE FEATURE: JAPAN'S COLOSSAL PENSION CRISIS

Japan's aging crisis is by far the worst in the developing world, and few people have thought through the massive implications of this fact for Japan's economic, societal, and foreign policy. One of those who has is Nomura Capital Management expert Milton Ezrati, whose 1997 *Foreign Affairs* essay laid out the full scope of Japan's aging crisis.[28]

Within five years, Japan will have a demographic profile similar to Florida's. By the year 2015, 1 in 4 Japanese will be 65 or older; by 2010, it will have only 2.5 workers for every retiree. The ramifications of this process of aging will be immense.

- *Japan's standard of living will decline.* A smaller percentage of the population earning income will mean a lower national income. Ezrati estimates that "this demographic situation could ultimately cut the average Japanese standard of living by 18 percent." This equates, in Japan's slow-growth 1990s, to a decade of lost economic growth.
- *Japan's savings rate will plummet.* Japan's high rate of national savings has been critical to its economic strength, but it will not last. Retirees do not save, and Ezrati estimates a decline of 12 to 15 percent in Japan's personal savings rate. Meanwhile massive pension obligations will create a persistent government budget deficit of 5 percent or more. Together these effects will halve the country's overall savings rate.
- *Exports will decline.* As workers become scarce and wages rise, the trend of Japanese companies locating production offshore will accelerate. Lower production within Japan will cut into its trade surplus, already down to $77 billion from a peak of $130 billion in 1993. "It is likely," Ezrati concludes, "that within the next five years Japan will have a trade deficit"—an astounding reversal of fortune for the world's champion exporter.
- *Japan's economy will open up.* A retired population facing declining living standards will want cheaper imported goods, and thus Japan's policy of maximizing its trade surplus "will lose its rationale and eventually be reversed," Ezrati concludes.
- *Japan's foreign policy will become more active.* With production facilities located throughout Asia, Japan will want projectable military power to protect them.

Aging populations will have social and cultural as well as economic ramifications. Home shopping networks may expand as older people seek ways to shop that require less mobility. "Convenience and access," argues *Age Wave* author Ken Dychtwald, "may be just as important as the product itself."[29] Older populations also will encourage thousands of small revisions of existing products and services, from slower-moving commercial images on television, to nonslip bathtubs, to glare-resistant automobile windows, to automatically controlled household equipment such as lights.

In political and cultural terms, the growing dominance of the elderly in many developed nations could produce conservative, risk-averse governments precisely in many places (such as Japan) where the need for broad-based social reform is achingly clear. Tensions could grow between the old and the young workers paying huge tax bills to finance elder services. In a more positive vein, retired or semiretired people may expand their commitment to voluntarism, strengthening the emerging "social sector" that I'll examine in Trend Five. And shrinking workforces could make many rich countries view immigrants, and the economic potential they bring, more sympathetically. By about 2005, for example, immigrants may make up something like half of all new U.S. workers; without immigrants and the children they bear, the United States would be worse off demographically—both our workforce and the total number of children in the country would begin to decline a decade or two into the next century.

In the longer run, too, it is important to keep in mind that even the developing world is aging. Globally, the number of people aged 60 and older will jump from 500 million in 1990 to 1.4 billion by 2030, tripling in a single lifetime—and even with the developed world's aging trend, most of the new elderly will live in developing nations. In China, for example, the proportion of people over 60 will skyrocket from about 9 percent in 1990 to about 22 percent in 2030. The percentage of Indians over 60 during those same four decades will grow from 6.9 to 13.1; of Mexicans, from 5.7 to 15.7; of Brazilians, from 6.7 to 16.9.[30]

A number of factors make the developing world's aging crisis far more challenging than that of the developed world, even though developing nations won't hit the peak of the crisis as soon. Most developing countries are aging much more rapidly than the developed nations did, telescoping themselves into an aging crisis with less time to

ISSUE FEATURE: AN OLDER *AND* YOUNGER AMERICA

The headline-grabbing demographic trend in the United States in recent years has been the aging of the population and the attendant Social Security and Medicare crises. But this trend is already being matched by a very different one: America's youth populations are exploding.

TABLE 1.1
Changing Demographics: U.S. Generations, 1995–2025
As percentage of the overall U.S. population

	Pre-Boom	Baby Boom	Baby Bust	Boomlet	Post-Boomlet
1995	26	29.5	17	27.5	——
2005	17.2	26.7	16.2	26.6	13.4
2015	9.8	23.4	15.1	25.2	26.5
2025	4.3	19.4	13.6	23.9	38.9

In 2005, the "Baby Boomlet" will be between 10 and 28 years of age; in 2015 it will be 20 to 38 years old. By 2015, there will be *82 million* teenagers in the United States.
Source: Diane Crispell, "Generations to 2025," *American Demographics,* January 1995.

The aging of the population is produced by the juxtaposition of two generations: an enormous Baby Boom followed by a much smaller Baby Bust only slightly greater than half the size of the Boom. As the Boom ages, the population as a whole will skew in the same direction—and create a Social Security crisis. But behind the Baby Bust are two new generations, each expected to rival the size of the Baby Boom. (See table 1.1.) Already in 1997, the total number of children under 18 in the United States surpassed the peak of the Baby Boom; and while the *percentage* of the U.S. population under 18 won't be as high as in the 1960s (because the total has grown so much since then), the absolute number of kids is unprecedented.

This coming flood of youngsters has many implications. Trend Five examines its impact on crime rates; some worry, too, that even if teen pregnancy rates continue to decline, because there are more teenage girls, the absolute number of teen pregnancies will grow. Another implication may be overloaded schools:[31] Between 1996 and 2006, enrollment in U.S. high schools will jump sharply—over a third in California and nearly as much in Arizona, Nevada, Virginia, North Carolina, and Maryland. Nationwide, elementary and secondary education enrollment will surge from 52.2 million in 1997—already a record 800,000 more than in 1996—to nearly 55 million in 2007. College admissions will become more competitive, with the number of applicants per opening growing from 10 to 12 or 13.

prepare for it. Pension systems, health care, and other aspects of elderly well-being are not well prepared in most developing countries. And because they are often so poor, developing nations simply don't have the economic wherewithal—or the long-term financial savings—to deal with the crushing costs of an aging society.

The issue of aging in the developing world is one of those topics that won't fully mature during the next decade. During that period, most developing countries will only be approaching their true aging years; they won't have reached them yet. But the decisions they make during the coming decade—decisions about savings rates, about establishing and reforming pension plans, about health care—will play a crucial role in determining whether they are prepared for the aging trend when it does hit home.

THE NATURAL ENVIRONMENT

Given the thousands of books, reports, and essays written in the last decade about the environment, it takes a bit of moxie to try to summarize the issue in just a few pages—a task made all the more difficult by the bitter debates and intensity of feeling that crowd the issue. There is simply no way I can introduce this subject so briefly without deeply offending at least some of the experts who have given their lives to it. As with few other issues I examined, this one is so complex, multifaceted, and controversial that I was tempted merely to push you in the direction of a few good books on the subject and leave it at that.

I have a responsibility to do more, and so I'll try. But keep firmly in mind that my take on the issue is just one view, and the next few pages are bound to be seen by some very smart and sincere people as either dangerously sanguine or foolishly alarmist. More than any other topic I discuss, if you want to understand this issue and form your own opinions—and for the sake of our planet, you should—you'll need to delve much more deeply into the literature on it. (Two very good places to start, which represent different perspectives on the current debate, are the engaging books *A Moment on the Earth,* by Gregg Easterbrook, and *Earth Odyssey,* by Mark Hertsgaard.)

My own view is that the story of the environment is similar to that of demography—a story of two worlds, a developed world still polluting heavily but taking the first steps toward a sustainable future, and a developing world awash in terrifying environmental dangers. Our major environmental challenges over the next decade seem to me to be accelerating the transition to the environmentally friendly aspects of the knowledge era in the developed world while keeping economic progress in the developing nations from doing irretrievable ecological damage.

Developed World Trends

The basic truth about developed-world environmental issues over the next decade offers yet another paradox: Pollution and other environmental damage will continue on a massive scale even as the transition to knowledge-era economies opens the way to an environmentally sustainable future.

For example, the developed world, led by the United States, will continue to generate scandalous amounts of air and water pollution and waste of all kinds. As of 1992, the United States was pouring 19.1 metric tons of carbon dioxide into the atmosphere every year *per-capita*—8 times China's per-capita rate and 20 times India's.[32] While per-capita energy use will remain stable or decline in the United States, and energy use per unit of gross domestic product (GDP) will continue to fall, rising population and a growing economy will make for higher overall energy use—much of it in heavily polluting coal.[33]

And yet, air pollution, resource use per unit of GDP, and per-capita wood use are all down in the developed world.[34] (See figure 1.6.) These figures reflect the fact that knowledge-era economies are less abusive of the environment than their predecessors. Producing, disseminating, and using knowledge requires fewer resources and less environmentally dangerous activity than manufacturing goods; and as the relative balance between these two activities shifts further in the direction of knowledge, the environment will benefit. In developed economies, per-capita energy use and pollution is down dramatically over the last 20 years. In the 1970s, for example, it took 164 pounds of metal to make 1,000 soda cans; today it takes 35 pounds. Per-capita steel use in the United States is 40 percent less than its peak levels in 1920, and falling. Faxes and e-mail save the energy and pollution that would have been expended by the post office. The trick now is to expand on these hopeful beginnings to create economies that are truly sustainable.[35]

FIGURE 1.6

Levels of Air Pollution

(Ambient concentrations of particulate matter in sample cities;
micrograms per cubic meter)

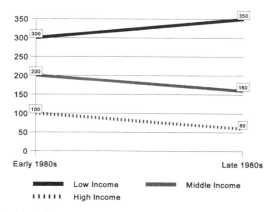

Source: The World Bank, *Monitoring Environmental Progress* (Washington: World Bank, 1995), p. 30.

This process will not be easy, and it will remain in its infancy during the coming decade. Indeed, in our time frame much of the environmental news about the developed world may continue to be bad, providing further proof of global warming and loss of natural species and furnishing constant reminders that a complete transition away from industrial-era transportation systems will take decades. Nonetheless, the potential for a better future exists, and the next decade will help decide how fully we embrace it.

The Emerging Notion of "Industrial Ecology"

Such a reconciling of society's need for short-term economic prosperity and long-term environmental health is the goal of a new field of scientific research and business practice loosely grouped under the label of industrial ecology. Its purpose is to integrate business into a holistic mode of thinking about society and the human and natural environment that takes ecological concerns seriously. This embryonic new paradigm has the power to reshape the way we think about our economies.

The environmental and economic writer Paul Hawken explains that industrial ecology sees businesses as part of an ecological system and argues that they can *increase* profitability if they view themselves in that fashion. Environmental health and economic growth are not exclusive—in fact, they can go hand in hand. Markets, as Hawken explains, "are superb at setting prices, but incapable of recognizing costs." The true social "cost" of the production of a hazardous chemical would include the price of environmental cleanup, health costs associated with illnesses produced by chemical spills or runoff, and so on. But chances are that the company making the product ignores all these factors when setting prices, because it isn't responsible for them.[36] The goal of industrial ecology is partly to make businesses aware of, and responsible for, the *full* costs of operations—including environmental impacts—and promote "closed-loop" manufacturing in which one company's waste becomes another's raw material.

A number of businesses have already picked up on this notion and are doing a better job of measuring the costs of such things as energy use and waste products and, by figuring them into their bottom line, deciding for profit reasons alone to opt for ecologically sound options. Using such approaches, as of the mid-1990s the company 3M had saved $500 million and reduced pollution 50 percent per unit of production since 1975.[37] British Petroleum is investing heavily in solar energy. Packing company Sonoco Products made a 1990 pledge to take back and recycle any used products customers wanted to return; leading U.S. carpet manufacturer Interface Inc.'s chief executive officer Ray Anderson in the early 1990s set a goal of zero waste generation and zero oil consumption.[38] And companies that implement energy-saving ideas, often culled from their own employees, save both money and the environment: Dow Chemical saw profits at its Louisiana division soar $110 million a year from such strategies.[39]

Increasingly, being good to the environment is not just good values or good politics—it is good business as well, and not only for financial reasons. More companies around the world are reaching for the public relations advantages of a "green" image. Toyota and Honda seem to be vying for the role as the world's most environmentally friendly carmaker; both are introducing hybrid-electric vehicles, Honda touts the gas mileage of its Civics in ecologically savvy commercials, and Toyota has hired botanists to develop genetically modified trees that absorb extra greenhouse gases.[40] Scandic Hotels, one of Europe's largest chains, recently has achieved impressive growth in part by setting into motion more than 1,500 distinct environmental initiatives, including the creation of a 97 percent recyclable hotel room—an "Eco-room."[41] The overall trend received a major boost in February 1997 when 2,000 U.S. economists, led by Nobel laureates Kenneth Arrow and Robert Solow, released a statement arguing that the United States could reduce its industrial emissions to slow global warming without damaging its economy and that carefully designed environmental policies using market mechanisms "may in fact improve U.S. productivity in the longer run"[42]—just as the industrial ecology movement argues.

Emerging Environmental Dangers

In the long run, therefore, the character of the knowledge era combined with the new understandings of the industrial ecology movement have the potential to radically reduce the damage done to the environment by the most modern economies. Even in the developed world, however, the transition to such clean economies will only have begun during the next decade. And if the developed world has not fully entered the knowledge era, as the Mexican case reminds us, developing nations are firmly stuck in industrial-era patterns of consumption and pollution. As emerging-market nations in the developing world grow dramatically over the next decade, the possibility of a renewed environmental disaster—both regionally and, as a product of rising industrial emissions, globally—is very real.

Increased energy use over the next decade will, for example, provoke a growth of the gases that allegedly produce global warming, the so-called greenhouse effect. Toward the end of the next decade, developing nations may surpass developed ones as consumers of energy, and many developing countries will rely more heavily on environmentally disastrous coal-fired power plants than most developed nations. The International Energy Agency suggested in 1995 that, largely because of developing-world growth, greenhouse gas emissions will grow 10 percent by 2000 and 40 percent by 2010,[43] even in the context of reduced emissions per unit of GDP.

The debate over global warming is intense, but one thing is clear: Increasingly, the fastest growing sources of greenhouse gases will be the developing world. Even by 1992, developing nations had over-taken the developed world in the emissions of carbon dioxide; their lead continues to grow, with the carbon emissions of developing nations expanding three times as fast as those of developed nations. China alone, if its current growth patterns continue, might by the year 2025 emit more greenhouse gases than the United States, Japan, and Canada combined.[44]

Global warming will almost certainly not have catastrophic impacts during the period under consideration here.[45] The massive coastal flooding and worldwide agricultural shifts predicted by some scientists may occur—but if they do, it will be well into the next century. The most recent International Panel on Climate Change estimate suggests a rise in sea levels of one-half a meter by the year 2100—a transition likely to be barely noticeable during the next ten years.[46] If global warming is a reality, what the next decade may bring is more severe weather—hurricanes, tornadoes, snowstorms, and the like—on a more regular basis, a trend some climatologists say is under way already.

Another dramatic development possible in connection with global warming during the next decade is the firm and unequivocal establish-ment of the validity of the theory itself. Today reactions to the idea of global warming are muted by the fact that, while the basic science underlying the theory is quite strong and has the status of a general consensus, the most critical policy-relevant links in the chain remain the subject of bitter debate. If new studies prove once and for all that human-induced warming is under way, the call for public policy responses would become intense.

An expanding human population and the environmental effects of its activities also appear to be causing the extinction of species. Biodiversity is important for a variety of reasons, from discovering new medicines to preserving the sometimes fragile network of plants, animals, and microorganisms that uphold local ecologies. Because we have only a very rough idea of the total number of species that exist, it is difficult to be sure how many are being lost to habitat destruction, hunting, pollution, and other causes. But the most recent U.N. Environmental Program report suggests that between 5 and 20 percent of some groups of plant and animal species could face extinction in coming decades.[47] Preventing major new rounds of extinctions represents a critical environmental challenge.

Long before the world faces the ultimate ramifications of global warming or species extinction, it will confront a series of regional environmental disasters in which localized pollution, resource degradation, or other factors spark catastrophes limited in reach but enormously destructive to human societies. These often manifest themselves as resource scarcities. But they can be exacerbated by changing climate conditions sparked by global warming, by periodic natural disasters, and by localized pollution that contaminates water and agricultural soil. One example is Russia, where environmental degradation from the communist era is a major roadblock to progress.

A Price Spike Economy

This chapter tells the story of natural resources and asks whether the world will have enough of them to meet demand over the next decade. Just as they are more environmentally friendly than industrial economies, knowledge-era economies are also less dependent on natural resources. Nonetheless, in selected areas, population growth combined with economic expansion will put new pressure on certain categories of resources. Combined with the growing prominence of just-in-time delivery techniques, these developments may well create a situation of recurrent price spikes amid generally stable resource prices.

FOOD

The experience of recent years tends to validate a relatively optimistic hypothesis, for example, about food supplies.[1] World food output has more than doubled in the last three decades; food supplies per capita have grown by a quarter even in many areas of the developing world, where the quality of most diets continues to improve as well; and the real cost of most food items has declined. During the 1980s, wheat production outside the United States grew at about 2 percent a year and rice production at 3.5 percent. Meanwhile, over 1 billion acres of potential additional cropland lie unused for lack of demand, much of it in the United States, Argentina, Brazil, Turkey, and Ukraine. A host of specific new varieties of plants, from short-season corn to high-yield

ISSUE FEATURE: CHINA AND FOOD

At the end of 1994 Beijing, already the world's largest buyer of wheat, was still exporting corn, but by 1995 it had become a massive importer—the world's second largest, after Japan. In 1994 China exported 10 to 12 million tons of corn a year; by 1996 it was buying millions of tons, driving world corn stocks to their lowest level in 20 years.[2] Alarmists pointed to the demand and predicted a regional or global food crisis.[3]

But the Chinese case is hardly dire. Reforms and superior technology have improved the yield of Chinese farms by 50 percent from 1978 to 1984. Continued reforms will open up more land to farming and encourage better use of existing land; new strains of seed will prove more insect- and disease-resistant; better fertilizers will boost yield. The International Food Policy Research Institute forecasts that "Chinese wheat, corn, and rice production will increase by 90 percent, 80 percent, and 54 percent, respectively, by the year 2020," and one U.N. agriculture expert suggests that Chinese cereal production will rise 70 percent between 1990 and 2030—even assuming a 12 percent loss in cultivated land.[4]

Nor have yields on Chinese farms reached a plateau. Satellite imagery shows Chinese cropland to be understated—and yields overestimated—by as much as 45 percent. *The Economist* explains that even "casual observation suggests that efficiency could be hugely increased down on the [Chinese] farm." Currently a quarter of the wheat harvest is lost through wastage and spoilage—and a 10 percent loss of wheat equals "all of China's wheat imports."[5] And land reform—granting farmers rights to their own land—would jump-start efforts to improve output.[6]

The Chinese case also suggests one of the most common responses to food shortages: trade. Countries that outstrip their local grain or cereal production base, such as China, can import these products from countries with excess production. Most estimates of global grain output to the year 2030 suggest that the world can easily respond to increased Chinese grain demands, partly because progress elsewhere will ease demand on surpluses: "If we have the right amount of input in agricultural research," explains researcher Gurdev Sing Khush in one example, "there is no reason why we can't feed the Indian population for the next 30 to 40 years."[7]

rice, promises to redouble the efficiency of many agricultural regions yet again. (See figure 2.1.)

Put another way by scientist Paul Waggoner: If in the next six or seven decades "the world farmer reaches the average yield of today's U.S. corn grower," a world population of 10 billion "will need only

half of today's cropland while they eat today's American calories."
"The potential to increase yields everywhere remains astonishing,"
agrees Jesse Ausubel. "On average, the world "grows only about half
the corn per hectare as the average Iowa farmer, who in turn grows
only about half the corn of the top Iowa farmer"; if world farmers can
add just 1.5 percent to their output per year, 10 billion people could
eat an American-style diet "and still spare close to a quarter of the
present 1.4 billion hectares of cropland"—an area equal to the size of
India.[8]

There is also a good deal of slack built into the system, slack that
can be eliminated if food supplies tighten more than they already
have.[9] Americans now spend an astounding 40 percent of their food
budget away from home in restaurants, compared to just 15 percent
in 1940. (Even with this growth of cash-intensive going out to dinner,
the percentage of U.S. disposable income spent on food has declined
from 21 percent in 1940 to 11 percent in 1995.) Higher food prices
might encourage Americans to eat at home more often, not eat less
nutritious foods. Or consider this: Only 21 cents of every dollar
Americans spend on food represents the cost of the food. The rest is
wrapped up in associated expenses, such as transportation, packaging,
and processing. A one-dollar jump in the price of a bushel of corn
could be offset by just 25 cents worth of savings in the other areas.

The general consensus of studies, then—including analyses by the
U.N. Food and Agriculture Organization, the World Bank, and others—is that food production can accommodate rising demand from a
growing and more affluent population.

Nonetheless, the world will not obtain these promising results
without intense effort, because a variety of factors will put more pressure
on food supplies. For one thing, higher living standards worldwide will
increase demand for high-quality food; the most likely source of sudden
food shortages is not population growth creating more mouths to feed
but economic growth creating more affluent mouths to feed. Worldwide, per-capita consumption of poultry, pork, and beef has grown 11
percent in the last decade alone.[10] Partly as a result, even the environmental optimist Dennis Avery explains that "We must be able to triple
the productivity of the world's agriculture over the short span of fifty
years to meet the needs of a larger and richer world population. Current
levels of productivity and knowledge cannot sustainably do the job."[11]

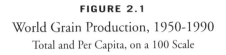

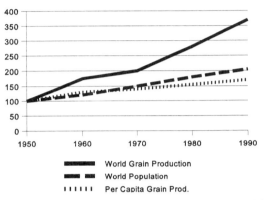

Source: Meadows, Meadows and Randers, *Beyond the Limits* (VT: Chelsea Green Publishing, 1992), p. 48.

More demand for cropland may reduce forests or fields available for animals and plants, thus accelerating species extinction. To get quick boosts in production, nations may expand the use of pesticides and cause environmental damage. More efficient strains of crops tend to require much more water, further exacerbating regional shortages. The loss of croplands through soil erosion, desertification, and overfarming is also well under way: Deserts have expanded 120 million hectares in twenty years; China has lost croplands equal to the size of farms in Germany, Denmark, and Holland combined; and 6 or 7 million hectares of land in developing countries go out of production every year.[12] At the same time, something like three-quarters of world fisheries are being fished beyond their sustainable capacity; "almost everywhere," *The Economist* concludes, "fish stocks have been plundered to the point of exhaustion."[13]

This trend once again aims squarely at the arc of crisis: Already 175 million people in Africa are undernourished, a number that could nearly double by the year 2010; in South Asia by that same year, nearly 200 million people may face starvation. For such impoverished countries in

---

ISSUE FEATURE: A VEGETARIAN FUTURE?

Because feed animals consume so much grain, diets rich in meat require three times as much of it to feed a person as do vegetarian diets. Thus a "shift away from eating meat to a vegetarian diet," writes Jesse Ausubel, "could roughly halve our need for [agricultural] land."[14]

Such a shift may indeed be under way. U.S. consumption of beef, for example, has dropped from 60 kilograms per person annually in 1976 to about 45 kilograms in the 1990s. The trend is especially powerful among younger Americans: 15 percent of U.S. college students call themselves vegetarians. Food industry analysts remain highly skeptical of the trend, but my hunch is that it's for real—and that it will carry important business implications. The demand for vegetarian food, alternatives to leather clothing, and other animal-friendly consumer tastes will grow. The next decade could, for example, witness the birth of "the vegetarian McDonald's"—veggie fast-food restaurants offering state-of-the art vegetable and meat-substitute foods, many of them low fat.

---

the arc of crisis, price spikes could be disastrous. This situation stands in stark contrast to East Asia and Latin America, where economic growth may reduce undernourished populations to 4 and 6 percent of the total by 2010, respectively; in developing countries as a whole, chronic undernutrition should fall to 11 percent of the population by 2010, down from 20 percent in 1988–1989.[15]

WATER

Growing worldwide population also will place new pressures on world water supplies. Already some regions—notably the Middle East—face a constant challenge of providing sufficient water for drinking, cooking, irrigation, and other purposes. Global demand for water increased 900 percent in the twentieth century; it increased by a factor of four between 1940 and 1990 alone[16] and is expected roughly to triple again by the year 2020. While the Earth is quite literally awash in water, only a tiny percentage—the renewable level of annual fresh-water deposits—is available for human use. "If all the world's water fit into a bathtub," explain Robert Engelman and Pamela LeRoy of Population Action International, "the portion of it that could be used sustainably in any given year would barely fill a teaspoon."[17] The story of water follows the same pattern as other resources: generally sufficient global supplies marred by regional inequities and shortages.

World Bank vice president for sustainable development Ismail Serageldin says that 80 countries, most in Africa and the Middle East, already face severe and life-threatening water shortages. (See table 2.1.) By 2025 water available to individuals in those countries will fall 80 percent.

The countries hit hardest by these trends are largely the same as those facing demographic tensions—the nations of the arc of crisis. The connection is hardly surprising; in many cases it is population growth that is contributing to resource depletion, including water.[18] In such countries, water shortages worsen inequality: Expensive, government-funded water projects often benefit the rich, so that the poor often end up paying more for their water than do the wealthy.

One especially dangerous implication of worsening water supplies in the arc of crisis is to imperil already constrained food supplies. Water scarcity will constrain agriculture in developing countries as much or more than land shortages, particularly because many new high-yield crops demand much more water than natural varieties and therefore will place added pressure on agricultural water supplies.[19] Economic development will lag as states find themselves unable to sustain growth because of water shortages. And increasingly, states may fight over declining water resources: Forty percent of the world lives in 250 river basins whose water supplies are subject to international disputes.[20] Tension over water supplies is already on the rise in a region relatively new to water-based conflict: Asia. Farmlands around Beijing are losing water supplies to urban uses, and as many as 300 Chinese cities are now short of water.[21]

Potential solutions to water shortages are sometimes obvious; they are always expensive. One option is conservation: Vast amounts of water are wasted in inefficient irrigation techniques, and many city water systems leak out up to half their supply in the course of delivering it. More efficient irrigation methods alone would save vast amounts of water—although not nearly enough, or quickly enough, to prevent a

TABLE 2.1

Water Scarcities in the Middle East and Africa

Forecast availability of water in 2025, in cubic meters per person per year,
with 1000 as the worldwide standard of sufficiency

900-1000 m³	600-900 m³	300-600 m³	<300m³
Ethiopia	*Egypt*	*Algeria*	Burundi
Lesotho	*Morocco*	Rwanda	Djibouti
Nigeria	*Somalia*	*Tunisia*	*Kenya*
Tanzania	South Africa	Israel	Libya
Haiti		Oman	Barbados
Peru			*Jordan*
Iran			*Kuwait*
Lebanon			*Saudi Arabia*
			Qatar
			Singapore
			Yemen

Nations in italics are expected to sustain a population doubling in the same period.

Source: Peter Gleick, "Water and Conflict," *International Security* 18, No. 1 (Summer 1993): 100-101.

water crunch in many areas of Africa and the Middle East. Eventually, with the development of renewable energy and new technologies, desalination may become a more widespread solution to water shortages, but not in the next decade. There are signs of hope: through greater efficiency (such as toilets and dishwashers that use less water) and other means, the U.S. Geological Survey recently estimated that use of water in the United States actually dropped almost 10 percent between 1980 and 1995, even as the U.S. population grew by 16 percent.[22]

In sum, water issues should retain the essentially localized character they do today. These local pressures will fall disproportionately on the Middle East and Africa—regions that, also because of rapid population growth and (in some cases) food shortages, will continue to be seen as the world's most serious zone of instability.

ENERGY

More people living at a gradually higher standard of living—especially in urban areas, where energy use is much higher than rural ones—will mean greater use of energy. By far the most important part of this growth will not take place in the developed world, where knowledge-era economies are more efficient in their use of energy than industrial economies. In the United States, for example, energy use per dollar of GDP has *declined* almost 30 percent in the last 20 years[23]; since about 1800 in America, "the production of a good or service has required 1 percent less energy on average than it did the previous year."[24] Instead, much of the new energy demand will be from developing countries whose economies are expanding but not as advanced—with the result that they reflect the industrial rather than the knowledge era.

Energy supply and price should not pose a major barrier to economic development over the next decade. Energy prices, including prices of crude oil, should remain relatively stable through 2010.[25] The major event that could break this trend would be severe instability in the Middle East.

Consider, for example, the forecast of the U.S. Department of Energy in its 1995 *International Energy Outlook*. (See figure 2.2.) It projects an increase in world energy consumption from 346 quadrillion British thermal units (Btu) in 1990 to about 440 quadrillion Btu in 2005 and 472 quadrillion Btu in 2010. This growth rate of roughly 1.6 percent per year represents a substantial decline from the 2.6 percent growth of the previous two decades, reflecting, the report notes, "the adoption of more energy-efficient technologies worldwide." Since the oil shocks of the 1970s, energy use has grown more slowly than economic growth in highly industrialized nations, with the result that, just after 2010, nations that are not members of the Organization for Economic Cooperation and Development (OECD) will surpass the highly industrialized countries as consumers of energy.[26] Total worldwide energy demand is expected to increase roughly 30 percent to the year 2005, 40 percent by 2010, and 50 percent or more by 2020.[27]

Within the energy field, there is little doubt that the most important potential uncertainties lurk in the status of that most hotly contested of natural resources: oil. The oil picture over the next decade is a paradoxical

FIGURE 2.2

World Energy Use, 1970–2010

OECD versus Non-OECD, in percent

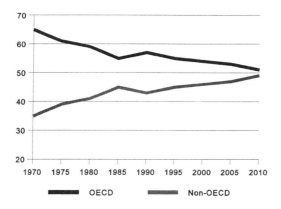

Source: U.S. Department of Energy, *International Energy Outlook 1995* (Washington, D.C.: U.S. Government Printing Office, 1995), p. 1.

one: probably low prices and reliable supply, but also a growing dependence on Middle East oil and the first tentative signs of the end of the petroleum era. Most forecasts would have oil supplies rise gradually to meet demand and prices remain under $30 a barrel (after briefly dipping as low as $12 in 1998) through 2005. But as with almost no other energy source, major surprises are possible—a price spike up to that $30 level occurred in 1996, for example—and we must understand the risks.

In general terms, because of continued good supply and relatively low prices, the U.S. Energy Department forecasts that world oil consumption will grow roughly 1.5 percent per year, just slightly off the 1.6 percent growth rate between 1970 and 1990. (See figure 2.3.) Some experts have forecast prices in the range of $18 to $28 per barrel by 2005 to 2010, compared with $18 in 1992—hardly a stunning increase, even at the high end of the estimated range.[28] Referring to such forecasts, many U.S. and Western analysts have begun to treat oil as "just another commodity," in the words of one recent *Wall Street Journal* report. "In the interdependent, free-trade 1990s," the *Journal* noted, "the big oil exporters need big oil consumers just as much as consumers need them."[29]

FIGURE 2.3
World Oil Prices, 1970–2010

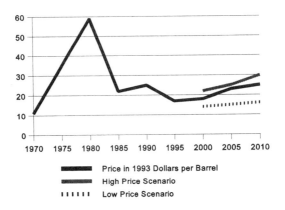

Source: U.S. Department of Energy, *International Energy Outlook 1995* (Washington, D.C.: U.S. Government Printing Office, 1995), p. 2.

Yet it may be too early to write off the threat of new oil shocks. For one thing, the next decade may represent the beginning of a reversal of the trend to more diverse suppliers. OPEC nations will account for most new oil production through 2010; early in the next century, the Middle East will account for half the world's daily oil supply. As of 1990, OPEC nations had 90 years' worth of proven reserves, while non-OPEC oil producers had just 17 years of reserves.[30]

Then, too, even if oil remains relatively cheap and its supply remains uninterrupted, the United States pays a significant economic price for its own imports—a substantially larger trade deficit. Already the U.S. trade deficit is $50-$70 billion larger each year because of oil imports, and the Department of Energy believes that this figure will rise to $100 billion or more as U.S. dependence on oil imports and the price of that oil both rise.

Two Energy Department officials recently summarized official forecasts. "Imagine a world in which the Persian Gulf controlled two thirds of the world's oil for export, with $200 billion a year in oil revenues streaming into that unstable and politically troubled region, and America was importing nearly 60 percent of its oil, resulting in a $100-billion-a-year outflow that undermines efforts to reduce our trade deficit. That's a scenario out of the 1970s which can never be repeated again, right? No, that's the 'reference case' projection for ten years from now from the federal Energy Information Administration."[31]

Rising oil demand in the fast-growing Asian emerging market nations provides another reason for worry. Recent estimates suggest that China's oil imports will grow from 600,000 barrels a day to 1 million by the year 2000 and 3 million by 2010; one oil company figures that China might be importing 7 million barrels a day by 2015—nearly as much as the United States does today, and half again as much as Japan's current imports. This pattern will be matched throughout the region: Between 1992 and 2010, oil imports in South Korea and Southeast Asian countries will rocket upward from a total of roughly 1 million barrels a day to over 5.[32] Asia's recent economic woes will alter these forecasts somewhat, but the general trend toward higher incomes—and greater oil use—is clear. If the per-capita oil consumption of China and India rose to the level of South Korea, for example, these two countries would together need 120 million barrels of oil a day, almost twice the total current world demand.[33]

One result of this accelerating oil demand will be an increasingly snug security nexus between Asia and the Middle East. By the year 2000, Asian nations will get close to 90 percent of their oil from the Middle East; by the year 2010, the dependence could hit 95 percent.[34] The strategic implications of this growing dependence could be both benign and dangerous. China and South Korea might insist more forcefully on the stability of the Middle East and put more weight behind the peace process—or they could fall into conflict over critical sea lanes through which oil supplies will pass and over areas in Asia where oil deposits are thought to reside.[35]

Beyond the dependencies of the next decade, by early in the twenty-first century the end of the world's "oil era" may finally be in sight. Many expert forecasts believe the world is approaching the peak production of recoverable oil, after which oil production would begin a long, slow decline to small levels. Royal Dutch Shell suggests that the peak will occur in 2030[36]; one estimate pegs it as early as 1998 to 2002, while most fall into the range from 2010 to 2025.[37] Again, these ideas are controversial—some analysts do not believe the world will come close to

SURPRISE SCENARIO:
ATTACKS ON MIDDLE EAST OIL SUPPLIES

Over the next decade, it is likely that the world's dependence on Middle East oil will increase. Mideast nations hold the majority of known oil reserves. The United States gets almost 20 percent of its oil from the region now; by 2000 the U.S. Department of Energy forecasts that something like 25 percent of U.S. oil will come from the Persian Gulf, and 30 percent by 2015.[38] European dependence on Mideast oil is currently at 30 percent, Japan's at 70 percent; and as we have seen, emerging-market nations in Asia will depend almost entirely on Mideast oil in the years ahead. Meanwhile, Persian Gulf states will remain equally dependent, with oil constituting 95 percent of their exports.

This scenario examines the potential ramifications of a military attack on Persian Gulf oil-fields that would halt production for a significant period of time—several weeks or more. The attack could be carried out with conventional arms, or with nuclear, chemical, or biological weapons, by predator states such as Iraq, by a major power, or even by terrorists. The attacker could choose simply to "close" the Strait of Hormuz—the narrow waterway at the mouth of the Persian Gulf through which millions of barrels of oil pass every day. But the oilfields themselves are certainly vulnerable. They are clustered in relatively contiguous bunches throughout the Gulf and would make inviting targets for a terrorist who managed to acquire three or four nuclear weapons. Quite obviously, the consequences of such attacks would be dire:

- *Severe damage to the world economy* as developed and developing economies alike felt the sudden energy pinch. The emerging-market nations of Asia would be devastated.
- *Intense international tension* as nations sought to punish the attacker and guarantee the security of future oil supplies. Territorial aggression, in the Middle East or Asia, would be possible—as would a cooperative global effort to weather the crisis.
- *The collapse of Gulf oil states* deprived for an extended period of time of the economic foundations of their rule—their oil wealth.
- *A sudden and dramatic boost to nonoil alternatives,* such as natural gas and renewable energy, so that even after the crisis oil need not return to its previous level of dominance in world energy use.

running out of oil during the lifetime of anyone reading this book. But a gradual move away from oil-based economics seems inevitable.

Energy statistics for the next decade betray two other important trends. One is the growing importance of natural gas. It generates little pollution compared to oil, and can be used for virtually any necessary energy application—even transportation, as evidenced by the clean-fuels taxicabs and post office trucks that dot the streets of America's big cities. Natural gas is very capital intensive to produce and transport, but many countries are plunging into the field nonetheless. Strategic concerns favor this fuel: Substantial reserves exist in many countries, so the world need not rely on a single vulnerable region for its supplies. Increasing natural gas use will help Russia and other former Soviet republics, which together sit atop 40 percent of known world reserves. Overall, the U.S. Department of Energy expects worldwide natural gas consumption to grow by nearly 50 percent from 1990 to 2010.[39]

Second, this period eventually may be seen as the beginning—the real beginning, after decades of fits and starts—of the age of renewable energy. Even cautious forecasts suggest that renewables will be the fastest-growing energy sources over the next decade, moving ahead globally at 2.3 percent per year—2.1 percent in the developed world and an impressive 3.3 percent annually in developing countries.[40] And these projections do not assume any technological advances that could render more widely usable renewable energy sources (such as photovoltaic cells) cost-competitive with traditional energy sources. Even without such an advance, the U.S. Energy Department forecasts that by 2010 renewable energy will attain only a 10 percent share of the energy consumption of OECD countries and about 7 percent in developing nations (for a world average of almost 9 percent).[41] And another decisive technological breakthrough may be around the corner, one that would shift energy consumption from fossil fuels into electricity: the development of inexpensive electric or hybrid-electric cars. (See the Surprise Scenario.)

To be sure, this trend will only be beginning in the next decade. The year 2005 or even 2010 will not inaugurate the "renewable energy era"; continued low oil prices, for example, will dampen the need for electric cars. But I believe that the next decade will witness the first not yet decisive convergence of the two factors that *will* eventually bring renewable energy to the fore: the advance of

ISSUE FEATURE: NUCLEAR POWER

Since the 1960s, when the first commercial nuclear power units entered service, through 1985, nuclear energy grew rapidly as a share of world energy. In 1970 nuclear plants generated 3 percent of electricity in countries with nuclear programs; by 1985 that figure had reached 25 percent. Since that time, however, nuclear energy's contribution has leveled off, and most projections see little growth in the next decade.

Fear of nuclear accidents, concerns and costs associated with the disposal of nuclear waste, and lower electricity costs attendant to power-sector deregulation have conspired to reduce nuclear energy's attractiveness in recent years. The U.S. Department of Energy expects world nuclear energy capacity to grow only 0.2 to 1 percent a year over the next decade.

As of 1993, 70 percent of world nuclear energy capacity resided in a handful of countries: the United States, France, Germany, Russia, Ukraine, and Japan. What growth in nuclear power occurs over the next decade will take place largely in Japan and developing nations in Asia such as South Korea, India, and Taiwan.

renewable energy technologies and the decline of fossil fuels as they become both more expensive and less environmentally acceptable.

The critical question is whether this transition occurs in time to avoid dramatic cost increases as world oil reserves are exhausted. This will not be answered in the next decade, but its eventual answer may be *determined* during the next ten years, by how far work on renewable energy progresses.

As technology and politics whipsaw the fate of oil back and forth, international markets will be watching closely—and reacting quickly. The reality of a knowledge economy acting on ideas and perception will be as true for oil as with anything else. "Perhaps the most dramatic change in international oil," notes the *Wall Street Journal,* "has been the emergence of a sophisticated crude futures market." Traders watch trends on a day-by-day basis and adjust oil prices accordingly.[42] This process has benefits, but it also carries risks; in the highly unstable oil market of the next decade, oil prices could fluctuate wildly and rapidly, sparked by alternating forces of glut and shortage.

SURPRISE SCENARIO:
HYBRID ELECTRIC CARS AND SCOOTERS

The emergence of a new breed of electric or hybrid gas-electric automobiles (as well as buses, trucks, motorized scooters and rickshaws) would revolutionize the energy picture in developed or developing nations. With a new Honda vehicle, the General Motors EV-1 and the Toyota RAV4-EV on the market now, this transition might hit sooner than some assume.[43]

In theory, the entire U.S. automobile fleet could shift to electric cars in roughly two decades, the time it takes for 99 percent of the fleet to turn over. That is beyond our time frame, and it is too optimistic in any case. Current estimates foresee only about 5,000 electric cars on U.S. roads by the year 2000. Still, electric-drive vehicles will inevitably replace gas-powered ones; the question is when and how.[44]

> A broad shift to hybrid electrics would be "the biggest change in industrial structure since the microchip."
> —Amory Lovins and Hunter Lovins

For this surprise scenario, I posited the emergence of lightweight "hybrid electric cars" that use gasoline to generate electricity and flywheels to store kinetic energy. Business strategist James Moore argues that the hybrid-electric car "appears to pass the value test" and says cascading change could quickly "undermine the current auto ecosystems."[45] An equally profound development would be the emergence of electric scooters in developing nations; gas-powered versions are terrible polluters, and tens of millions will be built in emerging markets over the next decade.[46] A major shift in the direction of electric-drive vehicles would have stunning implications.[47]

- *Reduced pollution,* especially in urban areas and developing nations, although this depends on the type of vehicles used and where their electricity comes from.
- Help render developed countries *less dependent on imported oil.*
- *Lead to a shift in manufacturing techniques* from steel to composite materials.
- *Have profound impacts on the global balance of power* depending on who mastered the new technology first. Auto manufacturing is the world's chief industry, and a new generation of big automakers could emerge in the developing world."[48]

As a result, the next decade should witness a series of recurring oil price spikes, a phenomenon that soon will be so well established that it might be possible to begin speaking of a price spike resource economy. Recent years have seen a number of sudden jumps in the price of oil— 17 percent in the spring of 1996, with crude oil rising to $30 a barrel by the end of that year. Natural gas sustained a short-lived but similar spike in 1996. Small inventories due to just-in-time delivery tactics, rising demand pushing the envelope of supply levels, and the emergence of a much more sensitive oil futures market are combining to make price spikes, in the words of a recent *Business Week* story, "regular events" occurring "often" and with "little warning." The implications are serious: higher home heating oil prices, for example (almost $100 in higher bills per home in the northeastern United States for the 1996-1997 winter); increasing transportation costs; and lower airline profits—$600 million less than they would have been in 1996 without the surge in fuel prices.[49]

A Foundation of
Human Perception: Culture

A final foundation of the next decade's trends is culture—that amorphous combination of values, habits, religion, language, and other factors that differentiates one people from another. Culture has been much in the news lately, its profile raised by political scientist Samuel Huntington's somewhat exaggerated thesis of a coming "clash of civilizations" and the arguments of people like Lawrence Harrison and political theorist Francis Fukuyama that culture is a major, and often decisive, determinant of individual and collective success.

Some readers will wonder at the inclusion of culture alongside such apparently quantifiable trends as energy and the environment. But if one is searching for the foundational issues on which the engines of history fashion their trends, culture must certainly rank among them: Culture plays an important role in shaping the everyday thoughts, beliefs, commitments, and decisions of all human beings. Some cultures will equip their people for success over the next decade better than others. Culture therefore ranks as a critical tectonic plate of history, no less so than resource supplies or the condition of the environment.

Many recent writers have pointed to the connections between culture and history. Lawrence Harrison, a former U.S. Agency for International Development official, argues that it is "values and attitudes—culture—that differentiate ethnic groups and are mainly responsible for such phenomena as Latin America's persistent instability and inequity, Taiwan's and Korea's economic 'miracles,' and the achievements of the Japanese."[1] Author Thomas Sowell suggests along the same lines that "Racial, ethnic, and cultural differences among peoples play a major role in the events of our times," because "a particular people usually has its own particular set of skills for dealing with the economic and social necessities of life."[2] Both authors advance dozens of brief case studies in an effort to support their overall thesis. Harrison contends, for example, that "[C]ooperatives don't work well in Thailand because Thais don't trust one another, and they know how to relate to one another only in a hierarchical way."[3] Sowell argues that "A disdain for commerce and industry has . . . been common for centuries among the Hispanic elite, both in Spain and in Latin America."[4]

Cultural analysis like this remains controversial. Some critics worry that it will lead to cultural determinism, even racism, judging people solely by their culture. It could also be used to dismiss the prospects for some developing nations because of their citizens' race. Yet in its basic sense, the application of culture to the trends examined here merely involves appreciating the basic insight of sociology: that, as phrased by Peter Berger in his classic *Invitation to Sociology,* people are not "also" social beings but are "social in every aspect of [their] being that is open to empirical investigation." Our specific society (and culture) "not only controls our movements, but shapes our identity, our thought and our emotions. The structures of society become the structures of our own consciousness."[5]

This basic connection between national culture and national success is a venerable idea. As we shall see, some cultures may be better equipped than others to succeed in the fast-paced, decentralized, flexible world of a knowledge era. After all, if we are to speak—as I will in Trend Three and thereafter—of a "human resources economy," we must understand the factors that influence the character of those resources, and culture is perhaps chief among such influences in its importance. Culture will therefore serve as a kind of prism for the knowledge era, shifting and refocusing its effects.

Culture also has profound effects on relations among countries and other large groups or institutions. Culture can affect economic relations between countries, such as trade agreements. It can foster misunderstandings in negotiations between countries or companies that, for cultural reasons, simply do not comprehend one another. And undoubtedly the most provocative and ambitious theory of culture and international relations to emerge in the last decade is Samuel Huntington's notion of the coming "clash of civilizations." Huntington predicts that the bipolar cold war is giving way to a multilateral competition among cultures and that the primary conflicts in the global system "will occur between nations and groups of different civilizations. The clash of civilizations will dominate global politics."[6] Huntington's notion, as we shall see, is exaggerated, but he points to a real phenomenon: the collision of global and local identities in the years to come. Trend Four takes this issue up in more detail.

In dozens of ways, therefore—social, economic, political, military—culture will exercise an important influence on the history of the next decade. Trends that might otherwise run in one direction might be bent or skewed by cultural institutions, practices, or preconceptions. But one thing cultural identity is *not* is static, exercising a predictable, unchanging influence on the members of its societies. In the fast-moving knowledge era, the engines of history to be outlined in Trend Two are reshaping world cultures more profoundly than at any time in human history—with results that are both hopeful and perilous.

A ROSTER OF CHALLENGES

In this section I've tried to review the issues that will be constants over the next decade. These processes will not change substantially or cause dramatic new changes in other challenges. They will provide the foundational basis for subsequent trends. And in most cases, I find transitional challenges that call for leapfrog strategies. In general terms, this section has argued that we should expect no great disruptions over the next decade in the areas of resources (including energy and materials), the environment, or culture.

Despite this relatively optimistic prognosis, the world will face long-term challenges that impose transitional requirements, such as the eventual decline of oil supplies. The strategies designed to deal with such transitions should begin to take shape over the next decade—yet the impetus to put them into place may be low, given the lack of major disruptions. The result is a clear requirement for long-term thinking with policy responses to match, guided by visionary leadership. Because

POLICY RECOMMENDATIONS: *TREND ONE*

1. *Inaugurate a major new worldwide program of research and development for renewable energy.* New and more economical renewable energy sources offer benefits in a host of areas: preparing for the decline of oil and natural gas; increasing U.S. and allied energy independence; and helping developing nations achieve rapid growth without destroying the environment.
2. *Continue and expand research in agriculture,* including biotechnology, to ensure that the required increases in yield over the next decade indeed occur.
3. Substantially increase the *investments in heading off disaster in the arc of crisis*—not merely short-term food aid, but long-term strategies for sustainability, including improved agricultural techniques and renewable energy sources.
4. Prepare for the failure of those efforts by working to develop a *standing international humanitarian disaster response unit* that combines civilian relief, police, and military functions.
5. Pursue *pension reform, savings enhancement, and debt reduction* to avoid capital crunches and budgetary crises when developed-world retired populations balloon.

government responses are becoming more and more anachronistic to the enormous speed and energy of the knowledge era, the required leadership will have to come from an unprecedented array of social actors, a theme I discuss in Trend Five.

This section also has argued that the next decade is likely to witness the continued emergence of an arc of instability running from Africa up into Libya, across North Africa into the Middle East, and along to the Indian subcontinent. Rapid population growth, water and food shortages, infectious disease, and cultural conflicts are all more severe in these areas than almost anywhere else on Earth, and the areas almost certainly will be the scene of major violence and instability. Again, long-term strategies are required now to begin heading off these possible outcomes—especially because the zone of instability has an unhappy degree of overlap with the nations three analysts recently nominated as "pivotal states" for U.S. strategy and national interests, states including Mexico, Brazil, Algeria, Egypt, South Africa, Turkey, India, Pakistan, and Indonesia.[7]

The policy recommendations box summarizes what emerges from this analysis—an imposing agenda, but no more imposing than the challenges we face on the cusp of a new millennium in each of the issue areas examined in this trend. And these, remember, are the *constants* of the next decade—the issues in which I expect the least change. Beginning with Trend Two, I'll trace the forces for transformation of the knowledge era—and the even more difficult responsibilities they hold for us.

The Engines of History

Being great implies flowing ever onward,
Flowing ever onward implies far-reaching,
Far-reaching implies reversal.

Tao Te Ching

In Trend One, I examined issues and processes that should remain relatively constant over the next decade. In this trend I turn my attention to the forces that will produce global change—the "engines of history" that are authoring the knowledge era. This trend reviews five of them— science and technology, socioeconomic processes, human needs and aspirations, social construction and evolutionary learning, and complexity—and then outlines the directions in which they are taking us. One of its major themes is that areas of instability will be concentrated in places where these inexorable motors of change collide with inflexible governments and other social institutions. Authoritarian societies, closed markets, and unreformed corporations face a precarious decade in which the engines of history will destabilize and transform them in dramatic ways.

4

The Engines:
Science and Technology

The advent of the scientific method has had a profound and stunning effect on human consciousness, an effect with which we are still coming to grips, and science is the fuel for all the engines driving knowledge-era history. "The truly revolutionary force in modern times has been science," the physicist Gregory Benford has argued, "far more than 'radical' politics or the like. This seems likely to be even more true in the future."[1] In this chapter, I focus on three specific categories of technology: biotechnology, renewable energy, and information technology. My goal is just to give a suggestive hint of the kinds of technological advances we can expect during the next decade, a subject treated in great detail by dozens of other books.

BIOTECHNOLOGY

February of 1997 brought news that stunned the scientific world. Biologists in Scotland announced that they had achieved what had until then been regarded as a near impossibility: They had cloned adult mammals, in this case sheep. The goal of the project was the creation of herds of animals genetically engineered to produce human medicines and organs and to provide test beds for medicines aimed at human genetic abnormalities.[2] The announcement of sheep cloning was just the most recent watershed in a field whose exploding research and potential will transform the human environment over the next decade: biotechnology.

Biotechnology involves the use and manipulation of biological agents to create new goods and services or modify existing ones. One key application is in the area of human health: The foundational endeavor of biomedical research today is gene mapping, and the most extensive gene-mapping endeavor under way is the Human Genome Project, which is on schedule to locate and functionally plot all the important genes in the human genome by about 2003. Scientists believe that its digital version would consume about 750 megabytes of space, which means, incredibly, that one laptop computer will be able to store the entire human genetic code. The result of this work, which will only begin to become apparent in the next ten years, "promises to be an explosion of new knowledge and power that will sever us from our human heritage and transform us in ways that we cannot yet imagine."[3]

Genetic mapping is designed in part to support genetic engineering—manipulation of genes once they have been mapped and their purposes better understood. Recombinant DNA technology has advanced efforts to understand the genetic basis of Alzheimer's disease, amyotrophic lateral sclerosis, and other illnesses, including AIDS, multiple sclerosis, Huntington's and Parkinson's diseases, sickle-cell anemia, breast and ovarian as well as prostate cancers, and hepatitis. Fifteen million Americans suffer from one or more birth defects; 80 percent of those defects have genetic causes; and more than 3,000 diseases, from Alzheimer's to hay fever, hepatitis, dermatitis, and testicular cancer, have genetic bases. Gene therapy works by introducing a fully functional and expressible gene into a target cell to correct an abnormality or dysfunction in that cell.

In other examples, transgenetic pigs have been engineered to manufacture two important human shield proteins, which may allow their organs to be transplanted into humans—a major motivation for the cloning research just described. Tests to implant the pig-generated organs in primates began in 1995.[4] Scientists have also linked a gene to some cases of hereditary breast and ovarian cancer as well as to incidences of nonhereditary ovarian tumors and breast cancers. One recent *Wired* magazine poll of experts predicted that "encouraging results from studies at cancer research institutes . . . suggest that after extensive refinement, an effective gene therapy for cancer will be available in 2000."[5] Many researchers probably would consider this forecast to be too optimistic—it is, after all, just a few months after the publication of this book—but it gives a sense of the rapid progress occurring in the field.

The first artificial human chromosome was created in 1997 and that progress all but exploded in 1998 with a host of new developments. Scientists announced in late 1998 that they had managed to encourage cells from human embryos—"stem cells" that can develop into any kind of specific human cell—to grow, and more than that, to grow into specialized heart, nerve, blood, and other kinds of cells. This development raises the hope of eventually injecting "new" nerve cells to heal the brains of victims of stroke, Parkinson's, or Alzheimer's disease as well as conducting a host of other genetic therapies. In December 1998 Japanese scientists revealed that they had successfully cloned cows, the third animal species (after mice and sheep) to be genetically duplicated; later, a South Korean scientist shocked the world with the claim—disputed by many scientists reviewing his work—that he had taken important steps toward cloning a human being.

Perhaps most disturbingly, the long-tenuous distinction between using healthy genes to heal sick patients and genetically altering human beings to prevent disease in advance began to waver. More and more scientists talked of altering fertilized eggs to change the basic genetic blueprint of a human being and help forestall cancer or diseases with heavy genetic components. Some even referred to fantastical notions like gene therapies inserted at birth that could be "switched on" with a drug later in life to preserve individual choice about whether to accept genetic therapy.

Another major application of biotechnology in the next five years will be genetically engineered food. Calgene, Inc., introduced in May 1994 one of the most exciting food products in history with its Flavr Savr tomato, a tomato genetically engineered so that it does not soften and rot in the journey from the vine to the market. Scientists used genetic manipulation to suppress the tomato's production of the enzyme responsible for rotting.[6] The Food and Drug Administration (FDA) has approved seven more vegetables, among them a potato that produces its own pesticide and a yellow crookneck squash with a built-in resistance to particular viruses, but it expects only 100 to 150

new products to be introduced in the next five years.[7] A recent poll of
experts by *Wired* magazine identified the year 2004 as a likely date by
which most produce sold in the United States will be genetically
engineered in the manner of the Flavr Savr.[8] Even more important
from a global food standpoint, genetic engineering also improves on
traditional efforts to optimize agricultural production: Some plants
are being engineered to be resistant to pests, with the goal of
maximizing yield and reducing pesticide use.

Biotechnology is not, of course, some magic wand that will wave
away disease, hunger, and environmental degradation. For one thing, its
turnover time is fairly long compared to the pace of information
technology, in part because of both the nature of the research and the
regulatory scheme surrounding it—and in part because of the profound
ethical questions that attend this field of science, questions that rank
among the most important and powerful ethical issues of the next ten
years. Our ability to make reasoned moral choices about our actions will
be tested as never before, because we will gain unprecedented control
over the natural environment.

Take perhaps the simplest issue: genetic testing. It is not too
long—perhaps within our ten-year time frame—before newborn
babies could come home from the hospital with a floppy disk or CD-
ROM full of their future medical history, based on genetic screening
conducted during pregnancy and after birth. What we do with those
disks will be one of the most wrenching ethical questions humanity
has ever faced. Would Americans want to be able to pull up their risk
for alcoholism, or heart disease, or Alzheimer's disease, on their
computer? Would they want their insurance company to be able to do
so? Such information will render today's risk-sharing practices in
insurance meaningless: Legislation before Congress to prevent insurance companies from rejecting applicants based on "preexisting
conditions" is only the tip of the iceberg in an era when a majority of
serious illness may someday be defined that way.

Even tougher moral challenges await us as biotechnology pushes
beyond testing into engineering and, eventually, creation—the ability
to "make" new life-forms by altering their genetic blueprint. The
situation might be simpler, author Charles Platt explained in *Wired*
magazine, "if there were some kind of normal baseline for human

beings, with defects lying below this level and enhancements above it. But life is not simple." Children with a genetic predisposition to obesity, he notes, are likely to die earlier than others (as well as suffering psychological burdens); "does this mean obesity is a disease that can be corrected in the germ cells, or would that be a form of enhancement? Poor eyesight may be a liability if a child wants to be an airline pilot; should *this* be erased from the germline?"[9] The potential for moral dilemma is obvious. What legal standard, for example, would both prevent the modification of fetuses and allow (as is now generally the case) their destruction in the form of abortion? Everyone knows, Gregory Benford writes, "that good looking people do well. What parent could resist the argument that [through genetic engineering] they were giving their child a powerful leg up (maybe literally) in a brave new competitive world?"[10]

Even today, "stem" cells from live human embryos, created through in vitro fertilization and for some reason not implanted in a potential mother, are used for genetic research. For those who believe that human life begins at conception, science has already begun experimenting on live human beings.

Biotechnology's advance also threatens to transform warfare into a nightmarish exchange of genetically engineered weapons—deadly biological agents released into an enemy's army or home front to wreak devastation on its people. Biological warfare and terrorism are already a reality, but new developments could produce toxins that are both more virulent and more resistant to exposure and thus longer-lived. Given the enormous investment required to build nuclear weapons and the advances of biotechnology, biological weapons may become the "poor country's nuke" of the future—the means developing states will choose to negate the conventional military advantages of the developed world.

All of this—the intense moral challenge posed by biotechnology, the risk of social stratification to which it contributes, and the dangerous new arenas of violence it spawns—again maximize the importance of a deepened and strengthened set of social values. The operative word is *responsibility:* responsibility in the use of biotechnology to test and alter humans and the natural world, responsibility in the control of biological weapons, and responsibility in monitoring the social implications of these new technologies.

RENEWABLE ENERGY

Every economy runs on energy, which must be derived from something. Traditional sources of energy used by early human economies—wood, later coal, eventually oil and natural gas—are nonrenewable; they will run out. Developing renewable sources of energy is therefore critical to avoiding a major economic crisis as well-known sources of fuel and electricity run dry.

Thankfully, a host of recent technological breakthroughs is making a reasonably smooth transition to a "renewable future" more likely than ever. In a span of between 50 and 100 years, oil became "the dominant fuel in a globe-spanning internal-combustion-based economic order," author Gregg Easterbrook reminds us, and "the transition to renewable energy future may happen as swiftly and emphatically."[11] This transition will be eased because these renewables produce electricity, and the percentage of U.S. energy demand composed of electrical power has grown steadily from 19 percent in 1960 to 36 percent in 1990 and a projected 40 percent in 2010.[12]

The impact of renewable energy sources over the next decade, as opposed to the next 50 or 100 years, will be limited. During that period, supplies of most major fossil fuels should remain plentiful, forestalling a major shift in the direction of renewables. As figure 4.1 suggests, even by the year 2010 renewables worldwide will comprise only about 9 percent of global energy consumption. But it is worthwhile to highlight this area of technology for three reasons: first, its eventual emergence as the world's dominant energy source is all but inevitable; second, the next decade will represent the true beginning (but only the beginning) of this process; and third, renewables are now close enough to being cost competitive that one major surprise—a sudden technological break-through to improve the efficiency of solar collectors, for example, or a geopolitical event that dramatically increases the cost of fossil fuels—could push them to the forefront of worldwide energy policy. Ultimately, a "renewable energy economy" will end up looking a lot more diverse than the common image of a "solar future": True renewables will combine with cleaner fossil-fuel alternatives such as natural gas, odd new renewable technologies such as biomass fuels and hydrogen-powered fuel cells, and a host of other sources of energy we cannot even conceive of today, perhaps even including nuclear fusion.

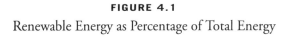

FIGURE 4.1

Renewable Energy as Percentage of Total Energy

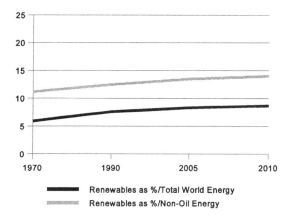

Source: U.S. Energy Information Administration, *International Energy Outlook 1995* (Washington, D.C.: U.S. Department of Energy, 1995), pp. 5, 79.

Nonetheless, in many ways solar power remains the "poster child" of the renewable revolution—and for good reason. The sun bombards Earth every year with 15,000 times as much energy as humans consume—13,000 times as much energy as is produced by burning fossil fuels and ten times as much as all the known reserves of coal, oil, natural gas, and uranium combined. The trick is to capture this energy efficiently. Photovoltaics have passed this hurdle: They have converted sunlight into electricity with efficiencies up to 30 percent. At that rate, the United States could meet its entire energy demand by using less than 2 percent of its land area (roughly equivalent to the size of Rhode Island—which seems like a lot but is actually no bigger than the amount of land area now used for mining) for solar collectors.[13]

The trouble has been building cells that can do this job without being enormously costly. But as the costs of other, diminishing energy forms go up, and as new solar technologies emerge, this gap will close. The cost of solar power dropped 65 percent in the past decade, and one estimate suggests that toward the end of the next decade, the cost of energy generated by photovoltaic cells—at roughly 40 cents per kilowatt-hour today—will drop to 10 cents per kilowatt-hour, competitive with many other forms of energy. Using federal tax subsidies to further reduce the cost to consumers, Enron and Amoco (which owns the photovoltaic cell maker Solarex, and has since merged with British Petroleum) are building a 100-megawatt solar plant in Nevada, whose energy initially will sell for 5.5 cents a kilowatt-hour—3 cents *cheaper* than electricity from coal, oil, or gas.[14]

If cost competitiveness is the race for renewables, then wind power is well in the lead. Wind contains enormous amounts of energy; one estimate suggests that the brisk breezes flowing above North and South Dakota alone could provide 80 percent of U.S. electricity needs.[15] With highly advanced technologies helped along by advances in the aircraft field (such things as lightweight yet strong materials and efficient propellers), the wind industry has made dramatic gains and is already among the cheapest forms of electrical generation in suitable areas.[16] Current wind power technologies aim at an energy production target of 5 cents per kilowatt-hour, a level already reached in some areas. By 2005 that figure might drop below 4 or even 3 cents per kilowatt-hour. California and Denmark alone boast more than 17,000 wind turbines, and California generates up to 8 percent of its baseline electricity from this relatively novel technology. By the middle of the next century, wind farms might produce as much as 20 percent of world electrical power;[17] this would mean that, in less than 15 years, one-quarter of U.S. electricity would be generated by zero-pollution, renewable energy sources.[18]

In a compelling 1999 *Foreign Affairs* essay, Senator Richard Lugar (R-Ind.) and former CIA Director James Woolsey made the case for yet another category of renewables: ethanol. Genetically engineered biocatalysts—enzymes, yeasts, and bacteria—will soon make it possible, they contend, to use any form of plant or plant product, including agricultural waste and cheap switch grass, to make ethanol. Even now, with inexpensive tweaks to their engines, vehicles can burn fuel with up to 85 percent ethanol. Much remains to be done—further scientific breakthroughs on the needed biocatalysts, for one thing—but Lugar and Woolsey say it's not hard to imagine the complete replacement of gasoline with ethanol in our lifetimes. The results would be astonishing: a shift in fuel wealth from oil-producing countries to farmers around the world and a dramatic reduction in greenhouse gas emissions, among others.[19]

ISSUE FEATURE: FUEL CELLS

Arguably the most important emerging renewable energy technology are fuel cells. These enchanting machines use hydrogen as fuel, electrochemically reacting it with oxygen to produce electricity. In its pure form, the fuel cell's only output is water—no carbon monoxide, no nitrogen, no greenhouse gases.[20] And the fuel cell's potential impact is so vast that some commentators have begun to speak of the rise of a Hydrogen Age.

In commercial power generation, fuel cells will offer localized, renewable power sources. A new company in China or India needing power could buy its own fuel cell rather than hooking into the local grid. Ultimately, this process may "lead to the emergence," as *The Economist* notes, "of hundreds of power-service companies, supplying local, tailor-made electricity rather than bulk utility-style power," one example of the pluralism of the knowledge era to be discussed in Trend Four. It could help provide the kind of renewable (and eventually, cheap) power needed to make desalination a reality.

> "Power plants are going to be just like furnaces. They're going to be appliances."
> —Joe Maceda

But it is in cars, trucks, buses, and other vehicles that fuel cells might make their biggest impact, displacing the gasoline-powered internal combustion engine and inaugurating a new era of low- or zero-pollution transportation. Many engines in development are hybrid ones, using methane to produce hydrogen (and thereby generating some greenhouse gases); Chrysler is developing a cell that would extract hydrogen from conventional gasoline. Even before its merger with Chrysler, Daimler-Benz was perhaps the farthest ahead—it bought a 25 percent share of the top fuel cell company, Ballard; it was developing a commercial fuel cell bus; it planned a fuel-cell-powered Mercedes in 2003; and by 2005 it expected to build 100,000 fuel cells a year.

Writer Jacques Leslie sums up the potential impact of fuel cells, saying that it's hard to overstate the implications of the new technology. "A drastic decline in air pollution, oil spills, acid rain, and greenhouse-gas emissions. An epochal geopolitical shift as global reliance on Middle East oil comes to an end and international trade balance are realigned. The emergence of quiet, decentralized electric plants sized according to need. . . . The disappearance of the electric grid is a possibility." All of this will be under way by 2010.

INFORMATION TECHNOLOGY

The most visible area of change within science and technology in the last few decades is that of information technology, and the next decade will witness dramatic new advances in this field—far more practical innovations than in the other two areas of technology.

In the next few years, massive supercomputers of astounding power will be coming into service, partly as a result of the U.S. Department of Energy's $940 million Accelerated Strategic Computing Initiative (ASCI). In December 1996, for example, Intel Corporation inaugurated a $46 million machine at Sandia National Laboratory, the first computer capable of calculation at 1 "teraflops"—a trillion calculations a second. By 1998 ASCI aims to produce a 3-teraflops computer; by 2001, a 10-teraflops machine; by 2002 or 2003, 100 teraflops; and by 2005, a computer capable of 500 trillion calculations per second.

Several other developments promise to revolutionize the information technology field once again. Together they will help create a "Pervasive Knowledge Network": anytime/anywhere access to voice or video communications, Internet or networked computer access, and entertainment. One such trend is the marriage of televisions, computers, and telephones, a phenomenon that will do more to formalize the knowledge era than any other single technological leap. More and more, information channels that we have come to think of as separate and distinct will merge, creating powerful and pervasive new networks of knowledge and entertainment.[21]

This revolution is just around the corner, and once it hits, it will revolutionize the nature of multimedia knowledge manipulation. Customers could sit at home watching a home shopping network, check the Internet for better prices and reliability reports, send e-mail to a friend who bought the product, and order it—all on the same screen, with the same keyboard. Education will never be the same once lectures, multimedia presentations, and data can be broadcast through a single video screen. The emergence of such technologies have put television on a collision course with the personal computer, with companies "on both sides of the fence . . . jumping into the convergence game."[22]

The infrastructure for a Pervasive Knowledge Network will be provided in part by the proliferation of new global satellite networks. A number of major computer and telecommunications giants are pouring

$50 billion into the hardware and software of these new networks, a process that *Business Week* recently described as "a high-stakes, space-age equivalent of the California Gold Rush." In the next decade alone, these ventures will throw 1,700 new communications satellites—more than ten times the number that currently orbit Earth—into space. Applications include satellite television (perhaps 30 million customers worldwide by 2002); high-end cellular phones with worldwide access, a projected market of 7 million customers and $7 billion in revenues by 2005; cheap wireless phones for underserved areas of China, India and Russia; and global, cheap, and superfast Internet access via satellite.[23]

Several other categories of technology, most of them supportive in some way of the Pervasive Knowledge Network, will gain tremendous ground in the next decade. One is miniaturization—the emergence of nanotechnology, partly in the form of "microelectromechanical systems" (MEMS), tiny machines with sensors, electronic brains, and motors all on a chip-sized piece of silicon. Nanotechnology will revolutionize manufacturing, medicine, and a host of other fields. One example is radios built on a single computer chip that could do the same job as the $500 wireless communications cards now installed in many communication devices today, at a fraction of the price. One researcher has suggested that these amazing machines could hit the market within five years.[24]

The really astonishing application of nanotechnology is in manufacturing, where assembly MEMS could build electronic components or other products molecule by molecule, with unimaginable flexibility, precision, and speed. Ultimately, this might mean ordering a toy online and watching it appear, as if by magic, on the MEM assembly pad next to your computer; building a car so precisely that you could fashion a 100-pound Cadillac as tough as today's cars; making solar cells at a fraction of today's costs; or building supercomputers the size of a sugar cube. Don't get too excited; these kinds of nanotechnology applications probably won't emerge for several decades.[25] But we will see the first strong hints of the revolution in miniaturization by 2010.

Inventions like radio MEMS will help spur a related technological trend—the shift to wireless communications. Wireless networks can handle more and more data: today, the best wireless systems are about equal to the high-speed ISDN lines installed in many businesses or homes; one estimate suggests that, within a few years, new wireless systems will have 40 times the transmission rates of today's fastest land lines. It's no surprise that the percentage of people using cellular phones is growing fast—up to 40 percent in Finland, 23 percent (and growing 70 percent a year) in Japan, 20 percent in America; and estimates are that half of all Europeans will carry them by 2005.[26]

Tiny chips capable of wireless communications will join with miniature video transmitters to make possible another revolution—a thoroughly sensing environment. "Cars could recognize when the front-seat passenger is a child and adjust air-bag deployment accordingly. Airplanes could have an army of chips standing watch over mechanical systems. . . . And heart surgeons could leave tiny silicon eyes in a patient's chest" to keep track of postoperative health.[27] Other applications include videophones, visually based security systems, rear- and side-viewing cameras in cars, and the end of film-based cameras.

"Virtual reality" also will begin to come into its own over the next decade—in such applications as telemedicine networks, which link distant medical facilities to a central medical center through computers, cameras, and video monitors and allow doctors to examine patients remotely as intimately as they otherwise would.[28] Virtual reality equipment has been used to treat abused children, people who fear heights, and patients who suffer from muscular dystrophy.

The overriding result of these intersecting developments in information technology will be the pervasive and instant access to information. Our current levels of access to the Internet and to entertainment options on cable or via satellite represent just the first hints of what will become a much more profound trend, completely transforming the context for a dozen social activities and institutions—from education to publishing to all forms of electronically delivered services to manufacturing to politics. The ramifications of the Pervasive Knowledge Network run out in a dozen directions: the tendency to undermine social authorities (examined in Trend Five); the requirement for new models of business management (Trends Three and Five); the growing danger of psychological overload for the citizens of our pervasively networked knowledge society (which I'll take up in Trend Six). All of which is to say that the advent of a society awash in information means more than scrolling the Internet for a cheap plane ticket.

The Engines:
Social and Psychological

The next decade's changes also will be propelled by a number of social and psychological engines that will transform the character of governments and societies around the world. These include socioeconomic modernization, human needs, and social construction.

SOCIOECONOMIC MODERNIZATION

A second engine of history, and a direct product of technological advance, is a slow progression—and a gradual, never-complete homogenization—of social and economic structures that arises in response to the demands of technology and the industries it spawns. The organizational requirements of modern societies, combined with the rationalistic decision-making procedures fostered by a scientific age, gradually push human societies down a historical funnel with a single, though differentiated, end point. It is no accident, then, that most modern societies look alike in their institutions and some of their customs. They are the products of the same historical engines.

Francis Fukuyama, writing in *The End of History and the Last Man,* proposes a two-part process of historical evolution. The first half of his theory has to do with the implications of what he terms "modern natural science," the world outlook and process created by technology. "The unfolding of modern natural science," Fukuyama writes, "has had a uniform effect on all societies that have experienced it," partly because it "establishes a uniform horizon of economic production possibilities." This process "guarantees an increasing homogenization of all human societies, regardless of their historical origins or cultural inheritances."[1] Fukuyama has merely offered the newest take on an old—and increasingly unquestionable—hypothesis: the "modernization" thesis that technological and economic advance draw countries through a fairly common set of developmental stages to a fairly homogenous end point.

Progress always has it doubters and victims; virtually no human advance has occurred without second thoughts. And we are surrounded today by people who hold such doubts about the knowledge era: people confused by its technology; workers whose careers are imperiled by its effects on the economy; members of communities or ethnic groups who see in the new era's globalism and increasing homogeneity a threat to their way of life. It is no surprise that radical socioeconomic change tends to foster instability and to produce cruel reactionary movements. History is not simply linear but *dialectical,* moving through a cycle of action, reaction, and finally a higher synthesis.

The writings of the grandfather of sociocultural studies, Arnold Toynbee, constitute perhaps the most famous—and ambitious—example of a dialectical and yet still progressive philosophy of history. Toynbee saw history as the rise and fall of civilizations.[2] But within this process he detected a powerful unifying and homogenizing trend whose roots lay in technological and economic forces. Toynbee wrote of the "uniformity which these separate civilizations display in their cultural character and their social structure," a uniformity produced by 4,000 years of parallel development culminating in the industrial age. The "most obvious ingredient" in this process "is technology," which encourages and demands similar socioeconomic institutions.[3] The result is some degree of cultural convergence among the advanced nations of the world. Over time, they tend to look, think, and act more and more alike, while preserving a healthy degree of cultural difference.

Toynbee summed up this process in a time line of history. Soon we would appreciate that "the great event of the twentieth century was the impact of Western civilization upon all the other living societies of the world of that day." A thousand years later Western civilization "may have been transformed, almost out of all recognition, by a counter-radiation of influences" from the rest of the world. And by the fourth millennium A.D. "the distinction—which looms large today—between the Western civilization" and other cultures "will probably seem unimportant. . . . [W]hat will stand out will be a single, great experience, common to all mankind": the experience of the congruence of cultures.[4]

Dozens of commentators have examined the emerging phenomenon of a relatively homogenous globalism or process of modernization, which we examine in more detail in Trend Four. Vaclav Havel has spoken of an "amalgamation of cultures"[5]; the Arabist Fouad Ajami agrees that "The things and ways that the West took to 'the rest' . . . have become the ways of the world. The secular idea, the state system and the balance of power, pop culture jumping tariff walls and barriers, the state as an instrument of welfare, all these have been internalized in the remotest places."[6] Toynbee's first phase—the spread of the Western idea—seems to be well under way.

As might be expected, this global convergence of values and beliefs is most apparent among the young. A recent survey of 25,000 middle-class teenagers around the world by the BrainWaves Group in New York found that "youths aged 15-18 share not only many tastes but beliefs, values and goals, many of which defy age-related and cultural stereotypes." Teenagers the world over want economic and personal success; see themselves as ultimately responsible for that success; respect achievement but not tradition; and increasingly value their families. Almost half expect to leave their country of birth to participate in the global economy. The world's teens "emerge from this survey as being more same than different, shaped by Western movies, television, music and higher levels of education, which has moved them away from their families and into a peer culture." BrainWaves managing director Elissa Moses says the world's teen population is "not homogenous, but it is linked"; anthropologist Alice Schlegel agreed that a "globalization of adolescent culture" is occurring rapidly: "This is not to say all cultures are going to become like ours, but there is a convergence" going on.[7]

HUMAN NATURE AND NEEDS

A third engine of history, as true now as in the past, is human nature— the needs, desires, and aspirations of human beings. Through their actions, individual as well as collective, people transform these needs into history, shaping their institutions and societies in the process.

Classical theories of international relations—and, by extension, theories of history—have proposed one of two very simplistic formulas of human nature. The most famous, and generally most widely held, has been the underlying—though, in fact, frequently exaggerated—pessimism of such writers as Thucydides, Thomas Hobbes, and Niccolò Machiavelli. Human nature, according to these men, is generally selfish, acquisitive, and aggressive. Human institutions—especially governments—reflect these tendencies. At the other end of the spectrum we find scholars for whom the reason and altruism inherent in humanity can produce systems of ever-increasing morality and law, both within and among nations.

A more sophisticated view of human nature may be available in the form of "human needs theory," the application of psychological and anthropological evidence about human nature to political problems. Rather than categorize human nature as inherently good or bad, conflictual or cooperative, human needs theory posits a number of core principles that human beings strive for in both constructive and destructive ways. As such it provides us with important clues to the way in which human desires constitute a major engine of history—and offers a framework for thinking about their practical implications over the next decade.

By far the most famous index of human desires is psychologist Abraham Maslow's "hierarchy of needs," outlined in Table 5.1.[8] Most other lists of needs contain ideas similar to Maslow's; reviewing a broad set of such lists, it is perhaps possible to outline a few basic categories into which most of the proposed needs would fit. I would suggest three: security (physical as well as economic, encompassing a craving for some level of order and certainty); relationships (the social category of needs—affection, community, belonging as well as ties to nature); and identity (dignity, self-esteem, recognition, and related needs).

Our appreciation of history as a dialectical process encourages us to look to those human needs most threatened by the instability attending the birth of the knowledge era. The need for security is an especially potent troublemaker: In its economic guise, it generates calls for protectionism by workers fearful of losing their jobs to the global economy; as a requirement for personal safety, it leads some in transition economies to seek out leaders who promise order and stability—

TABLE 5.1
Maslow's Hierarchy of Needs

1. Self-actualization, fulfilling one's potential
2. Esteem, achievement, recognition, prestige
3. Aesthetic needs—symmetry, order and beauty
4. Cognitive curiosity and desire to learn
5. Belongingness and love in social relationships
6. Safety and security; protection from danger
7. Physiological—simple bodily survival

Source: Abraham Maslow, "A Theory of Human Motivation," *Psychological Review* 50 (1943).

sometimes at the cost of freedom. The need for identity also can be problematic in transitional periods, when whole societies can undergo the sort of "identity crisis" that the psychologist Erik Erikson studied in adolescents, as their members struggle to forge workable identities from the fragments of the passing age and the hopes of the arriving one. Human needs thus cut both ways—they may, as we argue later, prompt the evolution of society in the direction of economic and political freedom, but they also powerfully underpin the doubts and worries that follow such change, doubts that manifest themselves in reactions to globalization.

And yet it is important not to underestimate the capacity for cooperation and altruism that exists in human nature. Scientists puzzled at the existence of selfless generosity in a world of self-serving evolution have discovered that prosocial behavior—some instinctive degree of cooperation, empathy, and altruism—is part of human nature, built into our genetic code just as much as anger or fear or hair color.[9] The reasons, from an evolutionary standpoint, are obvious enough: Some degree of cooperative instinct helps the species to survive and prosper, and this trait then comes to be reflected in individuals. Theories of history that rely on a cynically pessimistic view of human nature at best capture one part of a much more complex reality. As world politics, the fate of individual nations, and corporate competition proceed over the next decade and beyond, each will be shaped by basic human instincts that are at least as cooperative as they are competitive.

SOCIAL CONSTRUCTION AND EVOLUTIONARY LEARNING

For my fourth engine of history I adopt a slightly more theoretical bent. Two related ideas—social construction and evolutionary learning— offer an important perspective on the nature of history as well as its likely direction.

The general idea of social construction is simple. Human beings are social animals—we exist within the contexts of our societies. The insight of social construction theory is simply that our understanding of ideas and events is shaped by that social context. Notions like liberty, institutions like the nation-state, and habits like men wearing a tie to work are not dictated by some higher power; they emerge gradually from human interaction, from the sharing of perceptions and ideas, from beliefs we gain about one another and the society in which we want to live. The notion that it's wrong to kill is not a thing, like a stone; it isn't forced on us by an all-powerful race of aliens; and yet, in most societies most of the time, it effectively molds human behavior. Eventually, successful norms and principles become broadly accepted, and the society teaches itself—through schools, myths, customs, religions—that they are valid.

The process gains its real force over generations, when tentatively established norms move from the category of "We won't do this" to "This is not done in our society." A handful of people in a tribe may agree not to kill one another, but that commitment could be shattered with a single hammer blow. Once the process extends across genera- tions, however, and parents pass the message along to children, it attains much greater force: it becomes "the way things are done," and individual violations can be punished or written off without under- mining the norm.

It is at this point that the idea of social construction merges with and gains added strength from the related notion of "evolutionary learning." Human beings, and human institutions such as governments, are not static, unevolving entities. They experience the world; they draw conclusions and modify their perceptions; in short, they *learn*. Learning helps to explain and impel the behavior of individuals and institutions, for good and ill.

Evolutionary learning and social construction then reinforce one another. Learning establishes the basis of facts and ideas that social

ISSUE FEATURE: THE INTERACTION PRINCIPLE

The unifying theme for all human phenomena in the knowledge era may well be the idea of *interaction*. Encompassing related notions such as relationships, perception, and social construction, this principle might always have laid at the foundation of human experience—and perhaps, more broadly, all life. But it has now clearly come to the fore.

The thought behind the Interaction Principle is simple, although necessarily vague inasmuch as the concept is an embryonic one. Stated most boldly, it is that "Interaction is the foundation of all existence, and the health and success of any organism or group can be measured first and foremost by the quality of its interactions, within or outside itself." Relationships, mutual influences, and resulting behaviors constitute the essential stuff of human and natural life. This is another way of phrasing one of our themes from the introduction—the idea that process, rather than products or things, lies at the core of the knowledge era. Examples of the principle crop up in a dozen disciplines, several of them discussed in this trend:

- *Complexity theory.* This important new class of science, to which we next turn, could be described as the "science of interactions": It investigates the ways in which the often random intermixing of agents produces patterns of behavior that had not been intended.
- *Social construction.* Ideas, norms, and institutions that are socially constructed arise from human interaction.
- *Quantum mechanics.* This field looks into the microscopic basis of life where "things" seem to give way to a complex soup of forces and particles that amount to pure interaction.
- *Modern management theory and the virtual corporation.* Increasingly, managers are taught to see their work teams or companies, not as a collection of buildings or in-boxes but as a set of relationships.
- *Interdisciplinary and holistic approaches to issues.* Interactions among various disciplines are at least as important as the facts uncovered by the disciplines themselves.

What does the Interaction Principle mean? What lessons does it teach? It's too early to tell in much detail. But it could become one of the keys to unlocking the character and mysteries of the knowledge era.

construction then imparts, which in turn establishes a new basis for learning. Americans learn, over time, that Canada is a friendly trading partner that poses no threat. That fact enters into social understanding and is constructed through schools, families, and the media. Having learned and constructed that fact, Americans are then ready to learn something further: that they can and should, for example, develop a fully free trading zone with Canada. And the knowledge era magnifies both social construction and learning in striking ways. The speed with which social construction can work is strikingly evident in Europe today, recently growing debates about the future course of the European Union notwithstanding. Having learned the fruitlessness of war, the members of the European Union are attempting to transcend their past through a new social arrangement.

It's not entirely clear where precisely social construction will take us over the coming decade. But the phenomenon will be very much in evidence on such issues as globalization and the spread of democracy. And it reemphasizes one important theme of this book: That we are not the prisoners of an arbitrary history. Our own beliefs and choices will shape the future, for good or ill, through the reality we create.

6

Chaos and Complexity Theory

Many of the engines of history outlined in this trend are largely progressive or linear. But history does not always work like that. It is often unpredictable and apparently random—especially in the short term, which can be pretty chaotic even amid long-term trends. History is a little like an enormous line of marching ants: Examined through a magnifying glass, the line might appear chaotic, with ants scurrying this way and that after nearby pieces of food or droplets of water; it is only when looked at from above that the stream's direction becomes evident. The engines of history outlined in chapters four and five deal mostly with the long view. What model might offer the magnifying glass—providing models of how long-term patterns can emerge from apparently random and chaotic short-term events? The answer is an emerging body of thinking called complexity theory, our fifth "engine." This field examines what it terms "complex adaptive systems" and traces the role of asymmetrical and discontinuous change.

Complexity theory offers powerful tools for understanding how history works and the character of the engines driving it forward. It does not suggest that all linear thinking is wrong, nor does it aim to replace the clocklike, Newtonian paradigm—only to modify it, to gain a better understanding of its limitations and to uncover the behavior of nonlinear systems.

In brief, the sciences of complexity study how the actions of microlevel actors—genes, molecules, birds, human beings—add up to macrolevel effects. Their focus is how complex systems can emerge from the self-directed behavior of many individual actors. And their critical insight is that systems can exhibit characteristics that we would never expect or be able to predict from looking at the behavior of individuals alone.

The science writer Mitchell Waldrop, whose book *Complexity* is the most readable account of these new sciences, explains that the basic focus of complexity is "a system that is *complex,* in the sense that a great many independent agents are interacting with each other in a great many ways"—quadrillions of proteins, lipids, and nucleic acids that comprise a living cell, or billions of neurons that make up a brain, or millions of people that make up a human society.[1] Thus complex systems thinking is radically grass roots—it focuses our attention on the motivations of microlevel actors, whose actions add up to large group behavior. Rather than behaving like a well-ordered line of marching soldiers, complex systems operate like a swarm of bees: The whole operates not according to rigid rules but as the sum of the smaller actions.[2]

The odd thing is that often these apparently random interactions produce carefully ordered behaviors through a process known as self-organization. Flying birds, for example, react to the behavior of other birds, producing a graceful flocking action that no bird had individually planned. The Belgian physicist Ilya Prigogine won a Nobel Prize in 1977 partly for explaining this phenomenon: In nature, Prigogine argued, the second law of thermodynamics—the entropy law, of constantly degrading systems—isn't always true. When a given group of molecules or other living things is exposed to some energy or other spur from the outside, it can spontaneously create new and complex structures. Another example of self-organization, Waldrop writes, occurs when "people trying to satisfy their material needs unconsciously organize themselves into an economy through myriad individual acts of buying and selling; it happens without anyone being in charge or consciously planning it." And "these complex, self-organizing systems are *adaptive,*" Waldrop notes, "in that they don't just passively respond to events the way a rock might roll around in an earthquake. They actively try to turn whatever happens to their advantage."[3]

Another way of thinking about complexity is as a combination of basic laws (such as biological evolution's law of natural selection) combined with "frozen accidents"—in the case of biology, genetic mutations—that, once they arrive, are locked into place. The tendency is for complex systems to become more complex, because frozen accidents build on one another.

In the complex system of human society, both free-market economics and democracy might be frozen accidents, random mutations in social organization that serve the basic engines of history such as human needs. As Francis Fukuyama might put it, a random mutation that becomes frozen essentially "ends history" in its realm.

This analysis helps us to understand why some measure of accident and randomness, in human affairs as in the biological world, is to be welcomed: Randomness is a major engine of progress. Without it there would be no accidents to be frozen and fewer new and better ways of doing business. If progress and technological development depended only on planned advances and could not benefit from random new discoveries, the pace of history would slow dramatically, a fact that reemphasizes the role of freedom in allowing and encouraging progress. "The evolutionary potential of any system," writes the economist Max Boisot, "is ultimately linked to the existence of microscopic freedom"[4]; without that freedom, people have less opportunity to engage in the sort of random creativity that is at the core of evolution—another reason to doubt the success of centrally planned or mercantilistic countries, economies, or businesses.

These new sciences are helpful not so much because they can forecast the future or provide a comprehensive theory of world affairs but because they offer a powerful cautionary message. The reality of nonlinear, unpredictable patterns emerging even from very simple human instincts or behavioral patterns means that individuals and organizations always must work to break down unspoken assumptions, open their thinking to new possibilities, and draw in people and projects that help them to think in new ways. One clear message of complexity is that successful institutions will cultivate unpredictable thinking and actions as a complement, not a replacement, for traditional ways of doing business. (See table 6.1.) Why else, for example, would the highly successful head of a leading U.S. architectural firm rechristen his job title "Master of Madness"? "You have to get comfortable with being stupid, silly, crazy—*every day*," says Bill Little of Little & Associates. "Insanity's the best path to creativity that I know of."[5]

Brian Arthur, a Stanford economist, says that while the Newtonian clockwork approach to nature seemed analogous to Protestantism

TABLE 6.1

Complexity Theory: Recommendations

Wired Magazine *editor Kevin Kelly's "Nine Principles of Complexity"*

1. *Distribute being.* Decentralized operations; networked models.
2. *Control from the bottom up.* Empower low-level actors; pursue decentralization.
3. *Cultivate increasing returns.* Invest in advances and education to accelerate your competitive edge.
4. *Grow by chunking.* Build the system in pieces, not all at once.
5. *Maximize the fringes.* Focus on the randomness and unpredictability that leads to progress.
6. *Honor your errors.* Look for accidents that are competitive advantages.
7. *Pursue no optima; have multiple goals.* You can't forecast accurately; have alternative plans.
8. *Seek persistent disequilibrium.* Industry revolutionaries create turbulence to open spaces for their product.
9. *Change changes itself.* Static or incremental strategies often fail.

Source: Kevin Kelly, *Out of Control* (Reading, MA: Addison-Wesley, 1994).

(relying on an ordering principle), the "alternative—the complex approach—is total Taoist. In Taoism there is no inherent order. . . . The universe in Taoism is perceived as vast, amorphous, and ever-changing. You can never nail it down."[6] In that spirit, one of complexity theory's most important pieces of advice is to respect integrative work aimed at capturing a comprehensive complex adaptive system rather than some tiny slice of it. The Nobel Prize–winning physicist Murray Gell-Mann has said that, as important as the study of discrete subjects continues to be, "we need to supplement that study with interdisciplinary investigations of the strong interdependence of all the principal facets of the world situation. In short, we need a crude look at the whole"[7]—not a bad phrase to describe this book.

The message of complexity theory, and in particular its principle of self-organization, is deeply hopeful. Leading complexity theorist Stuart Kauffman has referred to "matter's incessant attempts to organize itself into ever more complex structures," even in the face of the entropy of the second law of thermodynamics. What this means is that "a kind of deep, inner creativity [is] woven into the very fabric of nature."[8] This will be more true than ever in the knowledge era: More interaction means more feedback, more complexity—and more potential for progress.

7

Where Are They Taking Us?

To this point I have surveyed the "engines of history." What remains is to determine what direction they are taking us—the kind of world being created by these forces of change. To those areas of the world that have not yet undergone the social and economic transformations I will outline below—for example, free markets and liberal polities—the engines of history will bring reform and instability. Meanwhile, in many developed nations that have passed through these transitions, the next decade will be a period of reaction and rethinking—questioning the basic assumptions of their social systems and asking if they might be improved.

LIBERALIZATION, ECONOMIC REFORM, AND ECONOMIC FREEDOM

In the context of the socioeconomic convergence described in chapter five, the recent explosion of free-market economies and the move away from state-run systems is no accident. The same homogenizing impulses of technology and economics behind the global cultural convergence also have sparked an institutional convergence. It is a kind of natural selection of economies—uncompetitive, state-planned systems decay and die, while thriving free-market systems survive. (See figure 7.1.) The result over the last decade has been astonishing—in some places (such as the former Soviet Union) it has implied the rejection of whole socio-economic systems; in others (much of Latin America and increasingly

ISSUE FEATURE: POSTMATERIALIST VALUES

The political scientist Ronald Inglehart has spent three decades uncovering some of the most powerful evidence for a homogenizing worldview. Inglehart's studies of world value surveys suggest that priorities change with development, that a detectable shift occurs from "materialist" values—keeping one's job, gaining more wealth quickly—to "postmaterialist" values that emphasize noneconomic aspects of life quality: freedom, ecological health, spiritual experiences. "Throughout advanced industrial society," he argues, "what people want out of life is changing," and in a direction leading to "the deemphasis of economic growth as the dominant goal of society and the decline of economic criteria as the implicit standard of rational behavior."[1]

Inglehart's findings are profound and have dozens of implications for the various trends discussed throughout this book. They include the following.

- *Socioeconomic convergence is a real phenomenon* inasmuch as advanced societies tend to reflect not only similar institutions and practices but also similar values.
- *Economic progress leads to political freedom,* as I will contend, because personal and political liberty is a leading example of postmaterialist values.
- *Political participation, in turn, grows more elaborate over time*—as I argue in Trend Five—because a greater proportion of the population has the skills and interests to take part. One result is a broad-based assault on traditional authorities.
- *The trend in business toward greater social responsibility is no fluke*—it reflects and responds to the demands of public opinion in postmaterialist societies.
- *The practical importance of human needs like identity and belonging becomes more powerful than ever,* magnifying those engines of history and intensifying the popular search for spiritual grounding, a subject to which I return in Trends Five and Six.
- *Shifts in cultural values, like other elements of historical transitions, carry a substantial price.* Cultural changes "take place slowly," Inglehart writes, "and the transition tends to be painful," in part because there is "a built-in tendency for cultural change to lag behind the environmental changes that give rise to it."[2]
- *Major war becomes less likely,* as this trend argues, because populations imbued with postmaterialist values see the enterprise as wasteful and pointless.

FIGURE 7.1

Economic Freedom in the World, 1975–2015

World rating, on a scale in which 10 is perfect freedom (Y1); and amount of global
GDP open to contestable trade, in $ trillions (Y2)

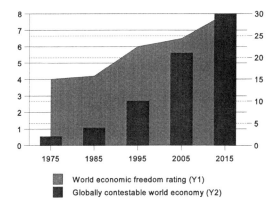

Legend:
- World economic freedom rating (Y1)
- Globally contestable world economy (Y2)

Sources: Author's estimates based on: (for world rating) various, including James D. Gartney and Robert A. Lawson, *Economic Freedom of the World,* available at www.fraserinstitute.ca/books; and (for contestable economy) Jane Fraser and Jeremy Oppenheim, "What's New About Globalization?" *The McKinsey Quarterly* no. 2 (1997):172.

Japan) it has demanded more subtle reform to clear away the barriers to progress and competition created by slow-moving, bureaucratic state structures. Even recent financial crises in Asia and elsewhere do not appear to have undermined the growing global consensus on the need for liberalization.[3]

The socioeconomic convergence of the knowledge era now has a powerful enforcement mechanism: the community of like-minded capitalist trading nations, whose rules of conduct *New York Times* columnist Thomas Friedman has referred to as "the Paradigm."[4] Even potentially aggressive states now need what only the democratic capitalist powers can provide—markets, investment, and technology. As a result, those democratic capitalist powers can impose rules of the road, global norms states must follow to gain access to those economic benefits. This global marketplace, former Citibank chairman Walter Wriston contends, "takes constant referenda on what in many ways is beginning to look like a global culture."[5] Historian Paul Schroeder calls this process "association/exclusion" and says it works "not by enforcing international law and punishing violators, but by forming and maintaining associations that reward those who conform to group norms and exclude those who do not."[6]

One can see this process at work today. Major trading nations, led by the United States, inform China of the steps it must take in opening its economy and other areas in order to qualify for admission to the World Trade Organization. A coalition of like-minded states, with backbone supplied by London and Washington, enforce tough requirements on Iraq to allow it even to *sell* its oil on world markets in the wake of the Persian Gulf War. To gain access to international political recognition and economic investment, North Korea is required to cap its nuclear program. As the trend continues, it will socially construct a reality in which military and economic misbehavior increasingly seems like more trouble than it is worth.

Despite the power of the forces pressing for homogenization, its actual achievement will entail immense transitional costs over the next decade—so much so that "counterglobalism" will be one of the basic themes of this period. It means a time of social and political discord, of psychological stress, of fertile ground for movements that express cultural identity in the face of onrushing globalism, a theme we will examine in greater depth in Trend Four.

This analysis places the recent argument of Samuel Huntington in new light. Huntington says that coming decades will witness a "clash of civilizations" as cultural values come to the fore. For him, culture could well be the fascism or socialism of the knowledge era—the world-historical value system to which people turn in difficult times, when their dignity and recognition are threatened.

And yet this connection highlights a seldom-recognized aspect of Huntington's model. In it, cultural identity is primarily an *effect*, not a cause. The ways in which culture "causes" conflict—a shrinking globe, the alienating features of rapid socioeconomic change, the reaction to democracy and consumer culture, and economic regionalism—are not primarily cultural events. They are not *caused* by culture; they stem from modernization and globalism, and culture is only a secondary force—a reaction to trends whose true origins lie elsewhere, trends running in the opposite direction from the cultural loyalties Huntington's model assumes.

As a result, civilizational tensions are often most intense where socioeconomic strife exists (such as the gap between the rich and the poor in India) and ease when economic conditions change (a decline in Japan-bashing in the United States attendant to Japan's economic slump). They are also likely to be especially destabilizing in those places that have yet to undergo the liberalizing transition. Such areas include not only the world's massive remaining statist economy—China—but also centrally directed capitalist practices in such places as Japan and France. The requirements of continued free-market reform in these areas will create the risk of instability and social stress. And those countries in the midst of the wrenching transitional process, such as Latin America and India and parts of East Asia and Europe, must deal with the resistance and backlash generated by this process of social change.

DEMOCRACY

The engines of history surveyed here also push the world further in the direction of increased freedom and democracy. They do this in a number of ways.

Expanded freedom is partly a product of the economic liberalization already described. Free markets generally produce free polities, at least in the long run. Rational economic forces alone, combined with a kind of Darwinism of social systems, should produce democracy: In a competitive world economy, planned or closed economies simply cannot keep pace with the innovative genius of free societies. Already a problem for undemocratic states by the middle of the twentieth century, this flaw became too obvious to ignore by its end.

Economic freedom creates expectations of liberty that inevitably seep into the political realm. This phenomenon has been replayed over and over again in developing nations, even within cultures—such as South Korea and Taiwan—said to be hostile to the idea of personal freedom. Now this process is under way in countries that are pursuing economic but not political reforms, including China and Indonesia. Chris Patten, Britain's last governor of Hong Kong, agrees that "In every country, as people get better off, travel more, learn to read, write and tap out their faxes, they will want to have a bigger say in the decisions taken in their name." A more "accountable and participative government is invariably the consequence sooner or later of economic growth and the opening of markets."[7] Ronald Inglehart's notion of postmaterialist

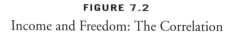

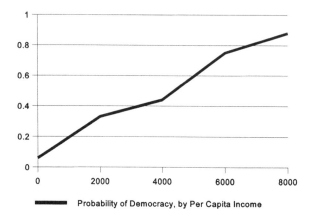

Source: Various, including Adam Przeworski and Fernando Limongi, "Modernization: Theories and Facts," *World Politics* 49, no. 2 (January 1997): 157.

values points in the same direction, contending that, as peoples' basic security needs are met in richer countries, they turn their attention to important secondary concerns—such as liberty, a desire for which seems to be inherent in human nature but that can only emerge reliably when more fundamental issues of personal safety, food, shelter, and other basic needs are met.

If economic progress does inevitably produce democratic progress, the practical importance of the connection is momentous. (See figure 7.2.) It has profound implications for China: If the adage is true that "the richer the country the freer," Hudson Institute scholar Henry Rowen argues, China is getting richer all the time, and we have powerful reason to believe the axiom that trade and engagement with China will bolster freedom. "The prospects for Chinese liberalization thus rest, above all, on continued rapid economic progress," Rowen writes. And because several researchers argue that most countries undertake the move to democracy when their per-capita incomes reach about $5,000 or $6,000, one can even forecast with some confidence the growth *rate* of freedom in China. "When will China become a democracy?" Rowen asks. "The answer is around the year 2015."[8]

Yet some scholars are disturbed by this tendency to turn a correlation into a causation. They suggest that development does not cause the emergence of democracy, but only cements it into place.[9] One can imagine, Francis Fukuyama contends, a highly successful technological society that is not democratic; there is no necessary connection between wealth and freedom. Economic convergence is not enough to explain the growth of democracy; "the progressive unfolding of modern natural science," Fukuyama writes, "could just as well lead us to Max Weber's nightmare of a rational and bureaucratized tyranny, rather than to an open, creative, and liberal society." The mechanism of history, then, "needs to be extended."[10]

So Fukuyama essentially adds the idea of human nature and human needs to the picture. Fukuyama emphasizes that we are social beings, and that our "sense of self-worth and identity is intimately connected with the value that other people place on [us]."[11] As a result, what we crave, as strongly as anything else, is what Fukuyama calls "recognition": respect, dignity, and the like. Then, because government is the collective agent that represents society, it becomes natural for us to demand recognition from government—a process that turns older ideas of individuals owing allegiance to and respect for autocratic or monarchical governments on their head. The desire for recognition, then, because it causes people to demand that governments respect their rights, becomes "the missing link between liberal economics and liberal politics"; and Fukuyama contends that, as a result, the world has reached the "end of history" because no political system could better satisfy the human need for recognition than democracy.[12]

By "the end of history," then, Fukuyama means something more specific than the end of global events. He doesn't mean that wars, trade disputes, energy crises, and other big things simply stop happening. He means something much more limited—the end of ideological competition among different forms of human society.

The results of this engine of history are clear enough: a magnification of the worldwide trend toward free markets and free polities already prompted by modern natural science. Human needs point in the direction of democracy, a fact that helps account for the amazing rise of free societies since roughly the year 1700. Democracies, republics, and

ISSUE FEATURE: DEMOCRACY IN CHINA

Whether modernization leads directly and inevitably to democracy or not, a wide variety of reasons exist to believe that the connection is real in China today.

Arguably the most important single law of the twentieth century was passed in Beijing in 1987. In that year, the Chinese government approved a decree allowing local villages to elect their own headmen and governing committees. This law unleashed a process of local democratization that is sowing the still-fragile seeds of democracy in mainland China.[13] Three-quarters of China's 1.3 billion people live in its 900,000 small villages; by 1997 the number of Chinese villages having held at least one election will reach 95 percent.

China's village democratization is an outgrowth of its economic reforms. Determined to increase efficiencies in farms and other village enter-prises, officials in Beijing realized that local Commu-nist Party hacks were often incompetent. "Villagers have a much better notion of village talent than the higher authorities," says the official who supervises the process. "If you allow the county government to choose a stupid idiot of a village chief, the whole economy will be ruined."

> Village elections mark "the Party's most sweeping abdication of power since the People's Republic was founded in 1949."
> —*The Economist*

    The victory of democratically elected representatives in Chinese villages is tentative, far from complete, and subject to reversal. Because of the process's role in promoting economic growth, however, the central government is pushing it: Lagging provinces "are getting a tongue-lashing from Beijing," *The Economist* reports, while "local governments are being 'educated' to surrender power." And a host of other indications of expanded freedom in China have emerged, from the expanded rule of law to the "self-liberalization" of Chinese mass media to more broadly available communications such as satellite television.[14] If these processes, along with the village democracy movement, inculcate the spirit of democracy from the grass roots in China, they will help bring the global democratic revolution to the world's most populous nation—and continue disproving the idea that "Chinese culture" is inhospitable to freedom.[15]

FIGURE 7.3

The Advance of Democracy

Number of democratic nations and percentage of total states that are democratic

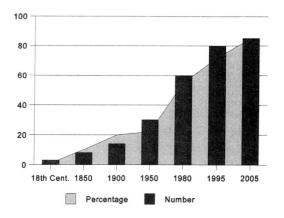

Sources: For eighteenth century through 1980, Michael Doyle, "Liberalism and World Politics,"
The American Political Science Review 80, no. 4 (December 1986); for the 1990s,
Freedom House; for 2005, author's estimate.

related forms of government, which flickered briefly in Greece and a handful of places after that for 2,000 years, have now become the global norm, as shown in figure 7.3. Not counting Africa and the Middle East, the two regional holdouts to freedom, a stunning *84 percent* of the world's nations are free or partly free.

And yet human needs also have a darker side. In the short run, deprivation of security can lead to calls for a return of undemocratic leaders to preserve order; we see this phenomenon especially in Russia today and in a handful of developing nations. And in the long run, the relativism of free societies, along with uncertainty and fear produced by the rapid change, can produce a wide-ranging anomie and sense of not belonging. If people feel that their needs for a job, for health care, or for safe streets are not being respected, their dignity may be threatened—and they may turn to protectionist, xenophobic, or violent movements in a quest for recognition.

History, however, provides us with reasons for optimism as well as caution. For, while the rise of democracy is a dialectical and painful rather than a linear and simple process, it is nonetheless *real.* And even skeptics of the causal link between modernization and democracy agree that prosperity helps to lock democracies into place, making them all but irreversible.[16] All of this carries powerful implications for how governments look at the world: As *The Economist* explains, the "vast and heartening progress" made by democracy during the last three decades implies, among other things, that "the realists' preoccupation with balance-of-power politics risks neglecting the underlying forces that move history."[17]

MINORITY AND GENDER EQUITY

An important fact about the connection between human needs and freedom is that it operates at all levels, not just the national. The urge for dignity and recognition frequently impels suppressed or minority groups within nations—whether identified by race, gender, or ethnicity—to demand equal treatment. Thus the last 100 years, in addition to a progressive evolution of national democratic governments throughout the world, have witnessed a growth of movements—many successful, some not—for minority and/or gender rights.

If this history is any guide, the next decade is likely to witness a renewed flowering of such movements in the developing world—as women achieve more equal status in the West, begin to achieve such equality in the developed nations of Asia, and take their first steps in that direction in much of the developing world. And the global "paradigm" of norms and expectations described earlier will increasingly make respect for minority rights one price of admission to world economic markets and political forums.

The universalization of roughly free-market economic models also will help expand minority rights and gender equity for a simple reason: competition. Companies and countries will search for every advantage they can get in the hypercompetitive global economy, and increasingly that will mean providing greater opportunity for minority groups to participate in the economic and political life of their countries or local communities.

One tragically classic example of discrimination impairing economic progress is the sad case of Alan Turing. Turing was one of the best scientific minds of the twentieth century, a man whose mathematical and engineering insights were critical to the invention of the computer. Yet in 1952, police investigating a burglary at his home in Britain discovered that he was homosexual, which was still against the law in that country at the time. There followed criminal charges, forced hormone treatments to combat his "unnatural" desires, and public censure. On June 7, 1954, at the age of just 41 and no doubt with decades of innovation ahead of him, Turing killed himself by eating an apple dipped in cyanide.

In the context of this case, IBM's recent decision to offer spousal benefits to the partners of its gay employees and Microsoft's efforts to drop its "boys' club" milieu and become more hospitable to women don't look so radical. Both companies just want to make sure they don't lose the next Alan Turing.[18]

What this all means is that the objective pursuit of economic self-interest by companies and governments alike will demand wider respect for minority rights and gender equity, in the developed and developing worlds alike.

THE DECLINE OF MAJOR WAR
AND THE RISE OF A GLOBAL SOCIAL CONTRACT

The engines of history just surveyed have two major implications for the future of conflict and cooperation in world affairs. One is to make major war, and especially war among the major powers, less likely. The other is to promote the halting emergence of more institutionalized and enforced international cooperation in the form of what we call a global social contract.

I'm not suggesting that wars will no longer occur, that the era of great-power politics is a thing of the past, or that U.S. international leadership is no longer necessary. The engines of history are only beginning to establish boundaries on the kinds of war that will be accepted, to lay the groundwork for better mediation of disputes short of war, and to strengthen the bonds of international society. As these processes emerge and even after they have developed, many nations will practice a good deal of hard-nosed *realpolitik*.

But the trend away from anarchic power politics is very real, and the first mechanism urging us in this direction is socioeconomic convergence. In a world of free-market economies, free trade will generally prevail; in a world of free trade, many of the things nations desire—prosperity, goods, capital—can be acquired without resort to force. A world of broadly capitalist trading partners and an open world economy is one that harbors few risks of zero-sum conflicts.

That the economic rationale for war has largely disappeared means that aggression by the major powers is extraordinarily unlikely; it does not mean that war is impossible. Major war can still happen through geopolitical rivalry, the aggressive moves of predator states, accident, miscalculation, or through some combination of those factors. But the rise of a global economy has overturned the assumption held by most ambitious national leaders of history through the nineteenth century: that their nation's economic and social fortunes could be improved by acquisitive warfare. One somewhat whimsical, but perhaps subtly significant, fact is that, as of 1998, no two countries with McDonald's had ever gone to war.

The expansion of democracy tends to have the same result. "Liberal democracy replaces the irrational desire to be recognized as greater than others with a rational desire to be recognized as equal," Francis Fukuyama points out. "A world made up of liberal democracies, then, should have much less incentive for war, since all nations would reciprocally recognize one another's legitimacy."[19] Fukuyama has added his voice to that of dozens of political scientists who, marshaling empirical as well as theoretical evidence, contend that democracies are less warlike than nondemocratic countries. Again as of 1998, no two fully independent and democratic nations had ever made war on one another; and as the world becomes increasingly populated by democracies, the incidence of war should decline. This effect becomes especially pronounced when democratic politics are married to liberal economics and postmaterialist values: Rich, industrialized democracies fully participant in the knowledge era have all the public disincentives to war mentioned by democratic theorists; their systems provide outlets for recognition and dignity; and they are rich enough to provide their citizens with a life of general ease—a standard of living that would be at risk in a major war.

Social construction and learning have similarly established for states the option of relying on general respect for sovereignty as an alternative to the "security dilemma" of constant competitive arms races. States have learned the value of mutual respect for sovereignty over time, the need for these principles to be respected—for the "fates of Napoleon and Hitler show what happens when they are not."[20] The exceptions to this rule—and the source of war risk that remain—are those great and medium powers still involved in the transition to high-income or democratic status as well as the "predator states"—undemocratic, territorially expansionist powers with an imperialistic ideology and a population willing to die for the pursuit of glory—that have long constituted a major cause of conflict.

Finally, the engines of history outlined in this trend may be propelling the world community in the direction of a gradually higher degree of unity and institutionalization of norms and rules of behavior—a global social contract. The human instinct toward self-interested cooperation helps to explain the emergence of society. Our genetic predisposition to preserve ourselves through reciprocal altruism, brought about by natural selection, helps to underwrite the bargain we know as the social contract: I'll trade my right to bash you and yours over the head for freedom from your assaults on me and mine, and together we'll set up a mutually agreeable mechanism to enforce this deal. All of which points to an intriguing question: If these forces can produce society at the national level, why not at the international level? If the human habit of self-interested cooperation in the service of security has produced national social contracts, why won't it produce a global one?

One can make a strong case that it will and that it is in the process of doing so today. Spurred by human nature, human reason, social construction, and evolutionary learning, we are in the process of establishing society in the international system just as we have within nations. This transition remains painfully slow, but it is accelerating all the time.

The size of social contract that we now understand by "domestic" is an order of magnitude larger and more complex than the state structures of hunter-gatherer bands, city-states, or the great empires of the pre-Christian era or the Middle Ages. At every stage—the 150-person tribe, the 5,000-person town, the 30,000-citizen city-state, the empire of several hundred thousand souls—skeptics could (and did) argue that the natural human ability to comprehend the value of the social contract on a larger scale had exhausted itself. All of those arguments proved false, in part because the critical variable in bringing about a global social contract (and a factor that harks back to the issue feature earlier in this trend) is *interaction*. Only when human beings interact with others can they establish relationships and proceed to cooperation. The advantages of cooperation generally become evident and take on evolutionary meaning only when reciprocal interactions occur frequently and over a long period of time. Only through interaction can the advantages of cooperation emerge: The reputational benefit of being seen as socially responsible, the economic boon of the division of labor. Only through repeated contacts can our undeniable xenophobia and other barriers to cooperation be overcome by establishing a history of reliable behavior and reciprocal trust.

Today such interaction and contacts emerge from the process of globalization—worldwide trade, communications and media, travel, immigration, multinational corporate activities, nongovernmental organizations whose activities span the globe, general worldwide awareness and the emergence of a global consumer culture, and all the other hallmarks of an integrating world—that slowly lays, brick by perceptual brick, the foundations for a global social contract. From this process of interaction emerges the instinctual desire and rational need to establish some form of order, some norms of behavior, some rules of conduct. The slow, fitful, dialectical result will be a form of international society and a strengthening network of global norms.

Evidence to support this process is overwhelming, at least in the economic realm. Institutions such as the World Trade Organization and regional free-trade areas such as the North American Free Trade Area, the European Union, Mercosur in South America, and the Association of Southeast Asian Nations were not imposed—they emerged naturally. Complexity theory helps to explain how this can happen: These arrangements represent a form of self-organizing order that emerges from the chaos of the state of nature, produced by inputs including human nature and social learning. Complexity theory allows us to see a form of global society as something simply reflective of how nature works. The "emergence of a global civilization," writes biologist and complexity theorist Stuart Kauffman, comes partly from global interaction. The resulting global civilization "is fast upon us. We will live through its birth, ready or not."[21]

POLICY RECOMMENDATIONS: *TREND TWO*

1. *Take chaos and complexity theory seriously* as metaphorical and analytical tools for understanding the knowledge era.
2. *Prepare for transitional instabilities* in countries that have not yet undergone the shift to free-market democracy—China, the Middle East, and others.
3. *Take steps to head off reactions* to the engines of change—steps including economic plans to explain and temper the impacts of globalization, expanded and more equitable access to new technologies, and economic and political support to nations in transition to democracy and free markets.
4. *Begin public debates now on genetic testing* and other ethical challenges of biotechnology.
5. Develop a new, long-range foreign policy vision that *takes seriously the insights of the global social contract model* of international relations.

A WORLD AWASH IN CHANGE

In a sense, the remaining trends in this volume involve sorting out the implications of the engines outlined in this one. Perhaps the most important, and disturbing, of those implications is the fact that the technological, economic, and social convergence under way in the modern world will generate profound instabilities. Countries undergoing the wrenching transitions to liberal economic and political orders could become the source of violence, external as well as internal. (The policy recommendations box outlines some of the necessary responses to these risks.) But the engines point in hopeful directions as well—surging interest in community identity and moral values. In particular, the concept of *responsibility* takes on major new importance at a time when people and institutions will be more responsible than ever for their actions and fates and when society as a whole must exercise enormous care in the application of new technologies. On the positive side of the ledger, the engines of history will help to answer these and other challenges in a number of ways.

In his wonderful book *Connexity,* Geoff Mulgan, head of London's Demos think tank and one of Europe's most visionary writers, phrases this collision of opportunity and danger in useful terms. It is nothing less than the next—and, he seems to imply (as I would myself argue), possibly decisive—phase in the age-old contest between freedom and order. Mulgan agrees that the engines of a globally interwoven era are liberating. "Earlier eras dreamed of the kingdom of God, or of absolute equality," he suggests, "but the most compelling dream of an age of connexity is freedom." And yet globalized interdependence, within and among states, also heightens our dependence upon and responsibilities toward each other. [22] This fundamental tension—between freedom and order, between individual and group, between part and whole—lies at the very core of the knowledge era, and its shadow falls over all the succeeding trends.

On the very first page of this book, I quoted Peter Drucker's statement that the societies of 50 or even 20 years from now will be very different from the ones we live in today. This Trend has offered the first pointed clues as to why that might be the case: a number of powerful trends are rewriting the language of economics, politics, military affairs, and a dozen other fields in profound ways. The next few Trends represent an effort to delve more deeply into some of these changes, and I'll begin by looking at the subject that represents the context in which most other changes will emerge: the knowledge-era economy.

A Human Resources Economy

When the ruler's trust is wanting,
there will be no trust in him . . .
When his work is completed and his affairs finished,
the common people say,
"We are like this by ourselves."

Tao Te Ching

Driven by the stunning technological advances of the twentieth century, the nature of economic activity—the essential character of what we know as an "economy"—is changing rapidly and radically. These changes carry profound implications for the organization and stability of modern society and the future of conflict within and between nations.

"Economic progress," notes former Citibank chairman Walter Wriston, is now "largely a process of increasing the relative contribution of knowledge in the creation of wealth."[1] Or, as the economist Max Boisot puts it, "we are moving towards an economic system in which information can no longer continue to be treated by economists simply as an external *support* for economic exchange; it has to be considered increasingly as its main focus."[2] Marshall McLuhan saw the trend three decades ago: "As automation takes hold, it becomes obvious that *information* is the crucial commodity, and that solid products are merely incidental to information movement."[3] And this new, information-dependent economy is based on a foundation of human resources, because people generate the knowledge on which it is based.

The central theme of this new economy is knowledge. We live in a knowledge era; our businesses increasingly operate in a knowledge economy.

This new economy is a story of paradox and contradiction: of micromarketing and global marketing, of empowerment amid alienation, of new opportunities for global cooperation and sinister new means of global conflict.

A New Kind of Economy

The single most important fact about all modern economies, and the greatest clue to their progress over the next decade, is that the nature of economic activity is changing. In its most important and fundamental sense, this means a shift to what many economic and social commentators have called an "information" or "knowledge" economy. I will also use the term "human resources economy" because, in this era as never before, people are the basic source of economic strength and growth—not land, not natural resources.

Whatever you call it, the new economy's primary good is knowledge, not natural resources or a tangible product. Most of its workers deal in knowledge—discovering, applying, or distributing knowledge. And the key to its productivity lies in making these information-based activities more efficient.

This transformation is not entirely new. As early as 1958, the economist Fritz Machlup calculated that the "information sector" of the U.S. economy already accounted for 29 percent of gross national product (GNP) and 31 percent of employment. During the 1960s economists following Machlup's lead, and using a variety of ways to calculate the size of the information sector, estimated that it accounted for over 40 percent of U.S. GNP.[1] The effect is broad-based: Better knowledge and the use of information-processing capabilities (such as computers) that work with knowledge enhance efficiency in all sectors of the economy. Economist Max Boisot argues that, in the U.S. economy between 1929 and 1982, education produced about 30

ISSUE FEATURE:
A "NEW ECONOMY"—FACT OR FICTION?

In the mid-1990s, the continued strong growth of the U.S. economy, the phenomenal rise in value of the stock market, and particularly the persistence of unemployment levels under 5 percent—all without triggering that 1970s' bugaboo, inflation—led some observers to speculate about the emergence of a New Economy that no longer follows the rules of classical economics.

New Economy devotees claim that productivity-enhancing technologies, efficiency-enhancing corporate restructuring, innovation-spurring deregulation, and cost-lowering globalization are working synergistically to open the possibility of an almost endless period of moderate growth, low unemployment, and minimal inflation. If they're right, the trend will have more than theoretical importance: bumping U.S. economic growth rate up from the officially-forecast 2.3 percent a year to 3 percent would boost the size of the U.S. economy in 2030 by 25 percent—helping to sidestep the social security crisis, providing bigger savings pools for investments, and having a host of other beneficial effects.[2]

> "Most of this [new economy] stuff is basically nonsense."
> —Paul Krugman

The New Economy movement has received a chilly reception from economists and government economic officials. Plenty of perfectly satisfactory interpretations, grounded in classical economics, exist to explain the recent behavior of the U.S. economy, these skeptics contend. "There are rather conventional explanations for what we see going on now that stop far short of saying that the world has been turned upside down," says Princeton economist Alan Blinder.[3]

Whatever one thinks about the New Economy, it does encourage reconsideration of what we know about modern economies. Combined with notions from complexity theory such as increasing returns, for example, the notion may indeed point to new patterns of economic cycles. Changing economic realities also provide more reason than ever to question old ways of measuring economic activity. And there can be little question that perception is increasingly driving economic activity: It is the absence of inflationary expectations, argues Goldman Sachs investment strategist Abby Joseph Cohen, as much as structural factors that explains the lack of inflation. Here we see an example of one of our themes—the role of perceptual reality in a knowledge era.

percent of productivity growth—and advances in knowledge accounted for over 60 percent.[4]

What, then, does this human resources economy mean in specific terms? It involves the development, exploration, storage, interpretation, and application of knowledge—not only the computer and telecommunications industries but also science, from research to engineering; education; media and entertainment; publishing in all its exploding varieties; health and medicine; financial and investment services; and such related fields as architecture, music, social services, law, psychiatry and psychology, advertising, and real estate.[5] The knowledge economy also means the *application* of many of these new areas to more traditional sectors of the economy, such as agriculture and manufacturing. Peter Drucker summarizes the dominance of knowledge industries—workers who make their living through ideas rather than physical labor—by tracing the decline of their competitors. In the 1950s, Drucker explains, people who worked "to make or move things were still a majority in all developed countries. By 1990, they had shrunk to one-fifth of the work force. By 2010 they will form no more than one tenth."[6]

As Trend One reminds us, the precise effects of the human resources economy will vary substantially by culture. Not all cultures are well organized to deal with its effects or take advantage of its opportunities. Hierarchical cultures, or those instinctively opposed to change, must alter their ways or be left frustrated by the side of the emerging human resources economy. Cultures with a strong disposition to xenophobia and a hostile suspicion of outside ideas and products will have to become more cosmopolitan and trusting in order to reap the full rewards of an increasingly integrated world economy.

The notion of a human resources economy is therefore much more fundamental than a mere overlay of computers and televisions on top of an industrial, manufacturing economy. A human resources economy is one that trades and deals in knowledge rather than goods, in ideas rather than things. It involves a radical transformation—although not a complete abandonment—of the economy we have known for the last 200 years. And it represents the emergence of human beings as the ultimate source of economic value.

Two such implications of a human resources economy are by now well understood. One is that such an economy uses fewer raw materials and energy than a manufacturing one—partly due to a shift in focus away

TABLE 8.1

The Growth of Services: Percentage of
World Production, 1960–1990

	Agriculture	Manufacturing	Services
. . . WORLDWIDE . . .			
1960	10.4	28.4	50.4
1990	4.4	21.4	62.4
. . . IN JAPAN . . .			
1960	13.1	35.1	40.9
1990	2.4	28.9	55.8
. . . IN EUROPE . . .			
1960	8.8	34.7	43.8
1990	3.0	21.5	63.8
. . . IN THE UNITED STATES . . .			
1960	4.0	29.0	57.2
1990	1.7	18.5	70.3

Source: The International Labor Office, *World Employment 1995* (Geneva: ILO, 1995), p. 29.

from manufacturing, partly due to efficiency, and partly due to new technologies—and thus benefits from largely stagnant commodity prices. "The raw material economy has thus come uncoupled from the industrial economy," Peter Drucker notes; it is now "quite unlikely that raw material prices will ever rise substantially as compared to the prices of manufactured goods . . . except in the event of a major prolonged war."[7]

The second, and probably most widely appreciated, implication of a human resources or knowledge economy is the growth of service industries. In a human resources economy, what is being produced is not so much goods as information, ideas, and concepts. Computer scientists develop new software; management consultants promote ideas; health care workers deal in medical knowledge. This is not to suggest that manufacturing disappears—obviously, those knowledge workers are still buying cars, bicycles, clothes, and houses; often, too, knowledge products demand manufacturing to support them (computers to run software, cellular phones to send signals). Increasingly, however, especially because of automation in the manufacturing sector, a very small percentage of the workforce can produce all the goods purchased by the population as a whole, just as a small number of farmers can grow all the food we eat.

The result of these trends, outlined in table 8.1, has been to dramatically increase the importance of the service component of all developed economies. In our time frame, the U.S. Bureau of Labor Statistics expects 23 million out of the 24.6 million new jobs created between 1990 and 2005 to be in the service sector.

But the knowledge era means more than just traditional services—it means an unprecedented emphasis on providing not just one service in isolation but a "holistic package of goods and services" to meet the consumer's total need,[8] something I call "elaborated services." Thus increasingly car dealers will not merely sell cars, they will offer a comprehensive service of auto design, production, servicing, repair, and replacement; they will become more involved in travel (as autos offer built-in guidance systems) and customized safety features; they will work more closely with insurance firms, perhaps even offering insurance themselves. Companies that now specialize in cable television will expand to offer Internet access, television and computer repair, movie rental, and other services. This trend of elaborated services is well under way in such knowledge-era industries as information and entertainment, and it represents a powerful example of two of this study's core themes: the decline of boundaries and disciplines in business and elsewhere and growing emphasis on holistic systems and networked enterprises.

In a world of competing service economies, the need to increase productivity in the service sector will become intense. Service-sector productivity growth will become the major engine of rising standards of living over the next decade.[9]

The drive for productivity can also become a push for automation: When banks learned that the average cost of a single customer interaction was 24 cents through an ATM machine versus almost three dollars through a teller, it did not take long for teller jobs to go into decline in favor of their electronic counterparts. One lesson: Service industries will face the same wrenching competitive pressures over the next two decades as their manufacturing industry counterparts did in the 1970s and 1980s.

9

The Reorganization of Work

The most sweeping implication of a human resources economy will be dramatic change in the nature of work. This change will encompass every aspect of business and labor, from the organization of corporations to the character of the workplace. It assumes great importance in the context of Trend Two's discussion of human needs: In the modern world, the need for identity and self-worth is intensely linked to work. As social and economic trends challenge traditional employment patterns, they also will challenge human identity in powerful, and potentially dangerous, ways.

THE NEW CHARACTER OF WORK

The human resources economy will carry profound implications for the character of work—its organization, timing, and nature. The principles of the knowledge era, principles such as speed, flexibility, decentralization, and empowerment, will change the workplace in fundamental ways.

This rapidly changing nature of employment has already produced much greater turnover and career shifts and has thus demanded greater flexibility on the part of workers. The idea of a single career for life with a major corporation is a thing of the past. Shifting career paths, serial careers, and less loyalty on both sides of the relationship are the norm. People's affiliation with their employers will be far more tenuous in such a world.

ISSUE FEATURE:
D'AVENI'S CONCEPT OF "HYPERCOMPETITION"

Hypercompetition, Dartmouth Business School professor Richard D'Aveni contends, is "a condition of rapidly escalating competition based on price-quality positioning, competition to create new know-how and establish first-mover advantage and competition for markets." The "frequency, boldness, and aggressiveness of dynamic movement by the players accelerates to create a condition of constant disequilibrium and change."[1]

D'Aveni's model is on display in the computer software industry: a series of rapid moves and coun-termoves that create *temporary* advantages. With shrinking product life cycles and accelerating technological innovation, companies focus less and less on attaining sustainable advantage and more on "developing a series of temporary advantages."

> "The goal of strategy is to disrupt the status quo."
> —Richard D'Aveni

Later D'Aveni says disrupting the status quo should be the top corporate goal. In a hypercompetitive world, he writes, there will only be two kinds of companies: "the disruptive and the dead." In such a world, chaos theory may depict the way business competition occurs. D'Aveni's insightful approach has a number of powerful implications:

- Leapfrog or transformative strategies become more important than ever.
- Businesses will achieve smaller profit margins under the pressure of price wars.
- Trust will come under new pressure—and "once trust is lost, it's very hard to recapture, especially in global markets where xenophobia makes foreign competitors suspect."
- A "logical approach is to be unpredictable and irrational," so as to throw competitors off their rhythm and distract them from your real intentions.
- Using the old strategy of attacking competitors' weaknesses "can be a mistake"—because those weaknesses won't last long, and you're shooting at a moving target.
- Antitrust laws badly need revising, because hypercompetition natu-rally produces actions and alliances that today would represent violations of those laws.

FIGURE 9.1

Declining Job Tenure: Median Years at Current Employer,
Male Workers, United States, 1983–1996

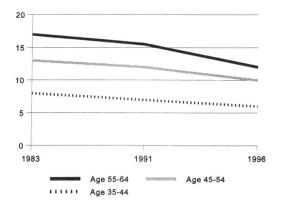

Source: Business Week, January 27, 1997, p. 20, citing the Employee Benefit Research Institute.

Forms of work—for some decades a relatively rigid 40-hour, five-day week—have become much less stable, uniform, and centralized; the new patterns include consulting, part-time and temporary positions, and the like. In 1993 more than 34 million Americans were part-timers or contractors, more than 25 percent of the workforce. This number may exceed 35 percent by 2000. One business revolution of the last two decades was just-in-time production; the new revolution may be just-in-time employment.[2]

Other new workplace arrangements are proliferating. One 1995 survey found 83 percent of responding companies using "alternative office strategies" such as telecommuting and "hoteling," giving employees temporary workstations that can be moved, combined, and recombined to meet the needs of changing work teams and projects. Another 1998 study found that almost 10 million people work outside their office at least three days a month, up from about five and a half million in 1993. At IBM, more than 20 percent of its 270,000 employees spend at least two days a week out of the office; within IBM's walls, over

20,000 employees already use shared offices, which has saved the company over $1 billion in real estate expenses.[3]

Whatever its real implications, this transformation of the workplace is coming—and fast. One recent survey of experts on workplace trends forecast that one-fifth of all U.S. workers will telecommute by the year 2003. This new workforce will have new needs, tastes, and worries—and businesses need to cater to all three.[4]

Admittedly, we have a long way to go before these patterns become the norm in U.S. companies or others throughout the developed world. Truly flexible work schedules have arrived at only a distinct minority of U.S. corporations. For example, while both economic and demographic trends scream out for flexible options to keep semi-retired older people involved in the workforce, one recent study found that fewer than 10 percent of U.S. companies offer such programs.

Then, too, alongside its opportunities for customized and tailored jobs, this trend carries risks of alienation. The *New York Times* reports that of 22 million part-time workers, 4.5 million want full-time jobs but cannot find them; meanwhile, the number of temporary workers—most without health or retirement benefits—has ballooned to 2.1 million, three times the number of a decade ago. The result is "a new and unstable work world in which [Americans] feel that the employer can call all the shots."[5] New, more flexible forms of work will require new kinds of workers—more educated, more accustomed to the rapid fluctuations of a hypercompetitive era, more willing and able to take responsibility for managing a complex, multifaceted, and serial career—especially the need for lifelong education.[6]

THE VIRTUAL CORPORATION

The knowledge era's ultimate corporate institutional form is that of substantially "virtual" organizations. The notion has been well captured by the British business expert Charles Handy.[7] It involves organizations that exist mostly on paper—employees who work independently and communicate by e-mail, phone, and fax but who don't always (or ever) share the same work space. Not many companies will try the virtual model any time soon and it might not work for some companies at all. Increasingly, however, it will become the norm against which the exceptions are measured.

The rationale for virtual organizations is as obvious as it is difficult for some to accept. Few organizations—whether businesses, schools, or government agencies—are defined by their physical work space. Most are, at heart, groups of people performing various functions, for which their offices may be basically irrelevant—and increasingly so in a human resources age where the emphasis is on people rather than their surroundings. As Handy points out, in a more competitive world, the office "will become an antiquated and very expensive notion." If there is an office in the future, he argues, "it will be more like a clubhouse: a place for meeting, eating, and greeting, with rooms reserved for activities, not for particular people"[8]—that is to say, a virtual organization.

The key engine driving this process is the way the various elements of the knowledge economy work together. Information technology encourages companies to automate and do business on-line. Gradually the core offices and personnel groups shrink away as efficiency dictates increasing elements of electronic business. And finally the corporation sees little need for a "central" office or activity at all; it becomes a dispersed, electronically linked organization—an "Amoeba Corporation," as business writer William Knoke has described it.[9] In a recent survey, several business experts told *Wired* magazine that they expect the first virtual company to join the ranks of the Fortune 500 by the year 2001.[10]

Even more fundamental is the change in the *character* of work that's taking place alongside the shifting organization of work. I'll go into this subject more fully in Trend Five, but generally knowledge era workforces are more decentralized, empowered, team-oriented, and nonhierarchical than their industrial-era forebears. They take seriously complexity theory's emphasis on discontinuity and innovation, and pay attention to the importance of human resources by investing in their employees in unprecedented ways. To a significant extent this trend ratifies the forecast of management guru Tom Peters, whose late-1980s bestseller *Thriving on Chaos* pointed to the importance of all these things.[11]

BUSINESS COMPETITION IN THE HUMAN RESOURCES ECONOMY

The nature of relations between businesses also changes in this new era. When corporations are fragmented among dozens of smaller subentities, bits and pieces of different—and competing—virtual companies can

ISSUE FEATURE: IDEALAB

Many elements of the new business paradigm are on display in a radical new business venture in Pasadena, California called Idealab.[12]

Founded by entrepreneur Bill Gross, Idealab is not so much a business as it is an incubator for businesses. Gross and about 20 core staff develop and review ideas for Internet-based companies; when they say yes, they provide $250,000 in seed money and take an equity stake. Everybody in the new firm gets some equity, at least 1 percent per employee. Idealab then spins off the new firm and lets it fly. And the resulting pattern represents a startling reversal of traditional business practice.

- *The focus on equity.* Gross insists that an equity stake, in addition to annual salary, revolutionizes employees' thinking: they feel ownership of their work; it creates a "story," with their company going up against someone else's, and thus generates drama and excitement; and it acts as a "self-selecting filter," attracting people "whose mindsets are well suited to high-risk, high-reward endeavors."
- *Spinning off the best ideas.* Most companies spin off dying units and hoard top producers. Idealab spins off everything—and that's something, Gross admits, "deeply discomfiting, something that feels like corporate apostasy." But it's also something that institutionalizes innovation, creativity, and all the other values of small companies.
- *Emphasizing teams.* If everybody has at least 1 percent equity, that means a maximum of 100 employees—a limit Gross likes. "[B]elonging to a small team exerts a basic emotional pull on employees," he writes. "When a company has more than 10 people and fewer than 100, it feels like a tribe—that primordial unit of human organization." No one has to be trained in team-building, because it comes naturally.
- *Networking.* The spun-off firms continue to share certain functions in common—accounting, legal, payroll, and so on—and Gross eventually gives all their CEOs a share in Idealab itself to encourage them to share ideas among companies and thus boost the overall value of the network. The result isn't just a bunch of separate entities but "a family of independent yet interdependent companies."

Gross sums up these lessons in what he calls "the new math of ownership": "the multiplicative effect of setting employees free and giving them significant equity has a net positive result." That simple phrase nicely captures the business principles of the knowledge era.

cooperate on specific projects. Business components, from one or several companies, will come together to serve shared interests and then go their separate ways.

A world of virtual corporations is increasingly a world of alliance projects, as groups of specialized companies come together in virtual alliances that then melt away. The behavior and strategies of businesses in this world will differ dramatically from the individualistic basis of competition of the industrial age.

Cooperative networks of virtual firms will compete with one another as strenuously and ferociously as companies do today—economic wars waged, for example, through increased use of industrial espionage and nationally supported economic intelligence.[13] Indeed, the knowledge era may create an unprecedented era of "hypercompetition," a phenomenon examined in depth by Dartmouth Business School professor Richard D'Aveni and discussed in the issue feature above.

Large corporations are increasingly dividing themselves into smaller, quasi-independent work units that aim to operate with the innovation and spirit of small companies. Airlines are realizing that their real core competency is in managing reservation and traffic systems; even flying the planes could one day be contracted out. The carmaker Volkswagen is leading an industrywide push to devolve as much assembly as possible onto subcontracting parts makers. U.S. banks are offering higher interest rates to "virtual" customers who bank remotely and never see a branch. And the ultimate extension of some of these notions of fragmentation and virtuality is on display in a fascinating U.S. company, Idealab, described in the issue feature.

Yet while they offer amazing new opportunities, virtual organizations also have important—and vexing—implications for the concepts of trust and responsibility. How will businesses trust employees they rarely see? How will responsibility be imposed on people who do their work outside the confines of an office?

This era, Anthony Giddens writes, "increasingly tears space away from place by fostering relations between 'absent' others," people who are "distant from any . . . face-to-face interaction."[14] Once human relationships have become so abstract, Giddens argues, people modify their means of interaction. They create money, for example, to allow regulated transactions between strangers and between people separated by thousands of miles. And they rely on "expert systems" of unknown

ISSUE FEATURE: CHINA'S CULTURE

Many observers don't notice the vast differences among Asian cultures. Chinese culture, author Joel Kotkin reminds us, is decentralized and family-based. Instead of being dominated by a handful of big companies, as in Japan or Korea, Chinese economies—whether on the mainland or on Taiwan—boast "a vast network of family firms with global reach," smaller and medium-sized companies that together amount to an energetic, innovative, self-organizing economic stew. In financial terms, Chinese capital also tends to be more diverse, circulating across borders in thousands of transactions rather than being dominated by a few large institutions.[15]

While the regime does prop up state industries for reasons of nationalism and national interest, moreover, Kotkin argues that individual Chinese investors are generally opportunistic capitalists first and foremost, and prideful ethnic Chinese second. This gives them an advantage in picking investments over the arguably more nation-building efforts in Japan and Korea. Taken together, all of this may suggest that Chinese culture might actually represent a pretty good fit with the economic demands of the knowledge era.

people schooled in very specific disciplines to keep many parts of the world working. As Giddens points out, all of these mechanisms of dealing with large, abstract society "rely upon trust. Trust is therefore involved in a fundamental way with the institutions of modernity" (or, to put it another way, "the nature of modern institutions is deeply bound up with the mechanisms of trust in abstract systems")[16]—and with the knowledge era. The advent of virtual organizations further complicates the issue of trust because virtual institutions are more dispersed and decentralized than traditional ones.

Not all cultures will take equally to these new ideas. Fast-moving, decentralized, autonomous corporate units may not fit easily into cultures accustomed to hierarchical social structures. Japan will probably need to make tolerance for change and individualism a larger part of its culture, for example.[17] France, which is experiencing a "brain drain" of talented young entrepreneurs fleeing the country's bureaucratized, hierarchical, anti-innovation culture, will have to change in similar directions.[18] In the long run, mismatches between the requirements of economic success and the traditions of culture will undermine those cultural habits, as a global process of socioeconomic evolution selects out those societies that cannot keep pace. And the angry reactions of countries and cultures forced to change their ways will be a major source of tension during the next decade, a phenomenon I examine in Trend Four.

THE END OF WORK?

The ultimate result of these trends may be a profound—and disturbing—assault on the very nature of employment and labor itself. Some observers suggest that the world has entered the early stages of a delaborization of the economy—as futurist Jeremy Rifkin puts it in the title of his recent book, *The End of Work.*

Peter Drucker pointed nearly a decade ago to the more and more evident "uncoupling of manufacturing production from manufacturing employment,"[19] and in fact today we see something even more dramatic: the uncoupling of jobs and employment from economic activity writ large.

Rifkin and others believe that this change is occurring for several reasons. First, automation and other forms of technological advance have dramatically reduced the number of people required to do many jobs. Second, knowledge-era businesses are seeking smaller, highly talented workforces rather than large, unskilled ones. Third, the knowledge era is not inherently job intensive: Peter Drucker explains that the costs of a semiconductor microchip consist of about 70 percent "knowledge" such as research, development and testing and only about 12 percent labor—compared to 20 or 25 percent labor costs in the most automated automobile plant.[20] Meanwhile, the "reengineering" movement in business management has sought efficiency and profit partly by slimming workforces.

The practical effects of these forces have been stunning and are most evident in the manufacturing sector. Between 1975 and 1990 manufacturing production remained at 22 or 23 percent of U.S. GNP, but manufacturing jobs declined from 25 percent of the labor force in 1960 to 16 or 17 percent in 1990. By 2005 Drucker expects it to fall to 12 percent.[21] And now service industries are beginning to experience the same technology-driven efficiency revolutions: In the 1980s U.S. service industries spent $900 billion on information technology, and the result was a new wave of efficiency that will gradually reduce employment.[22]

Many questions remain about how far this trend will actually progress. According to one recent, exhaustive study by the U.S. Labor Department, the rate of job destruction in the U.S. economy "has actually remained remarkably steady over the past three decades, and other surveys show that workers at all ages are staying in jobs longer than in the past."[23] Other workplace signs are also hopeful: Sixty percent of the 8 million new U.S. jobs created between 1991 and 1995 were managerial or professional; U.S. business spending on new equipment—a sign of future productivity—now stands at a robust 8 percent of gross domestic product (GDP); and people are responding to the need for education. The percentage of U.S. high school graduates going to college grew from 57 percent in 1986 to 62 percent today.[24] Manuel Castells finds it surprising that Jeremy Rifkin announced the "end of work" precisely when the U.S. economy was creating so many new jobs. "Work and employment are indeed being transformed," Castells argues, but "the number of paid jobs in the world . . . is at its highest peak in history and going up. And rates of participation of labor force in the adult population are increasing everywhere."[25]

One thing seems clear: While claims that the human resources economy spells the "end of work" are exaggerated, the shift to service- and knowledge-based drivers of the economy is producing substantial dislocations in employment. Reshuffled office space or adjustments to the work week are merely way-stations on a longer road whose implications for individual psychology and society are profound. Matching skills to jobs therefore emerges as one of the coming century's most imposing challenges.

1 0

Other Aspects of the New Economy

Another hallmark of the human resources economy is the growing dominance of *networked organizational forms.* No longer can we think of an economy as an immense soup of individual companies and people going about their independent projects. As virtual companies seek out cooperative ventures with their counterparts, as information highways and superhighways tie economic activity closer together, the metaphor for the new economy is the network.

Manuel Castells has made this metaphor the organizing theme of his book *The Rise of the Network Society.* The basic shift, he contends, is from vertical bureaucracies to horizontally organized companies (which parallels the general trend of all authorities in the knowledge era, as Trend Five suggests). Networks, he concludes, "are the fundamental stuff of which new organizations are and will be made," a trend that reflects the theme of process over product: specific business projects become the operating units, rather than a definable "company." The horizontal company, Castells concludes, "is a dynamic and strategically planned network of self-programmed, self-directed units based on decentralization, participation, and coordination."[1]

Networks are the logical result of virtual corporations and reflect complexity theory's ecological (rather than classical economics' clock-like) models. Business consultant James Moore has offered such a model in his book *The Death of Competition,* one that forces us to rethink the nature of business rivalry. The "traditional way to think about competition is in terms of offers and markets," Moore writes. "Your product or

SURPRISE SCENARIO:
GROWING AND PERSISTENT UNEMPLOYMENT

Since 1985 unemployment rates in developed countries as a group have held relatively stable at between 6 and 8 percent. European rates have been close to or exceeding 10 percent; American levels in the vicinity of 5 to 6 percent, Japan's under 3 percent. This scenario took the global challenge to employment and assumed continued sluggish growth in Europe, a substantial slowing of economic paces in emerging markets, market openings in places such as Japan that suddenly place at risk uncompetitive domestic service industries, and an acceleration of such workplace trends as automation that threaten a number of career paths.

The result was a surge in unemployment in the United States to 8 percent or more, roughly double current levels; a slight further inching upward of European joblessness; an official Japanese rate of 6 percent and more; and little or no job growth in developing nations to meet the requirements of their frequently burgeoning populations. In sum, this scenario looked at something on the order of 25 to 50 million new unemployed people in the developed world and perhaps an order of magnitude more than that number in developing nations, many of which are in the arc of crisis.

The implications of such an economic disaster would be stark:

*   *Social instability in developed countries,* and more and more alienated and jobless workers turn to extremist political causes. In the youth-rich and job-poor developing nations, this same effect could produce vast social violence.
*   *The growth of protectionist sentiment,* likely as expressed in the form of exclusive regional economic blocs—thus creating a vicious cycle in which improved growth in one region does not translate into a reduction of joblessness globally.
*   *Incredible new pressures on government budgets.* The strain would be especially severe in developed nations, because many will be grappling with the tremendous cost of bankrupt pension systems at roughly the same time.
*   *Risks of a knowledge-era depression as joblessness*—and alarmist media reports of it—create a cascading and self-fulfilling society-wide economic retrenchment.

service goes up against that of your competitor, and one wins." But this model "ignores the context—the environment—within which the business lies, and it ignores the need for coevolution with others in that environment, a process that involves cooperation as well as conflict." Businesses that learn "to lead economic coevolution" succeed by working to "seek out potential centers of innovation where, by orchestrating the contributions of a network of players, they can bring powerful benefits to bear for customers and producers alike." The trick is to break out of industry boundaries and "hasten the coming together of disparate business elements into new economic wholes." Moore urges us to recognize that we are witnessing nothing less that "the end of industry"[2]—by which he means the end of a time when businesspeople could think of their industries as unique, separate things. The idea of distinct companies is giving way to the notion of "business ecosystems"— networks that must be thought of as participatory human communities, similar to Arie de Geus's model of a "living company" that I discuss at the end of this trend.

THE CENTRAL ROLE OF FINANCE AND CAPITAL MARKETS

A further implication of a human resources economy is the growing role of financial services and capital markets in overall economy activity. One way of thinking about money is as a form of information, and so it is hardly surprising that the knowledge era has spawned global financial markets of unprecedented size and power. Today world financial decisionmakers often have decisive things to say about the success or failure of Europe's recovery, Japan's recession, and the future of emerging markets. Governments retain an important role, to be sure, but that role is circumscribed as never before by global finance.

Daily foreign exchange trading ran at about $10 billion or $20 billion in 1982; by 1992, it had reached $880 billion, and government bonds and equities added another $223 billion in daily trading.[3] Today daily foreign exchange transactions have ballooned close to $2.5 trillion per day.

A few observers are concerned that an economy so heavily influenced by finance is in a precarious situation. Some argue that speculative investments may spur short-term growth, but they do not lay the foundations for long-term prosperity.[4] Others worry that the norms set by global capital markets—the paradigm discussed in Trend Two—will crush local or national efforts to pursue social goals, such as ecological health. A country where business is more expensive because of environmental regulations is arguably one from which capital would flee—and the same principle would hold for union regulations, child-labor laws, antitrust standards, and other limits on unbridled corporate activity.

Another way in which a larger role for finance can be unhealthy to the global economy is by encouraging a more perceptual, rather than substantive or empirical, view of economic reality. Statements by economic officials in the major economic powers often carry more weight than accumulating evidence about the basic prospects for industrial and service enterprises. This trend is magnified by the power and influence of the media, its ability to manipulate economic facts into positive or negative "spin" for the day. We are, to some extent, entering a world of "virtual economics," in which the strength of an economy will be judged as much in perceptual as in real terms. Virtual economies, like the stock markets they mimic, could be more prone to sudden peaks and valleys, more susceptible to boom-and-bust cycles. This phenomenon is part and parcel of the knowledge era, and it applies to far more than just economics. In an era awash in information—and thousands of sources of it—perception becomes as important as reality, credibility as meaningful as strength, confidence as indispensable as resources.

Gradually, too, the *nature* of finance—even for individuals—is changing dramatically. Big investment firms and governments already conduct vast trades in cyberspace, with the push of a button. Eventually so will we all: The virtualization of finance is well under way; one estimate suggests that the number of on-line investment accounts will grow in the next 5 years from 1.5 million today to over 10 million and that on-line banking accounts will balloon from 1.1 million to almost 20 million. Financier David Shaw has plans for a bold new on-line financial service called FarSight, which will combine stock trading, bank accounts, credit cards, investments, even ATM machines—and, ultimately, car loans, home mortgages, and insurance—into a single, inexpensive package. Already several Internet-based stock trading companies, such as AmeriTrade, have cropped up, offering bargain-basement transaction fees and the convenience of anywhere-anytime access. This new technology, says one Morgan Stanley analyst, "allows end users to bypass the middleman. It allows them to bypass *us*."[5] Here again, the human resources economy undermines employment in a service industry—this time, finance and investment—while empowering individuals in stunning new ways.

WORSENING INCOME DISTRIBUTION

One of the most profound dangers of a globalized human resource economy is that it threatens to expand the gap between haves and have-nots in both developed and developing countries.[6] Several elements of the knowledge economy contribute to this result: a yawning gap between high-paying, high-tech jobs and low-paying service jobs; the social divisions fostered by the demand for highly educated workers in many new positions; and the stratifying effects of a global economy on developed economies. One basic fact illustrates this growing gap best: in 1979, U.S. college graduates made about half again as much as high school graduates; by the late 1990s, the premium on a college education was almost 90 percent, and climbing.

What is at stake is much more profound than mere income inequity. It is the danger that two groups could arise, groups with very different attitudes toward the global economy—two fundamentally different sectors of modern and modernizing nations. This emerging split has dramatic ramifications for politics, economics, society, and conflict; if unchecked, it carries a substantial risk of increased social and international violence. If *domination*, in the form of capitalist "exploitation," was the main theme of industrial-era critiques of capitalism, the primary theme of knowledge-era critiques could well become *inequality*.

One basic phenomenon underlying the risk of knowledge-era stratification is that knowledge-based skills tend to accumulate in social pools; the rich give their children a great education, they become wealthy, and the process repeats itself. (Figure 10.1 outlines one especially disturbing pattern in this vein: the immense disparity in college degrees acquired by children of wealthy and middle-class families in the United States.) "The most likely outcome" of the knowledge era, business expert Charles Handy concludes, is "an increasingly divided society," unless we take urgent steps to distribute knowledge and

FIGURE 10.1

Stratified Educational Achievement

Rates of College Graduation of Children, by Income, 1996

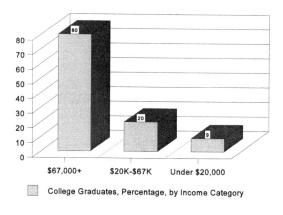

College Graduates, Percentage, by Income Category

Source: Washington Post, February 3, 1997, p. A6.

intelligence more widely.[7] Before his tenure as U.S. secretary of labor, Harvard economist Robert Reich wrote that America was cleaving into "symbolic analysts" and everyone else; the 20 percent would live lives of ease and wealth and "complete their secession from the union" in guarded suburban enclaves, while the poorest Americans "will be isolated within their own enclaves of urban and rural desperation" and the middle class, "gradually growing poorer, will feel powerless to alter any of these trends."[8]

I think that portrait is exaggerated, partly because tracking income and wealth distribution is a very tricky business. Some recent statistics support the idea that inequity is growing[9]; figures 10.2 and 10.3 offer a few of the basic statistics. A 1996 U.S. Census Department report concluded that "there has been growing income inequality over the last quarter-century. Inequality grew slowly in the 1970s and rapidly during the early 1980s. From about 1987 through 1992, the growth in measured inequality seemed to taper off, reaching 11.9 percent above its 1968 level." Put another way, in 1968, rich households (in the "95th percentile of income") had six times the income of lower-middle class

FIGURE 10.2

Change in the Gini Index of Inequality versus 1968, in percent

(higher numbers mean more inequality)

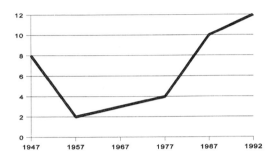

Source: U.S. Census Department, figures available at www.census.gov under "inequality."

households (at the 20th percentile); by 1994, rich households had over eight times the income of those in the lower-middle class.[10]

Skyrocketing pay at the top of the corporate ladder reflects the same trend. In 1979 U.S. chief executive officers made 29 times the average manufacturing salary; by 1988 they made 93 times as much, and in 1990, 113 times as much.[11] Some analysts had hoped that the explosion of mutual fund investing might deal with inequities, but the evidence suggests otherwise: The top 5 percent of American households holds 77 percent of all stocks; the bottom 80 percent holds just under 2 percent. "This was a slight gain from 1983, when the figure was 1.02 percent," writes economic analyst Robert Kuttner, "but it is a long way from people's capitalism."[12]

Shocking racial gaps show up in investments, threatening a further polarization of wealth. Only 14 percent of married black families owned stock in 1994, compared with 45 percent of all married families.[13] Racial inequalities also plague information technology ownership and use, a bedrock measurement of preparedness for the knowledge era: a recent study found that almost twice as many white families as black ones own computers, and whereas three-quarters of white high school and college kids have access to a computer, only about a third of black

FIGURE 10.3

Share of Household Income, in percent, 1967–1993

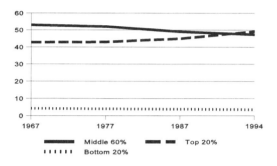

Source: U.S. Census Bureau, at www.census.gov

students do.[14] Racial inequality as measured in income has actually been declining in recent years, but that trend could slow or even halt if these underlying sources of inequality aren't corrected.

In a rapidly aging society, as the United States is today, is it perhaps even more disturbing to find that the level of inequality in accumulated wealth among people approaching retirement age is, in the words of one recent report, "simply enormous." A 1995 RAND Corporation study found that, among whites ages 51 to 61 in 1993, the richest tenth had nearly $1 million in assets per household; the middle tenth had only about $346,000; and the poorest tenth had but $88,640—including expected pension and Social Security payments. Among African Americans, the richest tenth had assets of only about $500,000, while the poorest tenth had just over $26,000—a shockingly low figure.[15]

In the developing world, we find the same process. The computers introducing new efficiencies in Latin America, for example, are putting thousands out of work and creating a new caste barrier between the technologically literate and those who are not. "Economists worry that the PC revolution will only exaggerate the huge gap between rich and poor" in the developing world, the Wall Street Journal notes. "If only the wealthy can afford computers, and computers become essential to the success of any business, then the prospects for the underprivileged will only diminish.[16] One wide-ranging interview project on Asian countries

TABLE 10.1

Inequity in Select Asian Countries, 1975–1993

Percentage of income held by the top 20 percent of households

Country	1975	1993
Indonesia	41	51
South Korea	41	45
Hong Kong	47	49
Philippines	48	56
Malaysia	54	56
Thailand	51	50

Source: Far Eastern Economic Review, December 21, 1995, p. 15, based on World Bank data.

found near the top of the list of public concerns the "widening income gaps between the rich and the poor, especially between urban and rural populations."[17]

Worldwide, between 1960 and 1990 the incomes of the richest 20 percent grew three times faster than those of the poorest 20 percent. In 1960 the richest 20 percent held 70 percent of the world's income; the poorest 20 percent, just 2.3 percent; by 1990 the richest quintile held 85 percent of global income; the poorest quintile, just 1.4 percent. Rapid economic growth and development has "created a conspicuous divide between rich and poor in some Asian countries, like China, and worsened it in others."[18] (See table 10.1.)

Not everyone agrees, though, on the scope of these changes or the existence of a problem—at least in the United States. Some analysts question the meaning of small shifts. John Weicher of the Hudson Institute notes that the share of wealth held by the richest 1 percent of Americans ranged from 32 to 36 percent in 1983, depending on which measures one used; for 1989 it ranged between 35 and 37 percent. "Those ranges overlap," Weicher writes, "so that it is possible to argue either that the concentration ratio increased or that it decreased." Moreover, because any economic surveys are subject to sampling error, "almost none of the changes in concentration, in either direction, is statistically significant."[19] During the 1990s, wages at the lower end of the income scale actually rose faster than those at the top; Americans see the need for higher education, and are seeking it in unprecedented numbers; and the relative pay of women has grown from an average of 60 percent of men's pay in the 1950s to 75 percent and growing by 1997, thus offsetting some education-related inequality.[20]

Others contend that the process under way in the 1980s actually involved the middle class enriching itself—and thus the hollowing out of the *middle* class is really a story of the growth of the *upper* class. Figure 10.4 indicates that the number of "rich" in the United States does appear to have expanded over the last two decades while the number of "poor" has held relatively stable.

Some analysts who have looked most closely at the data deny any trend toward earnings inequality at all. Robert Lerman of the Urban Institute notes that a common confusion is to measure equality by total annual earnings—which can vary for a host of structural reasons, such as changes in hours worked—rather than earnings per hour, a more accurate measure. By that standard, he writes, U.S. earnings inequality has not risen since 1984; in fact, it actually declined somewhat between 1987 and 1994—the Gini coefficient (a measure of overall inequality) fell by 5.5 percent, and the lead in earnings enjoyed by the very well paid over the very poorly paid shrank by 7.1 percent.[21]

While individual income inequity measured by hourly pay has not increased, Lerman adds, inequity among various U.S. families has—but for social and demographic, not economic, reasons. Higher divorce rates, greater numbers of single mothers, and other trends in family life skew the U.S. income picture by creating a larger number of less-well-off individuals and families than would exist if there were more two-earner households. This is not to deny the economic hardship faced by such families, only to indicate that economic factors—globalization, or the rise of the human resources economy—are not to blame for these shifts.

Lerman argues further that what we are witnessing is the creation of a "meritocracy" in which the economy rewards skills and education regardless of race or gender—without, so far, increasing inequities. Increasing "employer emphasis on skill," he writes, "ultimately could lessen wage differentials across all workers" by downplaying traditional

FIGURE 10.4

Rich and Poor in America: 1969–1996

Proportion of U.S. households with incomes
classified as "low" and "high"

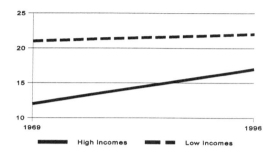

Source: U.S. Census Bureau, "Changes in Median Household Income," July 1998, at www.census.gov.

sources of bias and inequity "such as age, race, gender, family background, or where [workers] live." Lerman has found wage rate inequity by gender and race declining, which has offset growing inequity based on educational levels and related skills.[22] Yet as Lerman emphasizes, a meritocracy produces justice only if everyone has roughly matching access to education, training, and other determinants of skill—and the United States is far from such a situation today.

If new social disparities are indeed in the making, their implications will be powerful and dangerous. In the developed world, fearful workers might demand protectionist trade measures, slowing world trade and impairing economic growth. Legions of unemployed youth will stalk developing nations, unable to fathom the new knowledge era much less thrive in it. This growing threat of social unease is interwoven with the issue of globalization to be discussed in Trend Four: The middle class's concerns about jobs and wages mesh with political fears of interference in state sovereignty by supranational organizations and trends. As we have already seen on trade issues such as the North American Free Trade Agreement (NAFTA) and fast-track authority, one of the most urgent and important challenges facing governments over the next decade is to convince their citizens that the global economy works to their benefit.

THE FUTURE OF TRADE AND INVESTMENT:
SERVICES AND IDEAS, NOT GOODS

In a human resources economy whose core activities have moved away from manufacturing of physical products, it makes less and less sense to focus on trade balances of merchandise goods. Yet this is exactly what most trade experts and government agencies continue to do. The future is likely to demand something very different: a focus on trade in knowledge and information rather than in goods. This new kind of trade will be very difficult to measure except in one aspect: foreign direct investment—trade in money—which is a form of knowledge-based trade.

Electronic sales don't require as many employees and can be done from almost anywhere, facts that have accelerated the globalization of services. Anything that can be encoded digitally—software, text, music, video, and so on—can (and ultimately will) be delivered on-line, thus reducing transportation and shipping costs (and eliminating millions of jobs in those industries). A host of industries until now sheltered from international competition, from finance to banking and travel and retail sales, will soon feel the pressure of global economic competition.[23]

Another symptom of a human resources economy is therefore an increasing emphasis on service trade and technology transfer or intellectual property rights issues rather than trade in manufactured goods. Through means such as compulsory licensing, joint ventures, and forced technology transfer, developing nations are gaining access to Western technological know-how and research and development efforts—and thereby to the knowledge-based competitive advantages of the "new economy." Controlling the flow of this knowledge may well become the central focus of trade policy in the years ahead.

Average annual growth in commercial services trade between 1980 and 1993 was 7.7 percent, compared with 4.9 percent for merchandise trade, numbers that have led the World Bank to conclude that "The internationalization of services will likely lead the next stage of economic globalization."[24] Examples of services that are increasingly traded globally include software programming, back-office services, product design, research and development, and customer service. If outsourcing is a growing trend for businesses, it is increasingly taking on the character of *international* outsourcing—even for "services" as complex as

FIGURE 10.5

World Trade in Services, 1980–1998

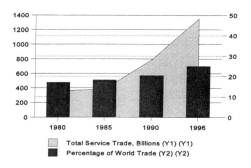

Source: The World Bank, *Global Economic Prospects* (Washington, D.C.: World Bank, 1995), p. 47; and World Bank, *World Development Indicators 1998* (Washington, D.C.: World Bank, 1998), pp. 198-99.

medical care.[25] Under the influence of the "death of distance" (to be examined in Trend Four), the share of world trade devoted to information as opposed to goods will rise even more dramatically.

SHIFT TO THE DEVELOPING WORLD

The broad trends under consideration here also will promote a relative shift of power, especially economic power, to the developing world, with the emerging markets in Asia as the centerpiece of the transition. The most basic reason for this change is differences in economic growth rates—a worldwide rate of 3 or 4 percent, about 2 percent in the developed countries, and between 4 and 7 percent in many parts of the developing world. Such a transfer of power eventually may precipitate a tectonic shift in the foundations of world politics; political scientist Robert Gilpin writes that "we are witnessing one of the most significant economic (and eventually political) transformations in modern history: the rapid and massive redistribution of world industry and economic power away from the rich, industrialized countries toward the newly industrializing economies (NIEs) of East and Southeast Asia."[26]

FIGURE 10.6

Developing Countries Share of World Output
(%, traditional and purchasing power parity standards)

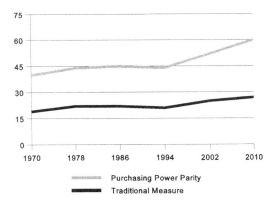

Source: World Bank, *Global Economic Prospects and the Developing Countries* (Washington, D.C.: World Bank, 1995), p. 63.

One especially powerful boost for developing nations has been the trend toward privatization and liberalization in formerly communist and autocratic societies. The decline of state planning has freed new entrepreneurial activities in many developing countries, fueled by vast amounts of foreign direct investment. The march of technology has allowed developing countries to leapfrog decades of economic progress and scientific research and begin to compete with the developed world in relatively short order. A grocery distributor in central Brazil bought a $3,000 computer to dispatch trucks, for example, and is delivering 30 percent more goods with a third fewer vehicles while reducing employment from 95 to 80. One of Brazil's largest banks, Unibanco, offers a system of banking-at-home via computer more advanced than almost anything in the United States. By 1997 it had over 43,000 customers and had begun airing ads featuring Microsoft founder Bill Gates.[27]

One of the most important implications of the human resources economy from the standpoint of the developing world is its emphasis on systems with small infrastructure requirements. This is true of both new wireless communications systems—which do not require the enormous expense and time-consuming process of laying thousands of miles of copper wire—and increasingly cost-effective soft energy alternatives such as solar and wind power. Developing nations are interested in both, and for obvious reasons: They can be installed locally without a huge nationwide grid and therefore will allow developing nations to pass over industrial-era communications and energy technologies.

Figure 10.6 spells out the broad results of these trends. By the year 2010, developing nations will account for 30 percent of world imports (versus 24 percent today) and 22 percent of exports (versus 17 percent today); measured in purchasing power parity terms, the developing world will account for over half of world output over the next decade. In sum, the rise of the developing world means that by 2010 more than 9 billion people in the developing world may have per capita incomes higher than those of Greece or Spain today.[28] One implication is a changing balance of U.S. exports: Roughly within our time frame, U.S. exports to emerging markets are expected to outpace exports going to Europe and Japan combined. U.S. trade policy will change to reflect these trends.[29]

The question for the future is straightforward: Is the developing-world boom sustainable? Will it persist over the long run, with developing nations maintaining an economic growth rate double that of developed nations?

First of all, we need to take a step back from the breathless pronouncements of an "economically multipolar world" and the growing "dominance" of emerging markets. Even by 2005 or even perhaps 2010, per-capita incomes in China and India will still be only a fraction of those of rich countries, and developed-world nations will still be responsible for roughly three-quarters of all imports and exports in the world. The "purchasing power parity" measurement of per-capita income, which measures economic activity in a nation by the standards of its own development level, tends to exaggerate developing countries' relative importance: A French company doesn't care what China's purchasing power parity level is if its people cannot afford to buy imported goods.

In fact, some analysts see a number of reasons to believe that developing-world growth will slow, though not collapse, in the next decade. Paul Krugman expects a "downward cycle of deflating expectations" in which capital markets become more reluctant to send money to higher-risk developing nations, and those nations in turn have a more difficult time selling the economic reforms necessary to reassure the financiers.[30] The 1998 Asian financial crisis will magnify this tendency. Then, too, developing nations that have begun to crack into high-technology industries, such as computers, may have a difficult time staying in the market in coming years, in part because few of them are laying a foundation of technological innovation: Research and development as a share of GNP, almost 3 percent for the developed world in 1990, was less than two-thirds of 1 percent for the developing world.[31]

A final barrier to continued emerging-market success is social instability inherent in rapid modernization. The countries of East Asia, researcher David Hitchcock writes, believe that they are confronting "enormous domestic problems of governance, ethnic tensions, corruption, widening income gaps, labor unrest, and stresses from rapid urbanization" and industrial dislocation—all of which occurs as the people of these nations "watch their own traditional ways and identity wash out under the waves of modernization, leaving many drifting without a compass in a sea of consumerism and impersonal materialism."[32] But there are other, potentially more powerful, reasons to believe that a human resources economy offers new opportunities for developing nations, and their gradual rise in power and influence seems all but inevitable over the next decade.

A NEW ECONOMICS

A change in the fundamental nature of an economy requires a reform in the economic theory used to analyze it. "We have an economic theory that can help us to understand and hence to manage the production and exchange of tangible objects like cornflakes and houses," explains Max Boisot, who has written extensively on knowledge-era economics, "but, as yet, no satisfactory economic theory to help us manage the production and exchange of intangible objects like knowledge."[33] An economic theory for the knowledge era would not abandon classical economics but would rethink some of its fundamental assumptions about profit, equilibrium, and rationality.

Knowledge-era economics will want, for example, to revisit classical economics' assumption of "diminishing returns"—the notion that

companies which gain leadership in a field eventually hit limits, whether
of resources or energy, and are overtaken by others in the field.
Economist Brian Arthur argues that a knowledge economy is characterized by *increasing* returns—"the tendency for that which is ahead to get
further ahead, for that which loses advantage to lose further advantage.
They are mechanisms of positive feedback which operate—within
markets, businesses, and industries—to reinforce that which gains
success or aggravate that which suffer loss."[34] Arthur (and others
working in the field of increasing returns, such as Stanford professor
Paul Romer)[35] explains that an economy operating on increasing returns
is characterized not by equilibrium but instability, because if a product
gets ahead, "increasing returns can magnify this advantage, and the
product or company or technology can go on to lock in the market."
The key to success in this world is predicting the Next Big Thing, and
rewards "go to the players who are first to make sense of the new games
looming out of the technological fog."[36]

These insights require modification of a second core principle of
classical economics—the natural equilibrium of markets. "What is
needed," Boisot writes, "is a far-from-equilibrium information economics which allows for innovation, evolution, and learning."[37] Not
surprisingly, much of the best work being done on these evolving
notions is by economists and others whose work is informed with
chaos and complexity theory.

The reference to complexity theory also should make it little
surprise that new models of economics rely on ecological understandings of business. "Technological products do not stand alone. They
depend on the existence of other products and other technologies,"
Arthur contends. "Unlike products of the processing world, such as
soybeans or rolled steel, technological products exist within local
groupings of products that support and enhance them. They exist in
mini-ecologies."[38] Business strategy increasingly requires networks of
interdependent companies, notions of elaborated services, and other
forms of ecological or holistic thinking.

As Boisot implies, new approaches to economics stress the crucial
role of *innovation.* In a nonlinear, rapidly changing environment,
innovation, rather than defending established market shares through
price competition or other means, takes on unprecedented importance.
This fact reinforces the message of Richard D'Aveni, Gary Hamel, and

others on the requirement for bold rather than incremental thinking in the knowledge era.

Finally, the impact of the knowledge era forces us to rethink classical economics' assumption of a "rational" consumer equipped with "perfect" information. Phenomena like increasing returns operate on the basis of perception as much as anything else, and economists studying the impact of the knowledge era tend to stress the role of corporate and government perception management, and of decisions based not on perfect information but on skewed perceptions, as crucially important economic trends—and ones that rely only marginally on the "objective" economic fundamentals.[39] This again reinforces the idea that the knowledge economy is based as much on perception as reality.

Conflict in the Knowledge Era

Finally, the advent of an information age is transforming the nature of conflict. Where previous armies focused on concentration of force and mass, today's most advanced militaries attempt to achieve a concentration of information. This is not an economic effect per se, but it stems from developments in technology that are commonly considered economic phenomena. It also works to break down the boundaries between economy and defense, between business competition and warfare.

"An unnamed U.S. intelligence official has boasted that with $1 billion and 20 capable hackers, he could shut down America," the historian Walter Laqueur explains. "What he could achieve, a terrorist could too."[1]

The question of violence within and between states over the next decade partly rests, very much as it always has, on the foundational issue of human needs. Great social and economic transitions such as the one under way today call into question the stability and regularity so critical to meeting those needs; around the world, the end of the industrial age has dramatically upset people's expectations about their jobs, incomes, families, countries, environments, and safety. In some cases, people turn for identity and security to violent groups, whether they are terrorist organizations, drug cartels, gangs, or militias. The growth of such small-scale violence—microviolence on a massive scale—is one of the fundamental trends of the next decade. The relative importance of this kind of warfare is increasing given the emergence, outlined in Trend Two, of a global social contract and the corresponding decline of major war.

152   GLOBAL TRENDS 2005

These groups will, in turn, experience enormous new potential for harm in coming years as a result of the ongoing revolution in warfare. Militaries are increasingly looking into the potential of computers, telephones, and broadcast media.[2] Computer viruses inserted into the stock market of an adversary could paralyze its economy. So-called logic bombs could have similar effects on the systems controlling air and rail transportation. Computer hackers could bring down the systems that allow Americans and others to use their credit cards, slicing billions of dollars a day out of the U.S. economy with a few keystrokes. Electronic warfare also has increasingly direct military applications: One U.S. Air Force investigator recently concluded that "We could not wage war without unclassified [computer] systems. We could not move people, food or anything without computers." In the future, enemies of the United States (or any knowledge-era power) will be able "to bypass confrontation with U.S. military forces and attack the United States directly by interfering with its national information infrastructure."[3]

The advent of an age of knowledge warfare—combined with the growing spread of the technologies for weapons of mass destruction, from nuclear to biological weapons—will signal a profound diffusion of the means of warfare, greatly increasing the harm that small groups can wreak on large powers. Through weapons of mass destruction, computer terrorism, or cable news–transmitted images of assassinations and bombings, small groups will be able to inflict substantial pain on the homeland of distant large states. Americans already confused about the rationale for intervening in a new Balkan war c. 2010 or 2015 will surely refuse to become involved when confronted by the risk of stolen Russian nuclear weapons being set off by Serb extremists in New York, or the potential that a handful of Indian or Chinese computer hackers hired by Belgrade could wipe out the savings accounts of millions of people in Chicago, Los Angeles, and Washington.

Yet an age of global information works simultaneously to draw nations into secondary issues around the world by exposing their populations to terrible images of starvation and repression and in effect shaming the governments into action. A nineteenth-century American populace reading newspaper accounts of a Balkan war (and not yet being accustomed to a leading U.S. world role) might regret the situation; a twenty-first-century populace seeing television images

ISSUE FEATURE: THE "LIVING COMPANY"

In his nearly 40 years with the oil company Royal Dutch/Shell, Arie de Geus cultivated a worldwide reputation as one of the most thoughtful strategic planners of his day. Now he has boiled down many of the lessons of his experience into a model for business culture and organization in a human resources era. He calls it a "living company."[4]

De Geus's particular angle is to examine the life span of corporations. He found that very few reached their potential—that most companies, as he put it, "die young." The reason? Because companies behave too much like classical economics tells them to: "Their managers focus exclusively on producing goods and services and forget that the organization is a

> Living companies "place commitment to people before assets, respect for innovation before devotion to policy . . . and the perpetuation of the community before all other concerns."
> —Arie de Geus

community of human beings that is in business—*any* business—to stay alive." In contrast, companies with extraordinary life spans shared a number of distinct characteristics:

- "*Conservatism in financing.*" Living companies "knew the usefulness of spare cash in the kitty" for snapping up sudden opportunities and did not overextend themselves.
- "*Sensitivity to the world around them.*" Living companies adapt well to change.
- "*Awareness of their identity.*" Employees in living companies have a clear sense of belonging to a meaningful whole; managers understand the company's goals.
- "*Tolerance of new ideas.*" Companies with long life spans "tolerated activities in the margin: experiments and eccentricities that stretched their understanding."
- Managers in living companies therefore will have a number of characteristics in common. They value people more than assets, because people represent the company's heart and soul. They give employees freedom to roam, tolerating new and unusual ideas. They promote a learning environment, and they nurture their organization as a community rather than using it to enrich a small inner circle of managers. De Geus contends that these values will be critical to surviving in a rapidly changing, hypercompetitive global economy.

POLICY RECOMMENDATIONS: *TREND THREE*

1. For businesses, *reorganize and rethink strategy to fit the requirements of the new era*—a networked, virtual, holistic, perceptual economy.
2. For societies, *take steps to improve the lot of the least skilled and poorest.* In America this means aid for the poor; in Europe, fewer regulations on businesses that want to hire them.
3. *Increase the focus on and place of education,* the linchpin of human resources economics.
4. *Get perceptually important elements of national economies,* such as budget deficits, *in order.*
5. *Rethink trade strategies* to focus on service industries and emerging market countries.
6. *Develop improved means of understanding a human resources economy,* including better measures of knowledge-era economic performance and a new economic theory.

---

of children being killed, women being assaulted, and soldiers being maimed may well demand action. Even if the public at large does not do so, images of war will help create political interest groups—as in the Bosnian case—that do. These thoughts reinforce the conclusion, reached in Trend One, that the United States and other major industrial powers will face an unending series of humanitarian, peacekeeping, and peacemaking challenges throughout the developing world over the next decade.

Evolving forms of information weapons and warfare also can blur the lines between military and economic conflict. How will we classify a crisis in which computers go down, economic activity comes to a halt, and gross national products plummet—a trade war or a "real" war? In recent conflicts, U.S. military leaders have hesitated to annihilate electronically the economy of a developing nation, even while they prosecuted a military campaign that killed tens of thousands of that nation's soldiers on the battlefield. The rise of information warfare will create demanding new strategic and moral dilemmas in the decade ahead. It also may create unprecedented interdependencies and vulnerabilities among developed nations; the U.S. government, like many others, buys many of the microchips and other computers components critical to its advanced weapons from international companies. In sharing ideas, products, and patents related to the core areas of the information economy, states also will be sharing military secrets. This fact can work for good—making war infeasible by establishing a network of interdependencies among the great powers—or ill, by prompting new protectionism and economic espionage.

THE NEW ECONOMIC RULES

The threads of the human resources economy weave together in a number of key themes—themes that lead to the policy recommendations summarized in the text box. Most broadly, economic theorist Kenichi Ohmae explains that, in such an era, "People are the only true means to create wealth." People—"and the values they do or do not carry with them"—make all the difference in economic performance.[5] It therefore follows that people whose culture values education, thrift, and hard work will thrive—and that intensifying economic competition will drive all cultures toward these social values even as it pushes them in the direction of democracy and free markets.

Companies that value their human resources—those that meet Arie de Geus's definition of a "living" company—will prosper and societies that respond to the demands of the human resources economy can engender new eras of growth and prosperity. If these requirements are met, then the economic promise of the knowledge era is considerable. Yet the risks of the human resources economy are just as profound as its opportunities: The knowledge era has the potential to harden socioeconomic inequities, banish developing nations from cutting-edge economic activity, and place weapons of frightening destructive power in the hands of terrorists and mischief-makers the world over.

Perhaps the single most important policy and social implication of this trend is the crucial importance of education. It makes sense that an era characterized by its emphasis on knowledge would put a premium on education. Societies will succeed or fail in this new age to a great extent based on the emphasis they place on educating their people. I return to this theme in the volume's conclusion.

In sum, the human resources economy offers incredible new potential alongside major risks. It can empower workers in dramatic new ways, but it also entails immense transitional pains. The human resources economy represents both the end of an old form of economy and the birth of a new one. It is in this transitional struggle, this tension between two ages, that we find the most important challenges of the next ten years.

An Era of Global Tribes

Though they may gaze across at a neighboring state,
and hear the sounds of its dogs and chickens,
The people will never travel back and forth,
till they die of old age.

Tao Te Ching

As should by now be apparent, the knowledge era is a time of paradox and contradiction, an age when theses and antitheses merge to produce unprecedentedly powerful engines of social change. Conflicting trends gain speed simultaneously, wrenching knowledge-era societies in two or more directions at the same time. Simple ideas are rendered complex by our age's amazing pace of change and the growing interdependence of its trends. Nowhere is this more apparent than in perhaps the most fundamental paradox of our time—the simultaneous acceleration of both globalism and pluralism, which I call an era of global tribes.[1] The world is becoming more cosmopolitan and more insular at the same time; accelerating global trade, awareness, and travel coincide with intensifying local, national, ethnic, and religious identity. "Our world and our lives," argues the political philosopher Benjamin Barber, "are caught between what William Butler Yeats called the two eternities of race and soul: that of race reflecting our tribal past, that of soul anticipating the cosmopolitan future."[2]

How is this so? What are the specific mechanisms by which globalism and tribalism emerge and grow? What are their effects on our lives? And most important of all, what future does their collision promise for humankind?

The Process of Globalization

"We live in a global world." This phrase captures the most common claim about the knowledge era: that it is a global phenomenon which tends to break down the barriers between countries in economic, social, and political ways. Measured in terms of consumer culture and interdependent financial markets, globalization is accelerating as a product of trade, improved telecommunications, and global media awareness made possible by the new information technologies.

But globalization is not a uniform phenomenon. It is more advanced on some issues, less on others. It is stunningly present in several regions of the world, almost nonexistent elsewhere. It constrains state power on a handful of key questions, such as finance, but leaves a wide swath of state authority on others. As the following chapters will suggest, the world of the next 10 years will be a regionalized, rather than a truly globalized, world in the most well-known yardstick of globalization: international trade. In other important ways, however, true globalization is indeed advancing and will become pronounced over the next decade. The rest of this trend examines these issues—the areas in which world economic and social affairs have yet to become global and those that already have.

THE WORLD ECONOMY: REGIONAL, BECOMING GLOBAL

To many observers, the primary feature of the modern world economy is its globalization. World economic activity is more globalized than ever

FIGURE 12.1

Trends in World Trade Integration

Growth of world trade, world output, and trade integration, 1971–2004

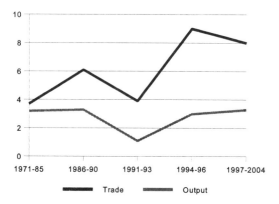

Source: The World Bank, *Global Economic Prospects and the Developing Countries*
(Washington, D.C.: IBRD/The World Bank, 1995), p. 15;
The Economist, March 28, 1998, p. 5; author's estimates.

before and is becoming more interdependent at an accelerating pace.
Thus Peter Drucker concluded in 1986 that "economic dynamics have
decisively shifted from the national economy to the world economy. . . .
This may be the most important—it surely is the most striking—feature
of the changed world economy."[1] (See figure 12.1.)

But the consensus on the scope and nature of globalization is far
from complete. Some economists argue that the importance of trade to
the U.S. economy is modest, noting that U.S. exports are equivalent to
only 10 percent of gross domestic product (GDP).[2] Others deny that
U.S. dependence on foreign trade is growing, pointing out that the ratio
of all U.S. trade (exports and imports) to the U.S. GDP has remained at
about 21 percent since 1980.[3] Scholar Vincent Cable, while recognizing
many economic aspects of globalization, notes that it is more evident in
some areas, such as finance, than others and warns against simple
projections: "History has taught us that much of what we regard as the
inexorable advance of globalization is, in fact, fragile and reversible."[4]

What, then, does "globalization" really mean in an economic sense? How far has it advanced? How "interdependent" has the world economy truly become?

Measuring global trade as a percentage of GDP is perhaps the simplest and most straightforward measure of globalization. If trade in goods and merchandise is growing faster than the world economy as a whole, then it is becoming more integrated.

The numbers support such a conclusion: World trade has grown faster than global GDP consistently since at least 1974. Between 1983 and 1993, for example, world exports grew a total of 70.5 percent while world output grew only 34.6 percent—exports grew over twice as fast.[5] (See figure 12.2.) This trend will continue: The World Bank forecasts economic growth in the Group of Seven (G-7) countries between 1995 and 2004 of about 3 percent and merchandise export volume growth of over 6 percent.[6] As a result of these trends, by the year 2004 trade in the developed countries will average 40 percent of GDP and, for the developing world, over 50 percent of GDP, while (as we saw in Trend Two) one estimate suggests that, during roughly the same period, the amount of global GDP open to competitive trading will explode from $4 trillion in the early 1990s to over $20 trillion. As we shall see, however, much of this merchandise trade remains within trading regions rather than traveling globally; its extent, both by types of products and country, is highly varied; and history has shown that integration through simple merchandise trade is reversible.

The second most common measure of globalization is foreign direct investment (FDI)—capital investments made by corporations in other countries, to build factories or service centers or to purchase existing foreign businesses. During the early 1990s the amount of FDI grew by leaps and bounds, and some observers characterize this as another sign of a globalized world economy. Between 1981 and 1985 total world foreign direct investment amounted to an annual average of $98 billion; from 1986 to 1990 the average annual global total of FDI jumped to $323 billion, and during the 1990s it ran consistently above $330 billion every year, reaching $440 billion in 1997. As a result, the "stock" of foreign investment—the running total of investment projects—had grown from $1.2 trillion in 1988 to nearly $3.5 trillion by 1997.[7]

Investment in developing countries accounted for the vast jump in FDI activity in the 1990s (although, as Figure 12.4 will show later, this

FIGURE 12.2

World Trade Integration, 1972–2004
(Export plus import merchandise trade volumes as share of GDP,
in percent; * years are projections)

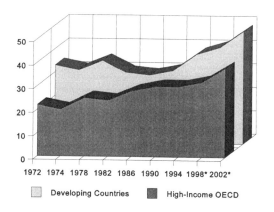

Source: The World Bank, *Global Economic Prospects and the Developing Countries*
(Washington, D.C.: World Bank, 1995), p. 18.

slowed in the late 1990s as a result of the global financial crisis). Foreign direct investment flows into developing countries reached $50 billion in 1992, an estimated $80 billion in 1993, and $150 billion by 1997. This growth in FDI is one basis for my opinion that developing states will own a larger share of world output.

Thus it would seem that the world economy is indeed becoming globalized. Trade and investment are growing faster than the world economy, which means that it is one characterized by relatively more international trade in goods and capital all the time. Yet the figures are not actually so clear:[8] A number of important qualifications to the data suggest that the world economy is not globalized to an unprecedented degree—and that in fact it may not be globalized at all but rather regionalized.

Neither trade nor FDI now stands at unprecedentedly high levels. The period between 1870 and 1913 has been described as a golden age of economic globalization, at least in Europe, where trade growth outpaced national growth, labor migration was enormous, and international capital flows were very large. One estimate, for example, suggests that the stock of long-term foreign investment reached $44 billion in 1914.[9] As outlined in the next issue feature, it would be wrong to say that the global economy of 1995 is no more integrated or globalized than was the world economy of 1913. Nonetheless, to claim, correctly, that we are on the road to a dramatically new level of globalization is not to argue that we have arrived.

A second qualification to economic globalism is that the vast majority of world trade—an increasing majority—goes on within the three major trading blocs of Europe, the Americas, and East Asia rather than between them. Between 1985 and 1993, U.S. exports and imports from North America grew relative to trade in other areas; European Union (EU) trade within Europe grew relative to other trade (an amount that seems set to increase with the introduction of the euro); and Japanese trade within East Asia rose relative to other trade.[10] In Europe intraregional trade accounts for almost 70 percent of the total. The trends are similar for foreign investment: From 1986 to 1992 almost 70 percent of investment in East Asia came from within the region[11]; overall, some 80 to 90 percent of FDI outflows from any given region stayed within that region.[12]

In fact, important economic currents are dictating a focus on areas much smaller than regions. Paul Krugman points to the "localization of the world economy": although "we talk a lot these days about globalization . . . when you look at the economies of modern cities what you see is a process of localization: A steadily rising share of the work force produces services that are sold only within that same metropolitan area."[13] This probably understates the real importance of economic globalization, but it is certainly true—as we shall see—that localization and micromarketing are key aspects of modern corporate thinking.

The key question about economic regionalism is: Where is it heading? Will deepened regional economic integration occur at the expense of true globalism, or serve as a stepping-stone toward global integration?

The obvious answer—and the correct one—is that it is too early to tell. Policy decisions by the major trading states will crucially effect the outcome; the conclusion of the Uruguay Round of the General Agreement on Tariffs and Trade (GATT), for example, builds a firewall

ISSUE FEATURE:
THE WORLD ECONOMY—1913 VERSUS 1997

The world economy today, measured by trade and investment, is global to an unprecedented degree—if only just surpassing 1913—for a variety of reasons.

First, it is more broadly based. The trade integration around the turn of the century primarily involved European countries; today's integration is much more widely dispersed. Second, modern trade flows much more freely than in 1913. Tariff rates on merchandise trade averaged about 20 percent within Europe in 1913; they

> The post-1945 surge in world trade "has lasted longer and has involved more countries than before 1914."
> —United Nations

stood at 30 percent in Japan and a whopping 44 percent in the still highly protective United States. By 1990 European Community trade agreements had reduced tariffs to 5.9 percent on average, while U.S. tariffs had slipped under 5 percent and Japan's official tariffs to an average of 5.3 percent.[14]

Third, world trade integration, measured as a share of GDP, has accelerated somewhat more quickly since 1945 than it did after 1870. Between 1870 and 1913 the average trade acceleration—the difference in the percentages of trade growth and economic growth—was 1.4 percent. In the 1950s it was 2.3 percent; in the 1960s, 3 percent; and in the 1970s, 1.6 percent. During the 1980s this rate of growth slipped to about 1 percent, but it accelerated again in the 1990s.[15]

Fourth and finally, merchandise trade as a percentage of GDP has indeed now surpassed the levels of 1913. It is accurate to say that we did not return to these levels until the last two decades—but now we have, and we have moved past them. Exports as a share of GDP have grown for most major economic powers. France's ratio of exports to GDP was 13.9 percent in 1913 and 17.5 percent in 1992; Germany's grew from 17.5 percent in 1913 to 24 percent in 1992; and the U.S. ratio grew from 6 percent to over 7.[16] If world trade as a percentage of world GDP continues to rise, the coming years will witness a series of stunning new heights in world trade integration.

against a dangerously intense regionalism in trade. Regional groupings could, for example, promote a broader global trade regime through gradual expansion: As the European Union spreads east, NAFTA south, and Japan's trade sphere south and west, the three regions could eventually blur and merge together. One current proposal would do exactly that between Europe and North America, creating a giant free-trade area among all the EU and NAFTA members. But the key underlying trend is that regional trade blocs are shifting the locus of economic activity away from insularity and toward a more cosmopolitan awareness.

OTHER ENGINES OF GLOBALIZATION: GLOBAL AWARENESS

The global economy itself, at least as measured in traditional trade terms, is therefore globaliz*ing* but not yet fully globaliz*ed*. The engine of economic interdependence that many believe to be pulling social and cultural factors in its wake turns out to be the caboose after all. Something more fundamental is at stake than mere trade, even if that trade serves as a sort of Trojan horse for the broader social and cultural changes that are afoot.

The political scientist Ernst Haas recognized decades ago the importance of a knowledge era in promoting global levels of awareness. He defined knowledge as "the sum of technical information and of theories about that information which commands sufficient consensus" to serve as a guide to public policy. Haas went on to note that, internationally, the sharing of knowledge among governments "is a form of cognitive convergence. When Soviet and American engineers agree on the properties of strategic weapons, and economists on the determinants of the business cycle . . . certain ideological differences are being bridged by converging modes of thought." He could locate "no single point of origin for this process, no single historical or sociological cause." Instead knowledge is "embedded in many social processes that are to be found in all economic and social systems" that have entered the modern era of science and technology. Having escaped the control of its originators, knowledge becomes "a kind of international public good." Haas even suggested that the term "consciousness" might be more appropriate for his notion than "knowledge."[17] *An emerging fund of global conscious-ness*—a perfect shorthand description of one implication of the knowledge era, and one that builds on the engines of global homogenization discussed in Trend Two.

Futurists Watts Wacker and Jim Taylor have made another fascinating connection here: the notion of "homophyly." This, they argue, is "the tendency of life-forms when touching to assume the properties of each other."[18] They suggest that it's true in biology; any husband and wife (or any friend of theirs who watches their clothing tastes) can tell you it's true in marriage; and, increasingly, it seems to be true in international affairs as well. And it implies that interaction, economic or otherwise, leads to homogenization—even on a global scale.

Thus the striking pluralism of knowledge-era society is developing alongside an expanded globalism and awareness of things and people *outside* our narrow groups. Information permits global awareness at the same time as it promotes self-awareness, fertile soil for thousands of ethnic movements around the globe. This global mentality is on display in increasingly specialized professions whose members may have more in common with colleagues half a world away than with their neighbors.

This process is made possible and impelled by science, which both creates the tools for global interchange and, through its methodology, makes such exchange a regular practice among members of its own professions. Modernity and the knowledge era, writes sociologist Anthony Giddens, is "inherently globalizing." Giddens goes on to define what he means by the term: Globalization can be defined "as the intensification of worldwide social relations which link distant localities in such a way that local happenings are shaped by events occurring many miles away and vice versa."[19] Global awareness is perhaps farthest advanced in consumer culture. People all over the globe wear American jeans, watch American movies, use French perfume, drive Japanese cars—and more than that, they increasingly possess a uniform consumerist mind-set that overwhelms the particulars of nation and culture.

Yet as we shall see, this advancing globalism does not undermine all nationalism. Giddens argues, for example, that while globalization might diminish peoples' allegiance to nation-states, it might also intensify their adherence to local forms of identity. There is, he writes, a "complicated, dialectical connection" between "the globalising tendencies of modernity and localized events in day-to-day life"; the result is a world that "interlace[s] the local and global in complex fashion"[20]—a world of globalism and tribalism, not only existing simultaneously but feeding off and accelerating one another. Czech president Vaclav Havel argues that humankind stands helpless before so many global challenges because "our civilization has essentially globalized only the surface of our lives"; and meanwhile, cultures that are "increasingly lumped together by contemporary civilization" seek autonomy and differences[21]—the paradoxical interplay of globalism and pluralism, a homogenous interdependence confronting a persistent longing for a unique identity and independence.

GLOBAL COMMUNICATIONS

Over the next decade, the cost of international communications— whether by phone, fax, or e-mail—will drop dramatically. In a world where it is just as cheap to call 3,000 miles away as it is to call next door, economic and social relations will be altered dramatically. One formula for conceiving of this dramatic change is as a *death of distance,* outlined in the next issue feature.

Technology is dramatically lowering the cost of telephony. One fiber-optic cable thinner than a human hair can carry 30,000 telephone calls and costs a fraction of old copper wire to install, use, and maintain. The resulting cost savings have been obstructed by national policies that charge stiff rates to let a call into or out of the country; this too will change. Developing nations are expanding communications networks with lightning speed; China is adding the telecommunications equivalent of a new Baby Bell every year.[22]

Cheaper global telephony will combine with wireless mobility to produce incredible communications options—the options, as I argued in Trend Two, of a pervasive knowledge network. Tiny mobile phones with the capability to send and receive video as well as sound will enable people to carry the world in their pocket—the ability almost instantly to reach anyone in the world from wherever they are, at low cost.

This trend will revolutionize service and knowledge industries, which will become far more tradable across national boundaries. Entertainment, education, and health care—three dominant service industries—will increasingly become global concerns. Indeed, any service that can be performed remotely and electronically, from toll-free

ISSUE FEATURE: A "DEATH OF DISTANCE"

The Economist magazine recently summarized the clear direction of global communications technologies.[23] "Over the next few years," it concluded, "the price of making a long-distance call in and between some countries will fall to the point where it costs little more to telephone from Hollywood to Glasgow than to nearby Beverly Hills. At the same time, telephone companies will begin to switch the basis of charging their customers from the length of time for which they talk to a flat subscription. Within a decade or two, most ordinary telephone conversations will cost nothing extra, whatever their duration or distance."

Imagine that transformation: Telephone calls will cost nothing extra, whatever their duration or distance. Imagine the implications for business, which can be conducted cheaply around the world. Imagine the results for personal relationships, which can be maintained over video phone links across the globe.

This process is already under way through the Internet, where phone companies are offering service for a flat rate of $15 or $20 a month. For that price, *Business Week* explained, "you can make all the calls you want" to anyone with the same setup "with no limit on length or destination."

The Economist sums up the ramifications of the death of distance this way. As a result of this trend, "one of the most important limits imposed by geography on human activities will eventually vanish," an event that "may well prove the most significant economic force shaping the next half century" whose "effects will be as pervasive as those of the discovery of electricity."

service numbers to keeping an eye on security cameras to doing someone's taxes, will be tradable. In the process, small towns far from urban centers will become new hubs of economic activity. Offering lower costs and greater safety, and suddenly capable of hosting major service operations with clients all over the world, small towns and rural areas will experience a boom in investment. As the economic analyst Michael Moynihan puts it, "The network revolution makes it easier to locate a business in a low-cost area but sell into a higher-cost one"[24]— though, as I argued in Trend One, cities are telecommunications and knowledge hubs and have not surrendered all their competitive advantages in the knowledge era.

FIGURE 12.3

Declining International Telephone Costs

Cost, in U.S. dollars, of a 7-minute telephone call from the listed
country to Australia, 1990–2000

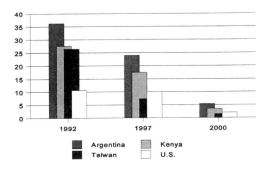

Source: Wired (September 1997): 132.

The tradability of services is one of the paramount economic trends
of the next decade. A student in Des Moines, Iowa—or Poland or
Bangladesh—will be able to flip on a television and tune into lectures from
Oxford University. A savvy consumer in Venezuela will open an account
with a German bank, monitoring it via a bank card swiped through a
reader on her television. Home shopping networks will go global.

One recent news story provides a stunning example of the new
global service economy at work. A hospital in Fairfax, Virginia, transmitted a digital recording of a physician's patient report to a typist for a
quick-turnaround transcript to save another night's hospital stay. It
shipped the recording at 7:00 A.M. and had a corrected copy back from
a proofreader by 11:00.[25] That doesn't sound too dramatic, until you
realize that the typist to whom they sent the recording is in Bangalore,
India—a specially trained transcriber who earns about $2,500 a year, less
than one-tenth the comparable wage in the United States.

GLOBAL ENVIRONMENTAL ISSUES

A second manner in which true globalism is advancing has to do with
the environment. Threats to the global ecosystem have drawn all of

SURPRISE SCENARIO:
THE RAPID EMERGENCE OF THE
"DEATH OF DISTANCE"

When flat-fee global communications becomes a reality, it will revolutionize major industries and accelerate the process of global awareness and communication already under way. One major question, however, is just how quickly this transition will occur. The small-scale Internet phone services currently available reach only a fraction of potential callers and suffer from the same problems of slow data exchange and signal fuzziness or dropping as does the overloaded Internet as a whole.

This scenario examines the results of a much faster than expected emergence of truly inexpensive flat-fee calling offered by major telephone providers. What if, for example, by the year 2005, companies such as Sprint, AT&T, and MCI offered businesses a global calling package for $30 to $40 a month—the same amount, no matter where or how often the business used the line? Such a rapid change in the assumptions guiding corporate decisions would have dramatic results for economies and societies.

- Pressures to *relocate service industries to low-wage areas* would increase dramatically, affecting companies in such industries as credit cards, banking, audiotext, computer servicing, and education.
- The resulting *challenge to employment* in developed nations would reduce service industry wages and perhaps spark a sudden wave of unemployment.
- *Protectionism in service trade* would emerge to join protectionism in manufactures as major challenges to the progress of global free trade. Populaces would demand safeguards against sudden job loss from foreign competition.
- The trend would pose a *social challenge for nondemocratic states* that are interested in attracting jobs and investment associated with globalizing service industries but concerned about the channels of communication it opens up.
- The importance of *foreign-language proficiency* would skyrocket, especially in developing countries, something that would cement English as the world's second language and provide competitive advantages to English-speaking developing countries.

humanity together in a new fashion, emphasizing our interdependence and mutual vulnerability.

Many environmental risks are regional or local rather than global. When a manufacturing plant releases chemicals into the local river, or when a drought ruins crop yields in an underdeveloped country, most of the effects will remain in the immediate area. Other environmental threats, such as nuclear power-plant accidents or overfishing, are largely regional in their impact.

Nonetheless, the sum of regional environmental issues adds up to a substantial global impact. Local food shortages reduce global supplies as well, depleting reserves available for other regions. At some point enough pollution of local waterways can begin to merge and create terrible global consequences. Moreover, the world faces several profound environmental challenges of truly global scope and impact, summarized in Trend One. These environmental threats constitute an important element of globalization—a mechanism for shrinking the perceived and actual boundaries of the world.

WORLD FINANCIAL MARKETS

So far I have described two traditional areas in which the world economy is becoming globalized, merchandise trade and foreign direct investment. Increasingly, however, globalization is being driven by new areas of economic activity that depart from these traditional measures. These new areas include financial markets (see figure 12.4; the decline in the late 1990s is a result of the Asian financial crisis, and is expected to be temporary)—stock and bond markets, for example, as distinguished from foreign investment in businesses or land—and multinational corporations. While neither is a new phenomenon, each has attained utterly unprecedented levels within the last several years. By 1992 the total size of world financial markets was $43 trillion.[26] And increasingly, financial markets ply their trade across borders: Over $2.3 trillion is now traded on world financial markets every day, a figure that swamps the amounts of money held in government reserve banks. For developed economies, cross-border bank lending equaled 4 percent of GDP in the early 1980s; by the early 1990s it reached 44 percent.[27]

FIGURE 12.4

Net Private Capital Flows

(Annual, in $ billion; 1980s figure is annual average)

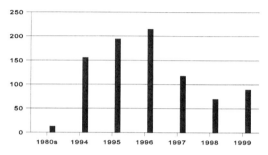

Source: The International Monetary Fund; data available at www.imf.org.

Even in the financial realm, globalization remains incomplete. In 1993 foreign owners accounted for only 6 percent of U.S. stocks and 14 percent of U.S. corporate bonds, and more than 95 percent of the stocks and 97 percent of the bonds owned by Americans were issued by U.S. sources.[28] But these numbers are changing rapidly, and financial markets are more heavily integrated and interdependent than any other aspect of the world economy—a fact that has created a major regulatory problem, because financial regulations remain largely national. Bridging the gap between international financial transactions and often anachronistic national financial laws is a major challenge for the next decade.

Global financial integration will take on an even more profound meaning when it is married to the revolution in electronic cash. Trend Three discussed the implications of a networked global financial system; as William Knoke phrases it, in the "age of digital capital" money "will flow so effortlessly across national borders that the world will effectively have one currency,"[29] because exchange and interest rates will be set globally. Less valuable currencies will become merely smaller denominations of the de facto global currency. At the same time, the digitization of money offers greater specialization and diversity, but on a global scale; a company plying E-cash "can gain direct access to millions of consumers and businesses—no matter what state or country they are in."[30] The

Bank of Japan could have depositors in Peoria and Basingstoke—and once again, people's identities, their sense of affiliation, will be drawn ineluctably upward to the international level.

GLOBAL PRODUCTION

Globalization is also accelerating under the influence of multinational corporations (MNCs). Like merchandise trade and investment, this is hardly a new phenomenon; truly multinational corporations operated in the British Empire hundreds of years ago. But the scope of MNC penetration of the world economy is surely unprecedented: "As much as one-third of world output," the United Nations recently noted, "is under the common governance of [MNCs] and hence potentially part of an integrated international production system."[31] By the late 1990s there were at least 450,000 foreign affiliate corporations in the world, and the largest 100 multinationals (not including banks and finance institutions) held $1.8 trillion in foreign assets, and $2.5 trillion in foreign sales—easily outstripping the combined GDPs of China, India, South Korea, Malaysia, Singapore, and the Philippines—by 1996.[32]

This amazing total demonstrates clearly how, at this stage, MNCs may at this stage be a much more powerful engine of globalization than traditional trade in manufactured goods and services. University of Michigan professor Marina Whitman has put it another way: "The assets of the world's five largest multinationals," she writes—General Motors, Ford, Royal Dutch/Shell, Exxon, and IBM—"rival the GNPs of such middle-sized countries as Indonesia, Saudi Arabia, South Africa and Turkey."[33]

An international integration of production is under way, in which one company will produce various components of the same final item— say, of an automobile—in different countries. This leads in turn to increasing intrafirm trade (trade between different parts of the same company rather than between companies), which is now estimated at over 50 percent of the international trade of the United States and Japan and 80 percent of British manufacturing exports.[34]

Yet to jump rapidly to the conclusion that MNCs are putting a globalized world economy into place would be an exaggeration. For one thing, MNCs' share of global output did not change much from 1980 to 1990, remaining at just over 20 percent of world GDP. Thus national companies, not multinational ones, still hold the bulk of world economic power. And it is wrong to assume that MNCs are becoming increasingly "stateless": Even international corporations obtain their corporate culture and identity from their home nation and tend to hoard their most important management and research activities there. Just a third of actual MNC production takes place outside the borders of their home country—a figure that dips to merely a quarter in the case of U.S. and Japanese companies.[35] U.S. companies conduct no more than 9 percent of their high-tech activity abroad; the figure for Europe is a little higher, but neither seems to be growing.[36] While the flow of top executives across borders has picked up in recent years, moreover, many MNCs still seem hesitant to place foreign nationals in top posts.

At the heart of the knowledge era, we therefore find an accelerating globalism, propelled by a variety of interdependent forces. But globalism is only half the story. For it is opposed and transformed into something quite different by a parallel trend—pluralism or tribalism.

Tribalism, Fragmentation, and Pluralism

If the knowledge era is an era of globalism, it is, paradoxically, also an era of pluralism—of fragmentation and diversity in careers, social and political groups, and religious organizations. In business terms, it is an era of niche markets, micromarketing, and specialized products. In social and political terms, it is a time of renewed search for identity in ethnic, national, and cultural affinities that magnify the differences among people and groups rather than, as in the case of globalism, emphasizing their similarities.

We will use the words "tribalism" and "pluralism" in all of their senses. The dictionary, for example, defines pluralism as "a condition of society in which numerous distinct ethnic, religious or cultural groups coexist within one nation." And this is indeed a primary result of the knowledge era: a proliferation of groups with which people identify, not only ethnic, religious, and cultural, but also corporate, electronic, and educational. In the knowledge era, society becomes more pluralistic than ever before. But the dictionary also notes that pluralism implies something else—"the belief that no single explanatory system or view of reality can account for all the phenomena of life."[1] Thus it is related to the end of universal beliefs and the breakdown of traditional authorities we will consider in Trend Five.

Tribalism manifests itself within all relatively advanced societies impacted by the knowledge era; but it also makes its presence felt between or among those societies. Tribalism in an international sense means a greater diversity of organizations, an increasing number of nation-states, and a growing menu of alternative institutions—international organizations such as the United Nations and global nongovernmental organizations such as Greenpeace—which share the stage of world politics with the nation-state. And it means a dizzying array of competing value systems by which global policy issues will be judged and according to which cultures will organize their societies.

If this sounds different from Trend Two's homogenous globalization, it is—to a point. Tribalism does not deny the reality of globalism. It suggests that globalism will have different faces, that cultures and nations will shape the broad contours of a unified future to suit their needs and tastes. And the reality of tribalism points to the inevitability of strong, sometimes violent reactions to globalism in nations undergoing rapid change.

THE NATURE OF TRIBALISM

As social critics Karl Marx and Jacques Ellul recognized, industrial society—the twentieth-century American and global economy of steel, automobiles, and other heavy industry—was characterized by such concepts as mass, uniformity, and conformism. The symbol of the industrial era was the mass-production factory: huge, impersonal, running on universal principles of rational bureaucratic organization. Supporting the industrial economy was the industrial-era school, which emphasized rote memorization, obedience, and punctuality, all values critical to the assembly-line worker.

In the knowledge era, this universal social organization has begun fragmenting into thousands of small groups, organizations, and loyalties. Fragmentation, pluralism, and differentiation rather than mass unity are the order of the day.

Pluralism is the obvious and immediate result of two large-scale social transformations. One is the growing scope of modern civilization in a knowledge era. In a complex, differentiated society, people do not rely on a single organization or group, whether it is a religion or community or political party, to prescribe most of their activities and beliefs. They instead belong to many overlapping organizations, including businesses, political parties, churches, and clubs; each has only a partial claim on individual loyalty. Thus, as the sociologists Herbert Spencer and Georg Simmel pointed out over 100 years ago, the size and complexity of modern civilization institutionalizes pluralism—another way in which the knowledge era represents a further development, rather than a reversal, of the modern era.

The second social transformation is the knowledge era itself. During the "modern" or "industrial" period from perhaps 1650 to 1950, expanding pluralism was camouflaged underneath social uniformities. But the knowledge era has now brought the natural pluralism of a complex society to the fore by providing individuals and small groups with the knowledge necessary to manage their own destinies, the awareness of their own uniqueness.

Robert Samuelson has written eloquently of the fragmentation that has come to characterize modern life. He cites one investigator who has calculated that the average American supermarket carries 30,000 products (up from 9,000 in 1976); cosmetic centers have 1,500 types and sizes of hair products; with cable television, an average household gets 30 or more channels (up from 6 in 1975, and soon to run into the hundreds); the number of FM radio stations has doubled since 1970. "Mass culture," Samuelson contends, "is receding before niche culture."[2] As the philosopher Gianni Vattimo has phrased it, this shift involves a transition from single, unitary utopias to plural, flexible "heterotopias": With the apparent collapse of "a central rationality of history," the information age "explodes like a multiplicity of 'local' rationalities—ethnic, sexual, religious, cultural or aesthetic minorities—that finally speak up for themselves."[3] Examples of such tribalism are all around us. In the knowledge era, self-identification tends to fragment in dozens of ways.

- *Self-identification.* A recent survey by *U.S. News & World Report* argued that the political attitudes of Americans had broken down into seven "tribes," from populist traditionalists to stewards, dowagers, liberal activists, and agnostics. "Today America is divided in new and different ways," *U.S. News* concluded. "There are scraps of evidence that old ties have frayed and loose new ones are being woven," but in a more plural, diverse manner. "There no longer is any center in American politics."[4]

- *Multiculturalism.* One of the most important social trends of our time, multiculturalism is tribalism writ large. Specific groups within society increase their self-awareness and celebrate their difference from others outside their racial or ethnic group even as they intensify the bonds of connectedness to those within their group.

The United States, for example, is well on the road to becoming arguably the world's first truly multiracial country. Demographers aren't sure precisely when the proportion of non-Hispanic whites in America will dip below 50 percent—some think around the year 2030—but when it happens, there will be no "majority" race, and America will become a collection of minorities. Over the next decade, the most powerful trend running in this direction will be the explosion of the U.S. Hispanic population: from about 30 million in 1990, the number of Hispanic-Americans will jump 75 percent by 2015 and could hit 100 million by 2050, by which time there will be more *Hispanic*-Americans in the country than there were *Americans* as recently as 1900. This will mean growing economic and political clout: one estimate suggests that Hispanic-Americans have $350 billion in purchasing power—more than the GDP of Mexico, and over a third of China's—and that it is growing by $1 billion every six weeks.[5]

- *The growing fragmentation of business.* The decentralization and "virtualization" of business outlined in Trend Three is also a form of pluralism. Such fragmented, shifting corporate structures are much more "tribal" than the hierarchical organizations of the industrial era. Their managers value decentralization, small work teams, unusual ideas, and product uniqueness.

Even the largest businesses are forced to think very small when designing their corporate strategy. This new technique has one focus: tailoring the good or service to the needs of the individual customer rather than mass-marketing identical products. Consumer tastes are partly fragmented along ethnic, regional, age, and other lines, and businesses are increasingly trying to "micro-market" their products to small niches of customers. This process reflects the virtual, amoebalike corporate structures discussed in Trend Three. Management expert Don Tapscott refers, for example, to an accelerating trend of "molecularization" through which "the old corporation is being disaggregated, replaced by dynamic molecules and clusters of individuals and entities," a shift from mass to "molecular" economics in which companies "forge a series of ever-changing alliances to achieve competitive success."[6] A number of writers have suggested that such corporate paradigms might produce an economic arrangement similar to the craft production models of earlier centuries—small, flexible, specialized firms with low capital cost and a high level of skill which have some features in common with the craft production of late-medieval artisans.[7]

- *The growing diversification of education and justice.* The one word that best describes the trend in education over the last decade is "pluralism": not just within schools, with a bewildering array of specialized classes and subjects, but pluralism among them, in the form of specialized schools for different subjects and various types of public, religious, nonprofit, and for-profit schools. Similarly in the arena of justice, many forms of dispute resolution have arisen in the past several years as an alternative to the monolithic public justice system.[8]

- *Government decentralization and federalism.* The effort in the United States to decentralize more and more government functions reflects this larger trend of fragmentation. It is bolstered by Americans' longing for stronger local communities, a reaction to other trends of the knowledge era. Similarly in Europe, the drive for "subsidiarity" and growing regionalism represent examples of the same trend.

Pluralism in government also goes to the heart of the growth of privatization efforts in recent years, summarized in table 13.1. Government itself is becoming a more plural, diverse activity. It is less and less a singular form of state-managed enterprise but encompasses larger numbers of flexible partnerships between government, nonprofit, and for-profit organizations. Trend Five examines this phenomenon in more detail.

TABLE 13.1

The Growth of Privatization

Percentage of selected services contracted out
by 3,000 U.S. county governments

Type of Service	1987	1992
Airports	30%	36%
Fire departments	22%	37%
Hospitals	34%	46%
Libraries	14%	23%
Public transit	37%	48%
Electric utility	74%	96%
Total of all services (ABOVE PLUS OTHERS)	24%	34%

Source: *The Wall Street Journal,* June 29, 1995, p. A16.

- *The fragmenting effects of media.* Marshall McLuhan recognized long ago the naturally pluralistic effects of mass media, effects that are accelerating under the influence of 150-channel cable systems and niche advertising.[9] One recent commentator agrees that the new media create a "segmented, differentiated audience that . . . is no longer a mass audience in terms of simultaneity and uniformity of the message it receives."[10]
- *A pluralism of religions.* In a time of diversity, religions become less monolithic, more local and diverse. In Japan, over 100 new religious groups form every year; by the end of 1993 there were over 230,000 splinter religions in Japan—an all-time record.[11] Theologian Richard John Neuhaus terms the world's fastest-growing religion—evangelical Protestantism—a "maddeningly diverse and rapidly growing world."[12]

This notion of diverse, plural, flexible, ad-hoc social groups is mirrored in philosopher Zygmunt Bauman's concept of "neotribalism." Today's tribes—be they corporations, sports clubs, social groups,

SURPRISE SCENARIO:
ACCELERATION OF REGIONALISM

One of the most important ways in which pluralism expresses itself is in the form of regionalism. In political, cultural, and economic terms, regions within countries often express a degree of independence and attempt to preserve some degree of unique identity. This scenario considers the potential for a sudden, cascading acceleration of regional demands for political and economic autonomy in three key regions: North America, China, and Europe.

In North America, such an event might involve a successful independence referendum in Quebec followed by similar demands for autonomy among some of the "nations" of North America[13]—the Pacific Northwest, central and southern California, and others. In China, the scenario posits that emerging differences between coastal and interior areas take on political manifestations and that the power of the central government declines past the point of being able to resist demands for autonomy. In Europe, regionalism is partly a product of the European Union's "subsidiarity" principle and is led by separatist movements in the Basque area of Spain and elsewhere.

Such a worldwide trend toward regionalism—and secessionism, as groups seek to create their own nations—would have a number of powerful effects.

- It would accelerate the *political and economic decline of the nation-state,* with all its implications. Social welfare policies would devolve from nations to regions.
- In the process, the rise of regionalism could spark a *movement toward a "new medievalism" in political and economic life,* with national and regional governments forced to share more power with private organizations, such as multinational corporations.
- *Trade issues would enter a new context* in which global accords negotiated among nation-states might no longer apply to autonomous regions.
- *Corporate strategies would need to be reformulated;* regionalism would encourage deepening of the current trends toward decentralization and globalization.
- The *possibility of national and cultural hostility* would be very real; at a minimum, social instability could result, perhaps even outright warfare in some areas.

political parties, or rural U.S. militia groups—are defined by people's varied forms of self-identification. Tribes "'exist' solely by individual decisions to sport the symbolic traits of tribal allegiance. They vanish once the decisions are revoked or their determination fades out. They persevere thanks only to their continuing seductive capacity. They cannot outlive their power of attraction."[14]

Here again we find the principle of virtuality extended to the sphere of civil society. It means that the groups to which we belong today, whether they are political parties, churches, or businesses, have a much more temporary and ephemeral hold on our allegiance than tribes of old. We find, too, another interesting parallel with chaos and complexity theory, which places substantial emphasis on the role of microlevel actors in creating complex or chaotic effects. A more plural, diverse world is a more complex one, and, to the extent that random innovations produced by small actors are a primary engine of progress, it is also a world that can evolve and change more quickly.

THE PLURALISM OF BUSINESS

The economist Robert Heilbroner, discussing Karl Marx, wanted to think of an analogy to demonstrate how revolutionary, how insightful, how against-the-grain was Marx's forecast of the rise of huge monopoly businesses. What Heilbroner came up with was this: "To claim that huge firms would come to dominate the business scene was as startling a prediction in 1867 as would be a statement today that fifty years hence America will be a land in which small-scale proprietorships will have displaced giant corporations."[15]

Thanks to the human resources economy, that second prediction may very well come true in a number of important ways. In an environment of diversity and pluralism, flexibility—the ability to respond to the rapidly changing demands and pressures of a fast-moving information society—becomes a key asset. Decentralized organizations are inherently more flexible than top-heavy, centralized ones, and this fact has created a sort of evolutionary selection in favor of pluralism. Trend Three outlined some of the new corporate structures that will emerge as a result of these trends, and Trend Five will review a few more. In such an era, hard-and-fast distinctions between "large" and "small" businesses no longer make sense. The truth is not so much that small businesses will predominate but that all businesses—large and small—will strive for the character of small businesses and the efficiencies of large ones. This means decentralization for large companies and networks and alliances for small ones.

The case for a small-business renaissance is a strong one. Peter Drucker has explained that "The entire shrinkage in manufacturing jobs in the United States has occurred in large companies. . . . In respect to market standing, exports and profitability too, smaller and middle-sized businesses have done remarkably better than big ones." The reasons? Advantages of smaller size include "ease of communications and nearness to market and customer."[16] Already, small businesses employ over half the U.S. workforce. In the 1980s Fortune 500 companies slashed 3.5 million jobs while small businesses created more than 20 million jobs. Thus, while in 1970 Fortune 500 businesses accounted for 20 percent of the U.S. economy, by 1993 they accounted for only 10 percent of U.S. GNP. New business incorporations hit a new record in 1994 of over 740,000.[17] Economists expect companies with between 100 and 1,000 workers to generate 40 percent of all new jobs during the 1990s; by 2000 companies with less than 500 employees will employ more than 70 percent of the workforce.[18] This trend seems certain to help further empower women: The Small Business Administration estimates that by the year 2000, women will own 40 percent of small businesses, and the best way of shattering the "glass ceiling" might be by starting out on the ground floor—and in charge.

But the issue is not as simple as the collapse of big businesses and their replacement with small ones. In a number of important sectors of the global economy, massive size and scope—not fragmentation—is the rule. In computers, for example, big is still beautiful because it costs upward of $1 billion to build a state-of-the-art silicon chip factory. This fact may be increasingly true in telecommunications, too; according to *The Economist,* "The economies of scale and scope in the transmission of information are such that, by the second quarter of the next century, only a handful of really big international providers may be left."[19] The same dynamics may continue to hold in such key industries as publishing, mining, agribusiness, and finance, where the revolution in global capital has strengthened the hand of big banks: Foreign exchange trading is increasingly centralized in a few major trading houses, in part because of the enormous cost of modern financial information systems.[20]

The critical new fact is that even big businesses that are staying big are also trying to become more like small ones, "decentralizing and reconstituting themselves as networks of entrepreneurs," as John Naisbitt puts it, becoming "confederations of small, autonomous, entrepreneurial companies." The corporate challenge today, IBM chief executive officer Louis Gerstner has said, is "how to incorporate small-company attributes—nimbleness, speed and customer responsiveness—with the advantages of size, like breadth of investment in research and development."[21] If large companies succeed in mimicking the advantages of smaller outfits while retaining the advantages of size—capitalization (having lots of money to invest) chief among them—the future may be kind to them. That such a trend toward bigness should emerge even alongside continued relative growth in the role of small businesses in the economy is merely another paradoxical symptom of a paradoxical time. The central message for businesses, then, is not so much big versus small but the paradox of trying to be *both* at the same time.

TRIBALISM'S TWIN: RELATIVISM

A relativism of values and norms, flowing directly from the pluralism and fragmentation of our society, also stands at the very the core of the knowledge era. It makes sense that a plural society would be one in which values, goals, and ideals become relativized: Each subgroup has its own ideas of the good life and the good society. And this has indeed occurred, with the result being one of the most profound ideological changes of our time, what the French philosopher Jean-François Lyotard has called the "death of metanarratives."

A "metanarrative" is a big word for a reasonably simple concept: a large-scale, universal ideology. The Western Judeo-Christian moral and ethical tradition is one example of a metanarrative; communism is another. They are based on a central concept or idea; they claim universal validity; they offer a coherent explanation of the world to those who hold them. And in a world of pluralism—a world, also, in which information necessary to challenge metanarratives is readily available—grand ideologies are collapsing. (One result is greater individual alienation as the faiths that order our lives crumble under the onslaught of information, a phenomenon I'll examine in Trend Six.) As writer Patrick Glynn puts it, behind "this new experience of cultural and intellectual fragmentation, lies a loss of faith in general truths, and even, at its most radical, a loss of faith in the very possibility of general truths."[22]

The revolution in travel and information abets this process. Famed sociologist Peter Berger pointed out 30 years ago that the unprecedented travel and geographical mobility of the modern world provided people with many different ways of seeing the world. Such a change implies "the awareness that one's own culture, including its basic values, is relative in space and time," an effect magnified by social mobility among classes. As a result, the "awareness of relativity, which probably in all ages of history has been the possession of a small group of intellectuals, today appears as a broad cultural fact reaching down into the lower reaches of the social system"[23] through the millions of people who now travel internationally.

Of the tangible effects of relativism, the most obvious is the now-famous crisis of values in the United States, the West, and indeed much of the world. Moral relativism has become commonplace. Many citizens of modern countries no longer sense clear moral codes governing their behavior—a perception at once liberating to many individuals and threatening to the social order.

Finally, a world of pluralism is a world in which culture—local, national, corporate, military, and otherwise—becomes increasingly important. Differing cultures become emphasized by the progress of pluralism and relativism, and many people's reaction to globalism and thirst for absolute values then intensifies cultural identity. But an unexpected implication of this line of thought might take some of the wind out of the "culture wars" thesis. An increasingly fragmented, plural world might seem the perfect environment for Huntington's "clash of civilizations." And so it might—except for the contrary influences of relativism, which saps the ability of religious or cultural ideologies to rally people to intercivilizational wars; and except for the simultaneous advance of globalism, which dilutes the fragmenting effects of different cultures. The principle of pluralism and tolerance combined with relativism means that people take pride in their culture, celebrate it, defend it against the encroaching tentacles of globalization—but seldom fight wars in service of it.[24]

Tribalism within Globalism

The two ideas surveyed earlier in this trend—pluralism and universalism, tribalism and globalism—are independently critical. But what is even more important is their interaction, the complex and profound dialectic produced by a world that is not merely global but plurally global; not merely plural but globally plural. Having now understood a little of what each of those two trends means, we can grasp some of the major ramifications of their blending.

Benjamin Barber argues that tribalism and globalism are "locked together in a kind of Freudian moment of the ongoing cultural struggle, neither willing to coexist with the other, neither complete without the other."[1] In the words of another writer, the "paradox of globalization" is that "rather than creating one big economy or one big polity, it also divides, fragments, and polarizes. Convergence and divergence are two sides of the same coin."[2] Patrick Glynn writes that the global-tribal clash "has every appearance of becoming the new bipolarity of global politics, the new dialectic of a new age."[3] South Korean publisher Kim Byung-ik explains that "The current globalization and universalizing trends" are at the same time "encouraging minimalization and individualism"; the world's task is not to choose between them but to find "a balanced compromise for overall harmony." Simultaneous Westernization and emphasis on Korean cultural traditions, Kim explains, should be viewed as the "harmonization of the two complementary desires within our collective mind—globalism and tribalism."[4]

ISSUE FEATURE: THE NET—GLOBAL OR PLURAL?

In Trend Two and elsewhere, we portrayed the Internet as a force for globalization. Like nearly all the trends of the next decade, however, this process is paradoxical, for the Internet is a global and tribal force at the same time.

Tim Berners-Lee, a British physicist who helped to invent the concept of a World Wide Web, says, "I don't think it's obvious whether the Web will become a great force for diversity or for the homogenization of the planet"; he very much hopes that "it will be both."

Umberto Eco agrees. The "triumph of American culture" in television and movies "is not going to happen on the Net," he told *Wired* magazine. It will be filled with non-English sites, or sites in English describing the ideas, norms and values of other cultures. This "is going to have a curious effect": It will sensitize Americans "to the need to embrace other cultures, other points of view."[5]

SOCIAL INSTABILITY AND TENSION

This explosive interaction leads to the most dangerous and powerful set of reactions to the engines of history as outlined in Trend Two. A process of slow, gradual, incomplete global homogenization is indeed under way—and hundreds of millions of people are paying an immense psychological, social, and in some cases economic price for it.

The results of Latin America's confrontation with the knife edge of the global-local paradox, for example, are disquieting. Economic and social reform and democracy have swept the region, sparking alienation and exacerbated economic inequities. Cultural and ideological reactions to capitalism are gaining strength. The great expectations that accompanied reforms in Argentina, Brazil, Mexico, and Chile have given way to widespread disaffection with reform. And in Asia, the collision between globalism and localism is producing a growing sense of unease with rapid change and a fear of losing traditional values and ways. One religious leader in Indonesia told researcher David Hitchcock that "we have not yet found the right way to be a modern people, a modern nation, to achieve modernity without losing our national identity."[6]

Modernization always produces social instabilities, frequently in the form of an embrace of tribal, ethnic, or ideological identities. It is no coincidence that German fascism arose as a romanticized ideology opposed to modern industrialism. The death of ideologies—or metanarratives—that we discussed earlier and the weakening of traditional authorities I survey in Trend Five exacerbate the impact of these strains by leaving people without a rock-solid reference point in a changing world. One of the most worrisome trends in this regard is the growth of the nationalistic, xenophobic right wing in European politics, which by the late 1990s was winning up to a fifth of the vote in some countries' parliamentary elections and trying desperately to legitimize itself by adopting the slogans and campaign tactics of more orthodox conservatives.

INTERDEPENDENCE

Both globalism and pluralism support the rise of unprecedented social interdependence. Mutual dependence flows logically from pluralism: Specialized workers are more interdependent than general ones. A late-twentieth-century molecular biologist is more dependent on others working in his or her field than a nineteenth-century "biologist," who was in turn more dependent than an eighteenth-century "scientist"—and in the twenty-first century, fields such as molecular biology will be again subdivided many times.

This fact is hardly new, of course. Nineteenth-century sociologists recognized both the growing differentiation of large-scale, complex societies and the mutual dependence this created. Herbert Spencer argued that increases in the size of societies led inevitably to great complexity, which in turn produced differentiation; and "once the parts have become unlike, they are mutually dependent on each other; thus, with growing differentiation comes growing interdependence and hence integration."[7] In the knowledge era, this process is advanced to a degree these older theorists could not have imagined. "The division of labor assumes a completely new form" in the knowledge era, Ernest Gellner has written. "It is not merely that there is far more specialization than there had been before: it is a qualitatively different kind of specialization."[8]

Even today's networked, empowered, diverse travelers of the information superhighway are thus more dependent than ever on a supporting social and organizational infrastructure. As Peter Drucker has pointed out, "Only the organization can provide the basic continuity that knowledge workers need in order to be effective. . . . The surgeon is not effective unless there is a diagnosis—which, by and large, is not the surgeon's task and not even within the surgeon's competence. As a loner in his or her research and writing, the historian can be very effective. But to educate students, a great many other specialists must contribute."[9] Such networked interdependence is the same phenomenon underlying Trend Two's notion of an emerging global social contract, the new era of business alliance described in Trend Three, and the growing importance of civil society that Trend Five examines.

A RESURGENCE OF MORAL VALUES

In periods of social transformation, traditional values—sometimes expressed in new forms—often make a comeback. This process, already well under way in the United States and throughout developed world, is likely to accelerate in the next decade. It may contribute to a resurgence in religious belief, expressed in plural rather than monolithic ways.

The theologian Richard John Neuhaus has referred to the twenty-first century as "the religious century." With the growth of evangelical Protestantism and Islam and the continuing strength of Catholicism, religion will strengthen in the next millennium. "According to textbooks since the Enlightenment," Neuhaus contends, "the story of modernity is the story of inexorable secularization. The great new fact at the edge of the third millennium is the desecularization of world history."[10] This spreading reassertion of traditional morals and values is often perceived as the province of the Republican right wing, but the impulses that give rise to it run much more deeply throughout the United States. The left has its own morals it is attempting to reassert—one could view, for example, the "political correctness" craze as a form of absolutism directed to the goal of equity and mutual respect.

One particular value held up by conservative politicians that seems certain to play an immense role in the knowledge era is responsibility—of personal, group, and national varieties. In an empowered and empowering era, there are fewer and fewer excuses; in an era at once highly individualistic and demanding of teamwork, people will be held accountable for their behavior, skills, and values as never before. We will hardly have time to celebrate the decline of the industrial era's nameless mass conformism before learning of the crushing burden of personal and group responsibility that has succeeded it.

In this context, the broad support for welfare reform and balanced budgets and the demand for greater individual responsibility is hardly surprising. And the diminishing state role in solving social problems, writes philosopher Zygmunt Bauman, "is conducive to the resumption by the agents of moral responsibility" that tended to be overwhelmed by a "unified, quasi-monopolistic legislating authority."[11] In such an atmosphere, as we shall see in Trend Five, corporations are increasingly recognizing the need to establish community service programs—and the clear benefits, measured in terms of morale and productivity, that such programs bring.[12] If people take these responsibilities seriously, the result will be the growth of civil society for which so many conservative and communitarian leaders have called.

Whether the majority of people and organizations in the advanced countries are prepared for this shift, however, is a different question. The transition toward "self-navigation" and away from the entitlement mentality of the last half century will be wrenching. I take up these questions in Trend Six.

RELATIVE DECLINE OF THE NATION-STATE

The trends of pluralism and globalism often have opposite effects, but sometimes they work together to undermine social institutions. Such is the character of their effect on the nation-state: they attack it from above and below at the same time, squeezing its influence and credibility perilously between the emerging global and local sources of identity.

In fact, the nation-state as an institution does not sit precariously on the brink of collapse. It is not likely to wither away substantially in our lifetimes, and certainly not in the next seven to ten years. Nation-states will remain the primary actors in world politics for decades to come. In fiscal and monetary policy, for example, states have always faced the constraints supposedly imposed by a new global world economy. In fact, global economic integration actually bolsters the role of the state in some ways: international capital and multinational companies respond to state actions, such as monetary policy and infrastructure investments.[13]

Increasingly, however, the nation-state it will be forced to *share* the stage of both domestic and international affairs with nonstate actors. Nation-states will retain starring roles, but their costars will be getting more attention—and their understudies will be waiting, more and more impatiently, in the wings. International institutions, nongovernmental organizations, global interest groups, multinational corporations, ethnic and cultural identities, consumerist universalism—these and more institutions and ideas will challenge the supremacy of authority of the nation-state.

And as much as some observers laud the decline of states as a step toward a more communal world, in fact the process carries very real dangers. Nation-states remain the world's primary reservoirs of democracy, social policy, and perhaps even peace. States have been the providers of social welfare to the less fortunate and undereducated. The existence of territorially defined states has nourished the idea that violations of national sovereignty are illegitimate—and thus helped to underwrite peace. Their decline could portend the confused, violent era of instability.

A GLOBAL AND TRIBAL ERA

It is impossible to capture the implications of the preceding analysis in a few simple statements. The phenomenon of "a globalized tribalism" is too complex, too contradictory, and indeed too unpredictable to allow an easy summary. It represents not a single and simple trend but a rich mixture of trends, countertrends, dangers, and possibilities that together form a dauntingly complex and unpredictable stew. A few ideas—and a handful of policy recommendations, summarized in the text box— nonetheless stand out as especially important. Globalization can be properly viewed only as "an economic, political, social, and ideological phenomenon which carries with it unanticipated, often contradictory and polarizing consequences."[14]

One such idea is the notion of trust. The knowledge era calls into question the traditional means for establishing confidence in other people. Globalism increasingly demands that we trust people we never see or, perhaps, hear; pluralism forces us to trust people close by who are very different from us—different in values, culture, or ethnicity. At the

---

POLICY RECOMMENDATIONS: *TREND FOUR*

1. For businesses, *success increasingly means being neither global nor local in outlook but both at the same time.*
2. *Prepare for a revolution in global service trade* caused by the death of distance.
3. *Rethink trade policy* with an eye toward the growing importance of services and multinational corporations.
4. *Continue and expand the emphasis in public policy on a renewed set of social values and community* as key foundations for societies in a global and tribal era.
5. *Enhance cross-cultural understanding* through dialogue at the governmental and nongovernmental levels to help avoid increased cultural tensions.

---

same time, our increasing reliance on virtual organizations is robbing us of the social interactions we have used to establish trust.

Another implication of the confrontation between tribalism and globalism has to do with responsibility. Both phenomena are pushing responsibility down to lower and lower levels and, in the process, are magnifying individual and social penalties for irresponsible behavior. In a pluralistic society, and at a moment when governmental institutions such as the welfare system have been discredited, the tendency of societies to express mutual and collective responsibility is on the decline. Individuals will be held more accountable for their personal choices. Similarly, the expansion of free trade is denying more and more corporations the protectionist umbrellas they have enjoyed until recently.

Finally, we can expect, as with any major social transformation, that both globalism and tribalism will provoke strong *socioeconomic and cultural reactions*—a process that has already begun. People will increasingly seek out leaders and institutions who offer a clear set of social values, as a reaction against excessive diversity and relativism; at the same time, they will retreat into local ethnic, religious, and national identities and economic patterns as a reaction against globalism. The conflict between these trends will be one of the major hallmarks of the coming decade, and I examine some of its psychological ramifications in Trend Six.

So far I have painted a portrait of a world awash in change—propelled ahead at dizzying speed by the most powerful engines of social change in history, witnessing the rise of a fundamentally new kind of economy, torn between the competing forces of globalism and tribalism. I've only begun to discuss the full measure of these challenges. For in this era of transition, at the precise moment when human societies need strong social institutions to guide them through to the knowledge era, those institutions are under attack from the very forces impelling the transition itself. The decline of industrial-era authorities magnifies the scope of the challenge we face; and it is the subject to which I now turn.

A Transformation
of Authority

*The people are hard to rule
because they have too much knowledge.*

Tao Te Ching

The transition to a knowledge era also holds dramatic implications for a
key concept of political and social life: *authority*. The acceleration of
history, of technology, and of social change implies weakened legitimacy
of all traditions and institutions, now a defining characteristic of our age.
This change involves something far more interesting than a mere
"decline of authority," a trend predicted and examined by dozens of
writers for decades. Instead, what we are seeing today is the transformation of authority—not merely the downfall of traditional authorities but
their replacement with different, knowledge-era institutions. Sometimes
the institutions are modified versions of traditional authorities; in other
cases, their influence is entirely new.

One critically important authority undergoing transformation is
the nation-state, and the philosopher Anthony Giddens has used this
institution to illustrate the process of decline and renewal at issue here.

What is under way, he writes, is not merely "the progressive loss of sovereignty on the part of the nation-state." Rather, the "loss of autonomy on the part of some states or groups of states has often gone along with an *increase* in that of others."[1] Thus this trend embodies a central paradox: authority is declining and reemerging at the same time. One change, however, is linear: the transformation in the *character* of authority. The authorities now rising up have little in common with the ones they are replacing: Knowledge-era authorities are diffuse and decentralized rather than monolithic, and they exercise their power through persuasion and influence rather than repression or mandate.[2]

The decline of old authorities, however, will not produce new ones overnight, and the hiatus between the two ages poses a powerful challenge. While nearly everyone recognizes that the set of familiar authorities—government, school, family, church, tradition—is under assault, political analyst James Pinkerton explains, "no consensus yet exists about what to build in its place. And so, as markets continue to crush old-style politics, and as the trend toward de-bureaucratization accelerates, older visions of community are mooted, and honored institutions are disequilibriated."[3]

One major theme of this trend is that a gap in legitimate authority demands a renewed focus on the *individual* as moral and social agent. Without clear and credible external authorities to guide them, people will increasingly need to learn to guide themselves. Self-control, self-guidance, "self-navigation": These and other forms of individual responsibility take on new importance in our era. A renewed emphasis on personal responsibility energizes a number of major public policy debates under way in the world today—the changing balance of "rights" and responsibilities, the value of individual liberty in societies that have seldom known it, the importance of welfare reform and the privatization of many paternalistic government social welfare programs.

This trend will not have the same effect on all societies. In some cases, such as the United States, the rights/responsibilities balance has shifted too far in the direction of rights, while in undemocratic nations such as China, Cuba, and Iran the crushing pressure of tradition and absolutist religion and ideology nearly eviscerates the potential for individual expression. But the broad principle is clear, and it comprises one of the major themes of this book: The key actor of the knowledge era, the basic root of authority in this new age, is the individual human being.

Phase One:
The Decline of
Hierarchical Authorities

The roots of the challenge to authority lay in the industrial age and even earlier. Already by the mid-1950s, the philosopher Hannah Arendt could argue that a "constant, ever-widening and deepening crisis of authority has accompanied the development of the modern world in our century."[1] But various aspects of the knowledge era—the widespread availability of knowledge, an accelerating fragmentation and pluralism, the speed of change, the requirement for dramatic business and government strategies that aim to destroy rather than preserve old ways of doing business—have achieved a critical mass and placed institutions based on hierarchical control achieved by tradition and inertia under a full-scale assault. Marshall McLuhan put it this way: "On the telephone only the authority of knowledge will work. Delegated authority is lineal, visual, hierarchical. The authority of knowledge is nonlineal, nonvisual, and inclusive."[2]

We see the trend of declining authorities in a host of places. It has always been a part of the American ethos, an ethos now spreading across the globe in the guise of a populist consumerism. It has always been part of the sensibilities of the young, and the world is becoming younger at a rapid pace. It has always gone hand in hand with liberal societies, and Trend Two chronicled the worldwide advance of political and economic freedom.

In the developed world, the reaction against statism is a powerful rejection of central authority; in developing nations from Mexico to China to Indonesia, one-party rule confronts movements demanding reform and freedom. The character of knowledge-era work reflects this trend: Workers are no longer supervised as much as encouraged and cared for; managers are not bosses as much as coaches and facilitators.[3] Even the character of the physical tools of work has the same effect: "While paper favors a hierarchy of information and lines of authority," writes philosopher Albert Borgmann, computers, with their logic of networked and distributed knowledge, "suggest a republic of information and a cooperative network."[4]

Thomas Frank, editor of the culture magazine *Baffler*, explains the result. Far from "feeling besieged by rebel youth movements of the 1960s, American business now routinely makes a practice of embracing the symbols, language and ideology of the counterculture"—a new business culture of speed, diversity, and change. As examples Frank cites corporate slogans of the mid-1990s: "Find Your Own Road" (Saab); "Sometimes You Gotta Break the Rules" (Burger King); "If You Don't Like the Rules, Change Them" (WXRT-FM, Chicago). This represents "an entirely new ideology of business that has come with the Information Age," one that flouts tradition in favor of "disorder, chaos and the meaninglessness of inherited rules"[5]—or at least appears to do so in order to sell products.

The decay of centralized, hierarchical authorities owes much to the phenomenon that lies at the heart of the knowledge era: the growing power of media, especially electronic media, which puts traditional authorities on the defensive.[6] In a world of proliferating media outlets, no one source—government or private—can claim to hold the truth. A *Washington Post* report noted recently that with 40 or 80 channels now available in most cities and with media messages being sent out over radio, newspapers, billboards, and on-line services, "the traditional voice of authority is gone, replaced with a soft cynicism."[7] An intriguing feature of the knowledge-era revolt against authority, therefore—at least in already democratic societies—is its passivity. Today's challenge to ruling groups and institutions is more about apathy and cynicism than street protests or violence. We reject authority as much by ignoring it as by opposing it.

The acceleration of history characteristic of the knowledge era chips away at authority as well. Charles Handy has written that, when change is incremental and predictable, "it is sensible to ape your elders." But under "conditions of discontinuity it is no longer obvious that their ways should continue to be your ways." The accelerating change of the knowledge era demands "a way of learning which can even be seen as disrespectful if not downright rebellious. Assume discontinuity in our affairs, in other words, and you threaten the authority of the holders of knowledge, of those in charge, or those in power."[8]

The sociologist Richard Sennett points out that "authority is not a thing. It is an interpretive process which seeks for itself the solidity of a thing."[9] And that interpretive process has begun to move in a new direction: The knowledge era, by radically expanding the ability of individuals to participate in that interpretive process, renders authorities unable to preserve a solid front.[10]

FOUR INDEXES OF DECLINING AUTHORITY

The philosopher Anthony Giddens has identified four sources of authority in the premodern world: kin, community (including the government), religion, and tradition.[11] The modern world undermines each of these in turn, a process that has accelerated in the knowledge era.

The Family

We are all aware of the sad statistics of threatened and decaying families in the United States. Births to unmarried American women, for example, doubled—soaring from 660,000 to 1.3 million—between 1980 and 1994. The number of U.S. households headed by a single mother reached 6.5 million by 1997 and was expected to exceed 7.2 million by 2010. Of the nearly 70 million U.S. children under 18 in 1996, almost 20 million of them—and a shocking 60 percent of African-American children—were living with a single parent.[12] What is perhaps not as well known is that this family decay is global: In many developed countries divorce rates doubled between the 1970s and the 1990s, and unwed motherhood is a global phenomenon.[13]

The price for this trend of family decay has been, and remains, substantial. As social theorist Barbara Dafoe Whitehead pointed out in a seminal 1993 *Atlantic Monthly* essay, children in single-parent families are six times as likely to be poor and two to three times as likely to have

ISSUE FEATURE:
DECLINING AUTHORITY—EVIDENCE FROM ASIA

No people seem more concerned with the knowledge era's threat to existing authorities than those of Asia, where strict social control has been a hallmark of many cultures for thousands of years. Researcher David Hitchcock has conducted hundreds of interviews with scholars, government officials, and businesspeople in over a dozen Asian countries, and his findings reinforce the conclusion that the crisis of hierarchical authority is a global phenomenon.[14]

Thai intellectuals, Hitchcock reports, worry that "there is no moral compass" governing the rapid modernization and democratization of their country. He cites the plaintive words of a popular Chinese rock musician, Cui Jian. Undemocratic governments confront a growing sense of popular empowerment and demands for more participation in decision making. Hitchcock catalogs the declining hold on popular imaginations of old moral value systems such as Confucianism and the disturbing sense that no new values are emerging to take their place.

> "Money beckons
> but we lack ideals.
> Although the air is clear,
> we cannot see far."
> —Cui Jian

A number of Asian nations have begun to reconsider the value of a hierarchical approach to social organization in an era that seems to demand the opposite. A senior official with Japan's NHK network worries that "Japan needs an entirely different approach politically, economically and socially," in part because "there is a sense of dissatisfaction, a lack of something, a stagnation, that maybe we've reached the end of the tunnel and found no visible light." This urge to reform extends, especially in Japan, to educational systems built on rote memorization and obedience to authority, a trend we examine in the volume's conclusion.

In short, Hitchcock reports, "Governance is a central issue everywhere" in Asia. Governments, businesses, and other social institutions hold increasingly tenuous power, while individualism and the demand for popular empowerment are on the rise. How to accommodate these elements of the knowledge era without sacrificing its bonds of social and family responsibility may be East Asia's most pressing challenge over the next decade.

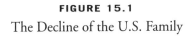

FIGURE 15.1

The Decline of the U.S. Family

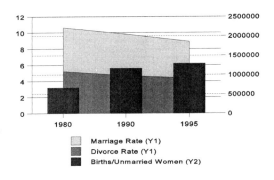

Source: U.S. Census Bureau and U.S. National Center for Health Statistics

emotional and behavioral problems as their counterparts in two-parent families. More than 20 percent of them will stay poor for seven years or more; several studies suggest that changes in family structure are responsible for about half the increase in child poverty since the 1960s. Daughters of single parents are 111 percent more likely to have children as teens and 92 percent more likely to see their own marriages end in divorce. In the United States, 70 percent of juveniles in detention homes come from broken families.[15]

David Hitchcock's interviews produced repeated comments among Asian scholars and officials that family decay is far advanced even in that region. The family in Asia "is gradually weakening," he writes. "Divorce rates, while still far lower than the United States, are mounting rapidly; drug use, crime and juvenile delinquency are on the rise. Child and spousal abuse is increasing." As wage earners migrate to burgeoning cities in search of jobs, they often leave children and families behind. In urban areas of Thailand, Malaysia, and Singapore, divorce rates have doubled in recent years.[16]

Evidence like this makes a larger point: Healthy families are indispensable to healthy societies. The institution of the family itself will not and cannot disappear—but it must be renewed to meet the new standards and demands of the knowledge era.

This recognition appears to be spreading: the decay of the American family has been arrested, at least for a while. The U.S. National Center for Health Statistics recently reported, for example, the first-ever decline in the percentage of teenagers having sex; a decline in the number of teen births during the 1990s in all states, with the largest drop among African American girls; a precipitous drop in the number of teens who already have one child having a second; and a decline in the overall divorce rate of almost 25 percent from the early 1980s to 1997, from 5.2 per 1,000 Americans to about 4.[17] But compared to earlier periods, these numbers remain high, and the topic of the developed world's fabric of family life continues to demand attention.

Community: The Nation-State

The knowledge era does not discriminate; it places every form of community—nation-states, nations within states, regional governments, and local towns and villages—under pressure.

Consider first the largest political and social community in the world today, the nation-state. Some of the more breathless pronunciations of the "death" of the nation-state, if they ever come true, certainly will not do so in the next decade. The vast majority of people in the world still identify themselves primarily as citizens of their nation, and people confronting social ills look most often to governments for solutions. Government spending remains at record-high postwar levels: 33 percent of gross domestic product in the United States in the mid-1990s (up from 31 percent in 1980), 50 percent in Germany (up from 48 percent), 54 percent in France (up from 46 percent).[18]

Nonetheless, the trend of reduced state authority is real, and it already has had a devastating impact on totalitarian regimes, helping to bring down the former Soviet regime and having the same effect elsewhere. In China, for example, respect for central authority is declining among the youth and among the regional and local governments, which are becoming more independent from Beijing's dictates. Even the regimes of the Middle East, long isolated from

ISSUE FEATURE: THE CHANGING ASIAN FAMILY

Parents who favor careers over children are not unique to the West. "In Southeast Asia, Korea and Japan," reports David Hitchcock, "middle-class parents are increasingly raising their children by cellular phone or pager." Business executives in the region "admitted to having as many as six members of their family who carry mobile phones." One recent poll found that an average father in Japan spends 36 *minutes* a day with his children. (Before Americans scoff too loudly, they should keep in mind that the equivalent U.S. figure is just 56 minutes—hardly a paragon of family life.) China's divorce rate has risen from 4.7 percent in 1981 to 12 percent in 1996; in Beijing it may have hit 25 percent.

In this environment, wives and children increasingly turn to public mentoring programs like Singapore's "Touch" community service and to friends, who are assuming greater importance as the family decays. And as in America, parents in Asia increasingly turn their children over to the influence of comic books and Disney cartoons—"probably the most influential force on moral behavior" among Japanese children, in the view of one Japanese scholar.

worldwide financial and technological trends, are increasingly feeling their influence.

Many of the trends outlined in other chapters contribute to this same process, creating a generalized crisis of authority that is a hallmark of the knowledge era. Globalization, for example, under-mines the ability of governments and international institutions to control and direct economic activity. As the Asian financial crisis of the late 1990s reminded us, global financial markets are launching a broad-based assault on government authority. Paradoxically, though, the role of finance also *increases* the importance of government action in other arenas. Markets respond to signs of economic strength, and sensible government policies are one major example. Thus privatiza-tion efforts, debt reduction, and other conscientious policies on the part of developing nations will attract investment. Finance, as the Asian crisis proved, responds to government action and is no substitute for it.

Thus, while the growing impact of financial markets restricts govern-ment authority and relevance in some areas, it magnifies it in others.

Nation-states are not withering away so much as they are sharing the stage with other actors. While it is premature to speak of "the decline" of the nation-state, it may be possible to discuss its "relative decline" in comparison to other social institutions, as I argued in Trend Four.

Community, Crime, and Social Stability

The relative weakening of the nation-state has been accompanied and abetted by a related phenomenon, the ebbing of community in all its forms. The growing "communitarian" movement contends that civil society, the network of communal institutions between the individual and the state, is in decline in the United States, the West generally, and throughout the world—and, like the family, must be rejuvenated. Harvard's Robert Putnam diagnoses the malady as a loss of "social capital," similar in importance to the more traditional economic categories of human and physical capital. For Putnam social capital "refers to features of social organization such as networks, norms, and social trust that facilitate coordination and cooperation for mutual benefit." Examples of such networks in the industrial world, such as neighborhood associations, churches, and families, are in decline, Putnam contends.[19]

To the list of afflictions undermining community we can add a crisis of public order. In developed and developing countries, an identifiable trend of widespread criminal activity is calling into question the ability of states to maintain order. The facts about crime, however—at least in the United States—are not as simple as commonly assumed. The story is not of more crime overall but of crime that is proportionately more violent. Recent years have seen a *decline* in general and violent crime rates.[20]

The crime issue is complicated by the fact that the United States keeps two sets of books on the issue: police reports and a national crime victimization survey, a survey of households conducted by the Justice Department. And as figure 15.2 indicates, until recently the two contradicted each other: Police reports showed crime growing immensely over the last 20 years, while the victimization survey showed crime declining in all categories besides motor vehicle theft.

Why the discrepancy? One reason is reporting rates: If they increased, police reports would show an apparent increase in crime when only the reporting level had increased.

SURPRISE SCENARIO:
A DRAMATIC INCREASE IN CRIME

Contrary to popular perceptions, U.S. crime rates have been declining for several years. Some observers, however, do not expect this to remain true for long. They look at the huge Baby Boomlet and post-Boomlet generations described in Trend One, which will add 500,000 new males ages 14 to 17 to the population by the year 2000. They recall evidence that younger people, especially young males, are more likely to commit crimes than older ones. And they become very worried.

This scenario examines the possible implications of a massive surge in crime, especially violent crime, beginning just before the turn of the century and extending for a decade or more beyond it. Juvenile arrests would grow from 125,000 annually to 250,000 or more. Homicides might jump from roughly 23,000 today to 30,000.[21] Such a nationwide crisis of law enforcement would carry a number of implications.

> "Experts agree that violent crime will increase in the years ahead, for demographic reasons alone."
> —Cheryl Russell

- Enormous new social costs as state, local, and federal governments rush to build more prisons, hire more prosecutors, and put more police on the street.
- An accelerated decline of urban areas and reversal of urban renewal efforts as new waves of violent crime sweep through the nation's major cities.
- Because personal security is so closely correlated with perceived standard of living, surging crime rates would spark a new sense of social crisis and decline that might support the rise of law-and-order demagogues who restrict individual liberty.
- Similar crises of public order could also arise in many other parts of the world. Reform efforts in Russia and China are already producing wealthy criminal classes; either of those societies could collapse into violence and chaos, undermining economic growth and democracy and turning both into less reliable members of the world community. And higher crime rates in developing nations of Latin America and the arc of crisis would discourage foreign investment and destabilize governments.

FIGURE 15.2
U.S. Crime Rates, 1974–1992
Percentage change in major categories according to police
Uniform Crime Reports and the National Crime Victimization Survey

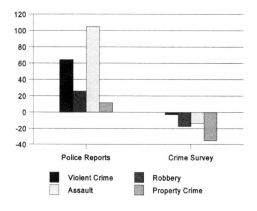

Source: Cheryl Miller, "True Crime," *American Demographics* (August 1995): 24.

Indeed, one comprehensive survey of the issue concluded that the overall reporting rate had climbed from 32 percent in 1973 to 39 percent in 1992, partly because Americans are older, better educated, and therefore more at ease when dealing with police. Most experts thus tend to favor the victimization survey as the more accurate report of crime levels.[22]

Confirmation of the trend toward lower crime rates emerged in October 1995, when the National Center for Health Statistics reported that the number of homicides in the United States fell in 1994 for the third straight year. In 1994 homicides registered a 7 percent drop, from 25,470 in 1993 to 23,730. Progress was especially striking in various urban areas: In New York the 1995 homicide rate was forecast to be nearly 50 percent lower than the record 1990 level of 2,245; in Washington, D.C., homicides in 1994 totaled 399, the smallest number since 1988. Even police reports for the first half of 1995 showed this trend continuing—a 12 percent drop in murders, for example, the

TABLE 15.1

No Enforcement

Percentage of U.S. criminals arrested who are convicted
and spend at least one year in prison

Violent felons	20%
Drug felons	10%
Murderers	49%
Rapists	29%

Source: Adam Walinsky, "The Crisis of Public Order," *The Atlantic Monthly* (July 1995).

largest decline in 35 years; a 5 percent reduction in all violent crime; and a 1 percent decline in reported crimes of all sorts.[23]

But the news isn't all good. Part of the reason for declining crime rates is the aging of the Baby Boomers. Younger people are more likely to engage in crime, and as the large Boomlet and post-Boomlet generations begin producing teenagers and young adults, rates could go up substantially.[24] "Listen closely," Princeton University scholar John DiIulio has written. "That ticking sound you hear off in the distance is America's crime bomb. The device is wired by irreversible demographic trends. The bomb is set to explode in the year 2000 when there will be about 500,000 more 14- to 17-year-old males in the population than there are today."[25]

There are other reasons for Americans to be concerned about crime even if rates are edging downward. One is that crime exacerbates social stratification and racial disparities. The homicide rate among African American youths has tripled since 1976; nearly 25 percent of black men ages 20 to 29 are in jail, or on parole or probation. Disturbingly, too, crime has become more violent: Police reports and the crime survey both show violent crime increasing as a proportion of all crime between 1974 and 1993—from 10 to 14 percent in police reports and from 15 to 20 percent in the victimization survey.[26]

Finally, the United States is plagued with a crisis of enforcement, as documented in table 15.1. Only 65 percent of homicides lead to an arrest, and over 90 percent of crimes are plea-bargained. If one murders a stranger in America today, the chances of getting away with it—the average chance of avoiding arrest plus the chance of avoiding conviction plus the rate of plea-bargaining a sentence without jail time—is a sobering *80 percent.*[27] Such ineffectual responses to crime magnify the already pronounced sense that existing social institutions are inadequate to the challenges of the knowledge era.

Crime is no less an issue abroad as it is in the United States. Indeed, for many developing nations, violent crime—and its usually nonviolent cousin, corruption—erect brutal hurdles to development and social stability. In Latin America, for example, as the tight controls of military regimes have given way to democratic rule and more lenient treatment of criminals, rising crime has become "a hemispheric trend," in the words of one regional business analyst.[28] In China, more than seven years after the demonstrations at Tiananmen Square, "crime—not political ferment—has arisen as the chief threat to order. . . . Experts here estimate that the rate of crime has tripled in the last 15 years."[29] Countries that cannot control their crime rate face a punishing array of economic costs: disappearing tourism, less interest from multinational corporations, and the domestic burden of police and jails.

A related international trend, corruption, could become one of the major strategic threats of the twenty-first century—imperiling reform efforts in Eastern Europe, Latin America, and China, keeping much of Africa mired in poverty, and ruining public confidence in government in large portions of the developed world. Corruption is especially insidious because it operates within the system rather than against it, making remedies more difficult. In Asia, David Hitchcock explains, corruption among politicians, bureaucrats, and businesses is "near the top of all countries' lists of concerns, except Singapore's." Several guides to regional graft cite China as the most corrupt—but in Thailand, many of those Hitchcock interviewed termed corruption "rampant," as did subjects in Korea and Japan.[30]

Increasingly, too, crime on the international stage displays a frightening new characteristic: It is highly *organized.* Global organized crime represents a growing epidemic of international criminal and drug organizations that have stepped into the breach provided by the decline of the state. In some countries, most notably Russia and, increasingly, China, thugs and mafia-like dons rule great swaths of territory with little interference from the state. These proliferating criminal gangs are forging new cross-border alliances against state-run law enforcement agencies.

Even as it raises the specter of exploding levels of crime and corruption, however, the knowledge era also offers new means—new authorities—for combating them. Technology will present one of the most important counterweights to crime in the next decade, furnishing dozens of tools to deter or prevent crime and catch criminals. Powerful new social actors also will devote part of their attention to fighting crime. Nonprofit organizations exist, and more will emerge, to help improve public safety. Privatized law enforcement groups will supplement the ranks of police. Businesses will do more to help guarantee the safety of their employees.

Religion

The same forces undermining the family and the community also have launched a powerful attack against monolithic religious orthodoxies. In most places, hierarchical religions do not command the same loyalty and authority they once did.

This does not imply the decline of religion, faith, or spirituality. Far from it: In fact, commentators as diverse as theologian Richard John Neuhaus and futurologist John Naisbitt point to a continuation and acceleration of religious influence. Both have referred to the next 100 years as a "religious century," characterized by the rapid, worldwide growth of faith.[31] Samuel Huntington calls this phenomenon "a global revival of religion" that has "pervaded every continent, every civilization, and virtually every country"[32]; Robert Fogel of the University of Chicago refers to it as the "Fourth Great Awakening" of American religious spirit.[33]

The next century will indeed be one of strong religious expression—but expression in a decentralized, personal sense rather than the centralized dogma of the past. As Naisbitt puts it, "Spirituality, yes. Organized religion, no."[34]

That may be a bit strong—many fast-growing churches are certainly "organized"—but the sentiment is on target. Most of the fastest-growing evangelical Christian churches, for example (some so large that they have become known as megachurches), are pluralistic in their organization and sensibility. This doesn't mean New Ageism—the churches being described here are clearly and avowedly Christian—but it does imply a growing tint of New Age-ish individualism and broad, holistic spirituality to all religions. Baby Boomers as customers, explains writer Charles Trueheart, "are accustomed to eclecticism, which is the embodiment of choice. In spontaneous imitation of that other late-century cathedral, the mall, the megachurch offers a panoply of choices under one roof—from worship styles to boutique ministries."[35] And the growth of these churches, as well as their unique quality, is tied up in the challenge to authority: The pastor of another modern church told Trueheart that people are turning to pluralistic forms of worship not because "we don't trust God; it's that we don't trust the institutions" of the old church.[36]

The enormous variety of New Age forms of spiritual expression also fit the pattern of decentralized religion. They offer individuals direct access to spiritual growth without the mediating institution of an organized church—although in some unfortunate cases, greedy pop-religious organizations move in to fill that void. The quest for personalized religions might produce a flowering of interest in Buddhism, Taoism, yoga, and other individualized forms of worship, especially in the West, in the next century. These forms of religious expression are the world's most "pluralistic" religions or forms of spirituality—individual searches for spiritual experiences.

Some students of the knowledge era have a tendency to view the decline of traditional religions and associated spiritual transformations dispassionately. Their implications, however, are anything but. "The history of the last few centuries seems to point an urgent lesson," the philosopher Karl Jaspers insisted. "The loss of religion changes everything. It destroys both authority and exception. Everything seems doubtful and fragile."[37] The gap between the pace of change and our human reactions to it is very much alive in the religious realm; creating new sources of spiritual grounding and moral values in pace with the emergence of the knowledge era is every bit as important as constructing the emerging society's social and economic institutions.

Tradition

In a time of rapid change, tradition is the first casualty. Old ways seem foolish and out of place rather than wise and helpful when everything good must be new, improved, better than yesterday's version. To the flexible, nonhierarchical citizen of the knowledge era, tradition is often a barrier to success and progress rather than a brace for it.

Our age's war against tradition is accelerated and given greater force by the emergence of a dramatically younger world population as cataloged in Trend One. The arrival of younger generations played a major role in many of history's great turning points—the Protestant Reformation, the late-eighteenth-century wave of democratic revolutions in Europe, the rise of fascism and socialism, and the anticommunist revolutions and tides of antistatist reform of recent years. The swelling numbers of young people in the world in the coming decade will further undermine the tenuous hold exercised by tradition in the developing world.

Richard Sennett argues that tradition no longer upholds authority because the tradition of the modern era is *anti*tradition. In part this is because free-flowing information encourages, even demands, that people constantly challenge and reassess the credibility of leadership figures. Sennett thus refers to the "essential feature of modern authority: figures of strength arouse feelings of dependence, fear and awe—yet [they arouse as well] the pervasive feeling that there was something false and illegitimate about the result."[38]

And yet, lest society fall apart, this trend must have its limits. Geoff Mulgan puts the problem well. "We have grown so used to struggling against authority," he writes, "that it is not easy to acknowledge that any institutions—whether they are firms or families, sports teams or nations—need some basis of authority" if they are to remain stable and act decisively and with a long-term view. Our challenge now, he says, is "to create the conditions for a fuller freedom, in radically new conditions, how to achieve what the Japanese call *kakumei,* the renewing of rules and order."[39] That's precisely what the knowledge era has in store for us—partly because the alternative is turbulent social instability and perpetual political crisis.

1 6

Implications: Social Instability and a Political Crisis

The most immediate and profound effect of the decline of old authorities is social instability. Whether measured in terms of crime, psychological distress, or the loosening bonds of trust and responsibility, the growth of social instability is one of the clearest trends of the last 30 years. Here, too, we find another example of the sort of transitional price we shall pay—are paying—for the advance into a new era.

Samuel Huntington predicted this result some 30 years ago. In his book *Political Order in Changing Societies*, he argued that modernization creates instability by forging a gap between the pace of social change and the ability of a society's institutions to keep up. Modernization, Huntington argued, "tends to produce alienation and anomie, normlessness generated by the conflict of old values and new. The new values undermine the old bases of association and of authority before new skills, motivations, and resources can be brought into existence to create new groupings."[1] Old authorities die out before new ones are fully ready to take their place. In the resulting breach grow alienation and social instability, in part because of the fierce competition to replace the old authorities in the social power structure.

In Huntington's formulation, this trend was fairly linear. Truly modern societies were stable, having reached a point at which new institutions emerged to take the place of the old. Thus his conclusion that "modernity breeds stability, but modernization breeds instability."[2]

TABLE 16.1
No Confidence in Government

Percentage of Americans saying they are angry or frustrated with the federal government:	
January 1995 *Washington Post*/ABC poll:	69%
April 1995 *Los Angeles Times* poll:	47%
May 1995 poll, after Oklahoma City bombing:	50%

Percentage of Americans who say the federal government is now a threat to civil liberties:	
April 1995 Gallup poll:	39%
April 1995 *Los Angeles Times* poll:	45%

Source: The American Enterprise (July/August 1995): 16.

In fact, modernity has turned out to be not a single place but a constantly shifting and evolving animal. Modernity has not arrived at a state of being; it remains in a constant state of *becoming*, all the while producing explosive reactions to itself. As the destroyer of tradition and the manufacturer of instability, then, the crisis of authority carries real dangers.

A key concern of our era therefore becomes finding legitimacy for more individualistic authorities in an unauthoritarian world. On what basis do governments rule? What justifies their authority? These are ancient questions—they represent the central inquiries of all politics— but they take on a new urgency in the knowledge era.

Politically, this instability and tension manifests itself in an unprecedented skepticism and even hatred of governments, a political crisis of the first order that is on display throughout the developed world. (See table 16.1.) The same disease infects a host of developing countries, including China, as well as Eastern Europe and Russia, where rising corruption and political instability are chipping away at citizens' confidence in their government. Governments in Western Europe, plagued with persistent unemployment, unaffordable welfare states, and economies strangled by regulation, confront two opposing camps of disaffected voters: educated elites who demand reform and working-class laborers who demand a defense of the status quo.

In the process, political parties tend to fragment. It is no wonder, then, that in the United States, party membership and affiliation is at its lowest point in decades; that some two-thirds of Americans identify themselves as politically independent; that a similar majority favors one or more new parties to challenge the orthodoxies of the Democrats and Republicans. And it is no wonder that, abroad, ruling parties of long standing—the Liberal Democrats in Japan, the Institutional Revolutionary Party (PRI) in Mexico, former president Suharto's party in Indonesia, the Congress Party in India—are fragmenting and losing their grip on power. In developed nations, this means weaker governments; in developing ones, it can mean civil war. And the same question arises as for all manner of declining authorities: What institutions will rise up to fill the gap left by fracturing political parties? Will the process be as simple as new parties (a "third" party in the United States) emerging to push knowledge-era reforms? Will the character of existing parties change? Or are political parties themselves truly anachronistic; will they remain in name only, hollow shells that provide convenient rallying points for diverse, shifting, fragmented coalitions of interest groups?

In addition to political instability, the decline of old authorities, when combined with the rapid change and uncertainty of the knowledge era, produces dangerous levels of personal anomie and alienation. The decline of hierarchical, industrial-era authorities is an arrow pointed at the heart of the human need for order and stability. Without careful attention, this need could once again become history's great mischief-maker, leading people to turn for reassurance to despots who promise order in exchange for obedience.

Phase Two:
The Rise of New Authorities

The story of authority in the knowledge era is not one of simple decline or deterioration, nor of the permanent victory of alienation. The forces of our time are enormously constructive as well as destructive, fashioning new institutions at the same time as they shatter old ones—and the new institutions often are more empowering and reflective of greater freedom than their predecessors.

Crises of authority are not ends in themselves; if they were, human society would have descended into chaos long ago. Instead, authority tends to renew itself through crisis, by bringing to the fore new sources of social order—a dialectical process very much under way today.[1] In the most basic sense this is true because people seek order and security in their lives (an instinct mentioned in Trend Two as the basis for social contracts, domestic as well as international). The decline of *all* authority would be seen as a threat to individual human well-being. Hence as old, monolithic, bureaucratic authorities decline, in their place arise new social movements.

In practice, this wrenching transition will be complex and unpredictable. The exact shape of the new authorities has yet to become clear. We can, however, say a few things about their likely character; table 17.1 lays out some of their characteristics. The winners in the contest for authority in the knowledge era are likely to be private groups such as nongovernmental organizations and businesses; reformed, privatized

---

TABLE 17.1

Characteristics of Knowledge-Era Authorities

1. In their *organization* they will be decentralized, small, and flexible—
   most often specialized, single-issue groups. In an age of micromarketing and diversity, few broad-based institutions will succeed.
2. In many cases their *physical structure* will be virtual instead of concrete;
   many will consist of far-flung, pluralistic conglomerations working
   together.
3. Their approach to *power* is not coercive; they seek influence rather than
   control or outright power. These new institutions are centers of
   information and knowledge competing for allegiance rather than
   rigid authorities as we have known them.
4. Their *method of acquiring influence* is through performance, competence, and effectiveness rather than brute force or tradition.

---

national and local governments; civil society institutions such as clubs
and guilds; and, ultimately, individuals. This conclusion points toward
a confusing new social structure, one in which power is more evenly
shared between public (governmental) and private sources. Partly this
means a pluralism of authority in keeping with the tribalism described
in Trend Four. Partly it means worker and voter empowerment, in ways
I will describe. Partly it means decentralization of government and
business operations to mold themselves into the kind of authorities the
new era demands.

Participation is the basic theme of these new authorities, and it is a
trend that finds strong support in complexity theory. By stressing the
creative potential of the interactions of individual actors, complexity
points to the value of a social order that allows for—and demands—
deep participation on the part of its members. Margaret Wheatley, who
grounds her business management ideas in complexity theory, explains
that "the movement toward participation is rooted, perhaps unconsciously for now, in our changing perceptions of the organizing principles of the universe."[2] The transformation of authority structures
through which we are living holds the potential to unleash immense new
amounts of human creativity and productivity, to underwrite long-term
economic growth, and to allow for unprecedented personal fulfillment.

But that potential arrives with corresponding risks and dangers that we leave unattended at our peril.

THE VIRTUAL STATE

At the most fundamental level of authority—the nation-state—the existing version will give way to a less centralized, more flexible and adaptable institution. Political scientist Richard Rosecrance has called the resulting institution "the virtual state." Far from disappearing from the scene, he argues, "the nation-state is becoming a tighter, more vigorous unit capable of sustaining the pressures of worldwide competition." Putting aside territorial aggression and other counterproductive tasks (as Trend Two suggested they should), states are focusing their efforts on economic competition, "downsizing—in function if not in geographic form."[3]

What downsizing means in economic terms is abandoning the effort to keep the factors of production—resources, factories—within a nation's territorial boundaries. In a globalizing economy, those things are increasingly mobile. So instead of trying, in mercantilist fashion, to remain self-sufficient, the virtual state works to attract capital and investment. To lure such capital, virtual states make themselves into attractive areas for investment, with highly educated populations, modern infrastructures, moderate tax rates, and tough but reasonable environmental laws. "Like the headquarters of a virtual corporation, the virtual state determines overall strategy and invests in its people rather than amassing expensive production capacity. It contracts out other functions to states that specialize in or need them."[4]

These ideas should sound familiar to anyone acquainted with the work of management guru Michael Porter. What Rosecrance has done is described a context in which Porter's notion of the "competitive advantage of nations" will become more important than ever before. Porter described a world in which nations, like companies or individual entrepreneurs, had to compete for investment and jobs in a world of global capital and multinational corporations. He and Rosecrance both emphasize the same social activity of states as the central state responsibility, the one function at which the virtual state must excel in the knowledge era: *education*. I return to this theme in the volume's conclusion.

PRIVATIZATION AND THE SOCIAL SECTOR

In this context, the explosion of interest in privatization—in the United States and worldwide—appears as not merely the collapse of authority: it is the rise of alternative authorities more efficient than government.

A move is underway, for example, to begin the privatization of the U.S. Social Security system, which will become insolvent without changes in benefit policy. The issue is not just an American one: Countries all over the world that face pension crises may look to private schemes, following the lead of privatization plans in Chile and Argentina. Even public welfare programs could be privatized to some degree: In the United States, federal welfare reform legislation of 1996 returned many welfare functions to states—and the states are turning to private firms to help them meet the challenge. Companies can often perform job-search and training functions more efficiently than government agencies.

A similar explosion of privatization and nongovernmental activity constitutes one of the most powerful global trends of the 1990s. Massive transitions to private economies are under way in formerly government-planned and socialist states from Latin America to Eastern Europe to East Asia. And the nongovernmental organization (NGO) activity even in undemocratic countries is astounding: Beijing's Ministry of Civil Affairs traces NGO growth from 100 in the 1950s to 200,000 today, including groups dedicated to family planning, AIDS, the environment, and small business.[5] As they change the landscape of authority in China, these groups are combining with the village democracy movement to advance the principle of self-rule and, ultimately, democracy. Table 17.2 chronicles the rise of the social sector worldwide, and its growth may help to reinvigorate the civil society so many commentators agree is essential to the functioning of large, free-market democracies.

The growth of social service groups will be constrained, however—at least in the United States—as long as the pattern of charitable giving continues to be weaker and more narrowly focused than it needs to be for the knowledge era. A few recent statistics tell a disturbing story in this respect.

For one thing, the richest Americans give the least, as a percentage of their income, to charity. And much of what they do give goes to universities: Of *Slate* magazine's list of the 60 top charitable donors in

TABLE 17.2
The Rise of the Social Sector:
A Snapshot of U.S. Nonprofits, 1990, in the Arts, Humanities, Environment, Health, Human Services, World Affairs, and Religious Affairs.

Number of Nonprofits:	1,375,000
Economic activity as percentage/U.S. GNP:	7 percent
Employment:	9.3 million

The economic activity of U.S. voluntary groups is roughly half the scale of the U.S. government and exceeds the GDP of all but seven nations.

- A 1992 Gallup survey found that in 1991, over 94 million Americans, 51 percent of working Americans, gave volunteer time to groups. At an average of 4 hours per week, the value of this labor (at a rate of $12 per hour) would be nearly $200 billion.
- As Baby Boomers age, contributions to charitable contributions can be expected to increase: Average household spending on cash contributions may grow from about $950 in 1993 to over $1,200 by 2002.
- It's the middle class who give. Internal Revenue Service data show that in the 1980s taxpayers with adjusted gross incomes of $25,000 to $30,000 increased charitable giving 62 percent, while those with incomes over $500,000 reduced giving by almost two-thirds.
- The Union of International Associations recognized over 14,500 nongovernmental groups that operate internationally, over 5,000 of which have formal members. In 1992, NGOs alone provided $8.3 billion in aid to developing countries, 13 percent of total world aid. More than 54,000 private associations were formed in France in 1987 alone, compared with 11,000 per year in the 1960s. There are over 275,000 charities in the United Kingdom. Over 4,600 Western groups work in the developing world with 20,000 indigenous organizations.

Sources: Kevin Phillips, *Boiling Point* (New York: Random House, 1993), p. 143; Jeremy Rifkin, *The End of Work* (New York: G. P. Putnam, 1995), p. 241; John Palmer Smith, "Scope and Dimensions of the Nonprofit Sector in the U.S.," unpub. briefing, 1995; Lester M. Salamon, "The Rise of the Nonprofit Sector," *Foreign Affairs* 73, no. 4 (July–August 1994): 111; Peter J. Spiro, "New Global Communities," *Washington Quarterly* 18, no. 1 (Winter 1995): 47, 49; *American Demographics* (January 1995): 19; and Peter Drucker, *Post-Capitalist Society* (New York. Harper-Business, 1993), p. 176.

America for 1996, fully 44, more than two-thirds, gave entirely or almost entirely to universities—this despite the fact that, in the words of *Slate*'s Jodie Allen, America "is already richly endowed with institutions of higher learning." Precisely zero members of the "*Slate* 60" gave any money to social service or welfare organizations, where the need is arguably greatest.[6] These sad facts reflect a larger social trend: While overall charitable giving increased 5 percent in 1996, donations to social service organizations helping the poor fell by 6 percent. People are giving less to antipoverty programs and more to museums, libraries, public broadcasting and the arts.[7]

Creating an effective social sector partly independent of government control will therefore require a revolution in charitable giving in the United States and elsewhere. Needed are both larger amounts of giving and giving more targeted to areas of need rather than areas of strength. Such a revolution cannot be brought about through tweaks in the tax structure; only a change in values—a new appreciation for the role of and urgent need for charitable giving in an era of smaller government—will suffice. One hopeful sign is that the 1996-1997 nationwide survey of new U.S. college freshmen found the highest level of voluntarism on record. (See figure 17.1.) Career interests also seemed to be shifting in promising directions: Interest in teaching hit a 23-year high, the number planning a career in business hit its smallest level in 20 years, and, at just 3.3 percent, the number of freshmen planning to go into law dropped to an all-time low.[8]

NEW BUSINESS STRATEGIES

The fast-moving knowledge-era business strategies described in Trend Three also launch their own attacks on tradition and authority. Richard D'Aveni's notion of "hypercompetition," for example, presumes that disrespect for old ways of doing business is essential for success. Another recent model of business strategy—London Business School professor Gary Hamel's notion of "strategy as revolution"—makes the same case.

Hamel argues that true business strategy "*is* revolution; everything else is tactics." Many firms, he argues, are running out of incremental improvements to make, while cutting-edge firms realize

FIGURE 17.1

Volunteerism in the United States, 1984–1996

Percentage of college freshmen who say they performed
volunteer work in the past year

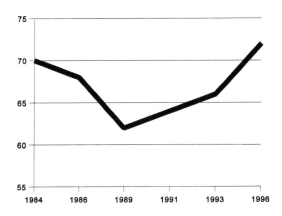

Source: Washington Post, January 13, 1997, p. A6.

that incrementalism is a road to obsolescence and decline—and that innovation is the new coin of the business realm. So he urges companies to become disruptive, to seek radical new ideas and build creativity into their genetic codes, and to recognize—as I mentioned in earlier trends—that rigid dividing lines between industries are becoming obsolete as the best companies try to create new alliances and service packages that transcend industry boundaries. Hamel also suggests that "Strategy making must be democratic," in part because the "capacity to think creatively about strategy is distributed widely in an enterprise. It is impossible to predict exactly where a revolutionary idea is forming; thus the net must be cast wide."[9]

Here again we find an argument for complexity theory's endorsement of some degree of randomness, unpredictability, and apparently "irrational" moves in business strategy. As an engine of progress, randomness has an obvious value, and businesses should keep this in mind as much as evolutionary biologists. Random movement, note science writers Peter Coveney and Roger Highfield, "leads to innovation—the discovery of smart and unexpected solutions to very hard problems." In a "competitive situation," scientist David Ruelle agrees, "the best strategy often involves random, unpredictable behavior."[10] For corporate leaders, the overall lesson is clear: Beginning with cutting-edge knowledge-era industries and spreading to the whole economy, successful businesses will *favor innovation and change over sustaining declining or current advantage.*

NEW MANAGEMENT STYLES

Modern management theories aim at one primary goal: placing more and more control in the hands of workers at the expense of management. Thus the decline of iron-fisted control by top and middle management has given way not to anarchy but to new business practices such as team-building and open-book management. Human resources economics demands a radical transformation of labor-management relations: A knowledge economy makes it impossible to preserve the very hierarchy implied by that phrase.[11] This recognition already has spawned a whole series of management reform efforts; reengineering, total quality management, work teams—one movement has followed another, while none has grasped the overall requirements of information-age management.

One writer—John Case—recently outlined one central organizing idea of management reform. He calls it "open-book management." Case explains that industrial-era business required employees akin to robots—people who would go to work and do the often-repetitious job they were given without questioning or contributing. The information age has turned all those precepts on their heads. Corporations increasingly need payrolls full of employees, as Case puts it, "thinking and acting like a businessperson, an owner, rather than like a traditional hired hand." The result "changes—fundamentally—the link between the employee and the company."[12] Note again the emphasis on people as resources, the overriding theme of the new economic era. Currently these revolutionary, democratizing philosophies of management are limited to a few insightful companies, but one recent poll of top executives found that over 60 percent agreed that "consensual management" models will dominate corporate America in the next decade.[13]

"Sick of it or not," writes the management consultant Frederick Harmon, "empowerment of workers will change the form of every organization in the twenty-first century. Empowerment is not a fad that failed. It is a core idea of the future that forces antiquated organizational forms to adjust to both societal change and the expansion of workers' attitudes."[14] At the same time, these trends do not absolve companies of leadership and coordination, and balancing these simultaneous requirements—for profound new levels of decentralization alongside the need for exceptional long-range strategic thinking and direction from the top—may be the overriding paradox for managers in the knowledge era.

A number of companies have moved to integrate these new management styles. In recreating itself as a nimble knowledge-era leader, for example, IBM formed a team called alphaWorks to shoot for quick turnaround time, short product development life cycles, and groundbreaking innovation. The alphaWorks culture is strictly entrepreneurial; staffers come to work in t-shirts and jeans, and their office sports a pirate flag and a poster that reads, "I cannot be managed by anybody." IBM hopes alphaWorks will change its wider culture from the inside and project a new image of IBM—young, hip, fast-moving, and creative—beyond its walls.[15]

With market capitalization approaching $200 billion and over 100,000 employees, Royal-Dutch Shell is one of the biggest companies on earth—and it's trying to get very small. Strategy and product development programs reach down into the grassroots of the company for ideas and solutions. When the company wanted to enhance service-station revenues in Malaysia, for example, it didn't send down a pre-printed brochure from on high; it convened small teams from a variety of functions, from marketers to truck drivers, set them to thinking, and followed up on the best ideas.

The Xerox company has also reinvented itself along the lines suggested in the last few trends. After a decade in the 1970s of declining quality, profits, and market share, Xerox officials got a wake-up call from a union shop steward named Frank Enos, who at the annual employees meeting in 1980 asked then-chairman David Kearns about a lousy new copier, the 3300: "David, why didn't you just ask us what we thought about this? We could have told you it was a piece of junk." Kearns determined to change the way Xerox did business.

Xerox now empowers its workers by giving them far more responsibility over product lines and rewards them with profit sharing and other bonuses. It pursues mass specialization with production lines than churn out tens of thousands of copiers a year—and nearly 50 tailored variations at the same time. It has a global network of plants and facilities and specializes its operations and products to the needs of local customers and communities. Its head of new business development, John Elter, got Xerox into digital copiers with sheer entreprenuership, by begging and borrowing money from other budgets; and he has tried to create a culture for his new product team that is, in the words of one report, "more like that of a Silicon Valley start-up than a lumbering bureaucratic corporation." Elter rented an office at a highway interchange and "slowly began building a staff of independent-minded engineers and PhDs. There were no private offices, no assigned parking spaces, no ties or titles. Closed meetings were banned in favor of open and ongoing brainstorming sessions."[16]

To be sure, these examples remain the exception rather than the rule. Chances are that you work in a company with a much more traditional, hierarchical, seniority-based and incrementally minded culture. Even economic theory, with its emphasis on market equilibrium, tends to discourage radical thinking: As the economist Max Boisot warns, "innovation is precisely what the neoclassical [economics] paradigm, given its orientation towards static equilibrium, has been unable to explain."[17] But all of this is in the process of changing—slowly, painfully, and in the face of a chorus of skepticism.

Worldwide, too, the implications of these ideas will be complex and differentiated, their impact filtered by culture. Cultures with traditions of hierarchical authority may try to reap the rewards of open-book management and its clones without truly respecting its principles by giving the appearance of decentralized responsibility without the reality. Countries or companies that attempt to maintain central control, that refuse to fragment into autonomous work teams and an increasingly virtual structure, will find themselves too sluggish to compete in the knowledge era.

DIRECT DEMOCRACY

The rise of new authorities also leads to a deepening of politics. Far from the claims of George Orwell's *1984* and other dark predictions of a totalitarian future, the knowledge era is a time of deepened political involvement, not technocratic authoritarianism—the result of greater pluralism and self-awareness and a media culture. Daniel Bell predicted 20 years ago that "post-industrial society will involve *more* politics than ever before,"[18] and he was right.

Joshua Meyrowitz has described the phenomenon well. In the knowledge era, he explains, information once filtered through a hierarchical series of representatives now reaches "directly from national leaders to the citizens' homes." Partly as a result, "We may be witnessing a political revolution of enormous proportions. . . . from a representative government of de facto elites to a government of direct participation with elected 'administrators.'" The change is hard to see, Meyrowitz notes, because "we refer to both of these systems as 'democracy.'"[19]

At the global level, the deepening of politics is evident in the spread of democracy described by Trend Two. It is nothing other than disintermediation—the death-of-middlemen principle—applied to politics. In its decision making, the knowledge era thus is characterized more by "unitary" than "adversary" democracy.

As explained by political scientist Jane Mansbridge, unitary democracy is that which is practiced by small social groups, based on an assumption of common interests and consensual decision making among equals. This contrasts with adversary democracy as practiced in the United States—the assumption of conflicting interests to be worked out through compromises and horse trading but ultimately colliding in elections that enforce majority rule through secret ballot. Mansbridge is not so simplistic as to assume that unitary democracy can replace its adversarial counterpart; the latter form, she recognizes, is the only one appropriate for large political units. But she believes that unitary forms of decision making can be expanded even in modern, complex societies; the challenge "is therefore to knit together these two fundamentally different kinds of democracies into a single institutional network."[20]

Unitary democracy will become more prevalent because it responds so well to the demands of the knowledge era. It is suitable for small, decentralized units. It deals with the crisis of authority and legitimacy by involving people in a consensual process of which they feel ownership. Psychologist Mihaly Csikszentmihalyi's "ideal social unit" would be "a group small enough to allow intense face-to-face interaction, one in which members participate voluntarily, and in which each person can contribute to a common goal by doing what he or she knows best"[21]— a prescription that matches strikingly the advice of Idealab founder Bill Gross, surveyed in Trend Three.

The trend toward direct democracy is being powerfully accelerated by new information technologies. The combination of television, telephone, and computer lines that is taking shape under the rubric of the information superhighway is changing the way Americans can participate in politics. Public opinion polling, direct referenda, ballot initiatives—all perhaps someday conducted via voting boxes attached to televisions—are bringing politics closer to the people. Lawrence Grossman, the former head of PBS and NBC News, writes in his book *The Electronic Republic* that "America is turning into an electronic republic, a democratic system that is vastly increasing the people's day-to-day influence on the decisions of state. New elements of direct democracy are being grafted on to our traditional representative form of government, transforming the nature of the political process and calling into question some of the fundamental assumptions about political life."[22] The *Economist* agreed in 1996 that "the next big change in human affairs will probably not be a matter of economics, or electronics, or military science; it will be a change in the supposedly humdrum world of politics. The coming century could see, at last, the full flowering of the idea of democracy."[23]

Closer citizen involvement in decision making offers a number of enticing possibilities. It could help cure the most important vice of much modern politics—the influence of powerful single-issue lobbies—by subjecting such lunacies as peanut subsidies and multimillion-dollar "highway demonstration projects" to the correcting influence of a general vote. "The big losers in the present-day reshuffling and resurgence of public influence," Grossman explains, "are the traditional institutions that have served as the main intermediaries between the government and its citizens—the political parties, labor unions, civic associations, even the commentators and correspondents in the mainstream press."[24]

Yet the expansion of public involvement in decision making is not always a positive thing. Thrilling calls for broader participation ignore a crucial intermediate step—the nurturing of civic virtues that will help people to use their newfound authority wisely. Successful participatory politics is an exercise in civic education as much as in electronic media. Whether such virtues still exist, or can arise, is a major question for the new millennium—a subset of the larger, overriding question of whether our societies possess the ethical norms necessary to weather the transition to this uniquely empowering historical era.

As with so many elements of the knowledge era, an increasingly remote information democracy also carries risks of hardening class divides and undermining deliberation in government. We have already seen how unequal access to computers and the Internet remains a problem in U.S. society, and a new politics built on electronic foundations could exacerbate social cleavages along similar lines.[25] Rapid-fire electronic decisions could be less deliberative and more subject to demagoguery than current ones. And localized government is not always less bureaucratic or more responsive than any other level; in the United States of the mid-1990s, for example, there are 13 million state and local officials available to meddle in people's lives versus just 2 million federal employees.[26] Once again, therefore, the practical results of empowerment offer benefits but issue challenges too: greater opportunities for individuals and concomitantly greater responsibilities to seize them honorably.

NEW ROLES FOR BUSINESS

Soon enough, we will no longer be able to think of corporations as strictly moneymaking enterprises. In a world of more fully shared authority, business's responsibilities relative to government will grow, and its activities will expand to fill the new space for action. As is always true with new authorities, corporate thinking will lag behind reality; business actions will not keep pace with business responsibilities. But the latter will grow and pull the former along with them—haltingly, irregularly, sometimes unwillingly, but nonetheless inevitably.

Charles Handy has discussed the changing "meaning of business." A business, he writes, "is no longer just an economic instrument." Part of the reason can be found in its purpose. "The principal purpose of a company is not to make a profit, full stop. It is to make a profit in order to continue to do things or make things, and to do so even better and more abundantly. *To say that profit is a means to other ends and not an end in itself is not a semantic quibble, it is a serious moral point.* "[27]

One recent poll found 95 percent of the American people agreeing with a sentiment long shared in Europe and Asia: Corporations owe a larger debt to society than simply making profits.[28] One reason why this is true is the growing recognition of an interdependent, networked society in which business plays a key role. James Moore's "business ecosystem" model, for example, along with such concepts as industrial ecology, stress that corporations are not narrow institutions distinct from the social contexts in which they are embedded. The recognition among business leaders that they cannot thrive if their surrounding ecology is perishing is already leading many companies to broaden the scope of their activities. "Ten years from now, I am firmly convinced," Moore has concluded, "business leaders will be actively and daily addressing social and environmental issues."[29] It is no surprise, then, that a corporate responsibility movement is already well under way, with research centers and action alliances, many of them funded and staffed by corporations, springing up around this theme worldwide. Astute business leaders increasingly know that their interests dictate that they take a hand in improving the health of that society, for a number of reasons:

- *The need for a well-trained workforce* to compete with foreign companies drives many business into strong support for education, in some cases to establishing their own training programs and in nearly all cases emphasizing the empowerment of women and minorities, whose untapped talents represent a key source of competitive advantage.
- *The importance of relationships in a tribal world.* The dean of Oxford University's new School of Management Studies, John Kay, achieved prominence in part through his 1993 book *Foundations of Corporate Success*, which argued that a firm's network of social and business relationships can provide it with a competitive advantage over other companies.

- *Competition to attract mobile, talented knowledge workers.* Firms such as DuPont, Eddie Bauer, Eli Lilly, Merrill Lynch, and Motorola pay rigorous attention to employees' family issues in part to be attractive to the best workers.[30]

- *Retention and productivity* rise when workers are better treated, better educated, and more in control of their own workplace. First Tennessee Bank estimates that its policies to make the workplace more family friendly led to its keeping employees twice as long as the industry average, to gaining 7 percent more retail customers—and to a 55 percent profit hike. Aetna Life and Casualty saved $1 million a year by extending unpaid parental leave to six months—thereby cutting in half the number of resignations by new mothers and reducing hiring and training costs.[31]

- *Public image and trust.* Increasingly, companies will compete for customer loyalty by establishing images of themselves as socially active, trustworthy businesses. As the knowledge era places more emphasis on values, businesses will increasingly be judged by their reliability as a civic partner.[32] One basis for "sustainable differentiation in the public's mind," argues Northwestern University business professor Philip Kotler, is "the company's civic character. . . . [I]n the future, as company products grow more alike, a company's civic image may be one of the most potent customer preference builders."[33]

In a human resources economy, companies that refuse to take ambitious steps to acquire and develop their human resources will fail. And those steps inevitably will encompass areas—child care, health care, elderly care, education, therapy, and on and on—that businesses have not traditionally felt the need to provide. All of these practices fit neatly into Arie de Geus's notion of a "living company," the model proposed in Trend Three as one of the keys to competitive success in the knowledge era. And the lesson, grounded in moral sensibilities, is sinking in: One recent survey of over 2,000 MBA students found that nearly 80 percent said it is a company's duty to weigh its impact on society, half claiming they would accept lower pay in order to work for a company they found "very socially responsible," and over 40 percent saying they would refuse altogether to work for an unresponsible business.[34]

None of this means that businesses will abandon profit making. The list of explicitly socially conscious corporations remains small; those same MBA students ranked customer service and product quality as the key qualities of a good company—and community involvement fifteenth. Nonetheless, over time, knowledge-era citizens are likely to favor companies that respond to the social, economic, and environmental demands of the age rather than simply seeking profit, and businesses will be forced to respect the new rules of the road.

THE EMPOWERED INDIVIDUAL

The crisis of authority is not a linear trend. It is not subverting all authorities but arousing the rise of new, more plural and decentralized ones. And it will help empower the most decentralized authority of all— the individual human being. As two commentators have recently put it, the knowledge era is the age of the "sovereign individual."[35]

Individual empowerment results partly from growing self-awareness among knowledge-era people. This era, as we have seen, is a time of diversity and individualism, a time of alienated yet empowered individuals, and a time of unprecedented information about the human condition. It therefore follows that it should be a time of intense self-awareness— which can take the form of either destructive selfishness or constructive self-reflection, among both individuals and groups. (See table 17.3.)

In its negative manifestations, self-awareness leads to self-absorption: the obsession with health and beauty; concern for one's own narrow interests; an unwillingness to sacrifice for the good of society; consumerism. Mihaly Csikszentmihalyi explains that, "with the advent of reflective consciousness, the ego begins to use possessions to symbolize the self."[36] In the absence of legitimate social institutions or myths, the production and purchase of new consumer goodies—fancy cars, the best new digital video player, computerized personal assistants—"turns out to be the major vehicle of social integration and peaceful coexistence" in the knowledge era.[37]

Yet the same urge to self-reflection can carry immense positive value as well. In a social context, it may help underwrite the values of tolerance

---

TABLE 17.3

The New Agenda of Choice and Responsibility

- Medical savings accounts
- School choice: vouchers, charter schools
- Individual retirement accounts and privatized social security
- Mutual funds and on-line personal investment and financial options
- Direct democracy through referenda and other means
- Self-management at work

---

and freedom. Curiosity about the self underlies many avenues of scientific experiment, some of which may result in cures for various diseases and birth defects. The same trends and technologies that produce alienation also serve to render individuals more powerful. The empowerment of the individual in what we call the knowledge era has been a major theme of Alvin Toffler's work, and it is present in many other analyses of the information age or the postmodern world. James Rosenau builds much of his theory of international politics around the notion that, to an increasing degree, "world politics are being shaped by powerful and restless people who can discern their remoteness from the centers of decision, who have the skills with which to do something about their situation, who are questioning of authority, and who are willing to accept the fast-paced cascade of events that mark the decentralized structures of the postindustrial world."[38] The cutting-edge business publication *Fast Company* has featured lengthy stories on the emergence of a "free-agent nation" in which employees work increasingly on their own, at their own pace, in their own way, for whom and on what they choose.[39]

But individualism has its downsides, and—as Trend Six makes clear—the gloriously empowering trends of the knowledge era also risk alienation and psychological overload. People, even the citizens of democratic and free-market countries, are not used to running their own affairs so comprehensively. It is inevitable that a reaction will set in as people reach out for the interpersonal ties that constitute a powerful category of human need. The urge for concreteness can take sinister

ISSUE FEATURE:
THE "SELF-NAVIGATORS" OF THE
KNOWLEDGE ERA

At least in the United States, younger people have begun to respond to the demands of the new "postauthority" era. One recent survey by the BrainWaves group in New York examined the rise and value systems of a new segment of the U.S. population besides traditionalists, yuppies, and Baby Boomers: the "self-navigators." The survey suggested that over a quarter of American adults, and perhaps an even higher percentage of teens, now belong to the self-navigator group.[40]

The value structure of self-navigators has a unique combination of elements. They reject tradition and authority—just 3 percent say that "living by time-honored traditions" occupies much of their thoughts, versus roughly half in the other three demographic groups. Self-navigators value achievement and success but temper these goals with a heavy emphasis on personal relationships. Indeed, self-navigators see such relationships as critical to establishing trust and the expectation of competence in a world in which confidence in traditional institutions has deteriorated.

> Self-Navigation "is not about individualism"; self-navigators "are self-reliant because they have to be, but they readily welcome the support of a network of human connections."
> —Brain Waves

Other values of self-navigators include self-reliance, a philosophy that "It's up to me to get what I want in life"; competence- rather than tradition-oriented values; and moderate political views: Self-navigators like the conservative emphasis on individual rights and responsibility and fiscal discipline and the liberal focus on humanism and diversity.

What does this new value orientation mean for the knowledge era? It is, first and foremost, a hopeful sign that people are responding to the demands of the new age—self-reliance tempered with compassion and a renewed emphasis on interpersonal relationships. And it creates even more momentum behind the opening for a new, moderate political movement of the sort I will describe. Finally, its title conveys as well as any phrase or thought the basic challenge of the knowledge era—it is, most fundamentally, a time of "self-navigation."

forms: Right-wing opposition groups, cults, and extreme forms of multicultural division offer clear and simple answers to the challenges of the knowledge era as well as membership in a tight-knit human community of fellow believers. While we remain "far from the social-political context of the 1930s," one scholar of global right-wing and fascist movements has concluded, nonetheless "in an amazingly short time the extreme right has made rapid gains" around the world.[41] Their continued advance, marching into the transitional gap between the reality of our social challenges and the ability of our social institutions to meet them, is one of the signal dangers of our time.

THE DANGERS OF TRANSITION

The threat posed by right-wing movements of anger and alienation is symbolic of the fundamental challenge posed by this trend. As old authorities decay and before new ones have arisen to take their place, a gap emerges—a gap in which solutions to pressing problems seem distant and in which social institutions seem slow-moving, slow-witted, corrupt, and hopelessly ill-equipped to tackle the demands of the new era. The result is a collapse in public confidence in all social authorities.

The philosopher José Ortega y Gasset described this process in the 1940s. Europe at that time, he argued, was witness to an "unimaginable spectacle. . . . I refer to the complete disappearance of law." And the problem was especially vexing because, he wrote, "we are not faced with another substitution of new for old laws" but, rather, for the "first time in the history of Europe what has happened is that the system of laws, of institutions is seen to be exhausted, without there having appeared on the horizon any new laws or institutions to replace them."[42] The response to such a situation—now as it was then—is as obvious as it is difficult: developing a clear, effective set of social values and norms. The conclusion argues that the reassertion of a robust and nonpartisan sense of ethical standards ranks among the key social tasks of the knowledge era; I suggest a few means of meeting them in the policy recommendations box.

One thing is certain. As the Italian political scientist Roberto Michels has written, "perhaps history is nothing but the struggle between different concepts of authority or between different groups personifying different

---

POLICY RECOMMENDATIONS: *TREND FIVE*

1. *Continue and expand the effort to create a new religious or secular sense of moral values* and responsibility in developed and developing nations.
2. *Increase the proportion of national budgets devoted to fighting crime and corruption* at all levels, as a critical foundation for social order in a transitional era.
3. *Increase support for elementary and secondary education* to prepare individuals for their responsibilities in an age of empowerment. Encourage dramatic reform in educational organization and practice.
4. *Take steps to encourage expanded charitable giving* among the wealthiest in society and direct it to the neediest areas.
5. *Respect the principles of "the competitive advantage of nations"* by preparing countries to attract investment through education, infrastructure, and so on.
6. *Increase opportunities for direct democracy* through referendums and other means.
7. For business, *adopt new corporate mission statements and strategies that embody broader responsibilities to the community,* for both altruistic and competitive reasons.

---

kinds and degrees of authority."[43] In the knowledge era, this struggle has become more brisk, more intense, and more constant than ever before. We have moved from a history of *periodic* authority crises into an era that represents a *persistent* crisis of authority. As this trend has made clear, the implications of these new authority relationships for social institutions will be profound. And it is a process that demands, more than anything else, the full emergence and development of one particular social actor: the responsible, self-aware, self-navigating, empowered individual. It is to that daunting challenge—the task of adjusting human psychology to the knowledge era—that I now turn.

A Test of Human Psychology

Understanding others is knowledge,
Understanding oneself is enlightenment;
Conquering others is power,
Conquering oneself is strength.

Tao Te Ching

It should be abundantly clear by now that the advent of a knowledge era, and the associated social and economic transformations implied in that transition, will place individuals under immense strain. Coping with change is never easy; coping with the sort of accelerated, comprehensive change that we face today could turn out to be the severest test that history has ever imposed on human psychology. This trend examines the character of that test, its social and personal implications, and the requirements for meeting it.

The special importance of human psychology in the knowledge era derives from the role our new age ascribes to the individual. More and more, decentralization and fragmentation to the point of individualism will be the order of the day. Society will increasingly hold individuals responsible for the choices they make, producing an acute sense of personal responsibility that will add to the psychological ordeal of the knowledge era. While most people understand that the knowledge era magnifies the importance of education, writes self-esteem guru Nathaniel Branden, what is not so well understood is that these facts "also create new demands on our psychological resources," asking for "a greater capacity for innovation, self-management, personal responsibility, and self-direction."[1] From the clash of opportunity and danger in the next decade emerges *responsibility*—personal and collective responsibility for our social and economic future. And from that responsibility can arise anxiety and alienation.

"When a culture is caught in the profound convulsions of a transitional period," the psychologist Rollo May wrote in 1983, "the individuals in the society understandably suffer spiritual and emotional upheaval; and finding that the accepted mores and ways of thought no longer yield security, they tend either to sink into dogmatism and conformism, giving up awareness, or are forced to strive for a heightened self-consciousness by which to become aware of their existence with new conviction and on new bases."[2] Here we find both the central psychological danger of the knowledge era and its fundamental duty: to avoid lashing out, turning to violent or separatist groups, or escaping into lethargy and inaction.

These same challenges are mirrored at the societal level. Sigmund Freud put the question well at the conclusion of his *Civilization and Its Discontents*. "If the evolution of civilization has such far-reaching similarity with the development of an individual," he wrote, "and if the same methods are employed in both," then would it not be right to conclude that "many systems of civilization—or epochs of it—or possibly even the whole of humanity—have become 'neurotic' under the pressure of the civilizing trends?" After stressing the important qualifications and limitations attached to any process of diagnosing "collective neuroses," Freud answered in the affirmative, as Carl Jung did after him.[3] Thus my project in the pages that follow: to diagnose the psychological burdens of the knowledge era and to discuss the treatments and cures available—for our empowering age does contain the answers to its own challenges, in the realm of psychology as in others.

"In Over Our Heads": Postmodern Life and Human Psychology

The transition to a knowledge era requires nothing less than a new level of human consciousness, one attuned to the abstract, virtual character of our age. The "role of the individual mind is changing," writes Merlin Donald in his book *Origins of the Modern Mind*, "not in trivial ways but in its essence."[1] These cognitive changes are accelerating for those of us who live in the knowledge era. Psychologist Robert Kegan agrees that the "demands of modern adult life may require a qualitative transformation in the complexity of mind every bit as fundamental as the transformation from magical thinking to concrete thinking to abstract thinking required of the adolescent," and suggests that the burden of our era "may be nothing less than the extraordinary cultural demand that each person, in adulthood, create internally an order of consciousness comparable to that which ordinarily would only be found at the level of the community's collective intelligence."[2]

It should be easy to imagine some of the practical results of these psychological pressures—for all of us face them every day in our homes, jobs, and classrooms. We are expected to understand our own career and life choices well enough to make them intelligently. We need to master dozens of advanced technologies and manage a lifelong process of education in support of our careers (or interests). We must pay our bills and complete complicated tax forms and manage a portfolio of insurance, retirement savings, and other investments. We are expected to administer our health care, wending our way through a maze of complicated options.

One of the chief effects of a media-saturated era is to undermine people's sense of *context,* their grounding in a familiar and stable situation. Partly the problem is one of fragmented information, which most schools at all levels unwittingly aggravate by failing to provide holistic overview courses of social change and by dividing learning into specialized disciplines. Partly, as we shall see, the problem is that amid the "death of distance," people lose a sense of place. Whatever the cause, the result is a sense of powerlessness and anxiety.

ANXIETY: THE PSYCHOLOGICAL VOID OF MODERN LIFE

The basic psychological predicament of our time builds on what may be the fundamental challenge of postmodern life: the absence of a central thread of meaning. Much of modern psychology, most especially that of Carl Jung, the existentialist school of philosophy, and postmodern writers of various stripes agree that modern, fast-moving technological society has deprived people of unifying stories and myths, whether religious, ideological, or ecological. Our growing knowledge has undermined old belief systems and authorities while our ever-expanding freedom provides us with an almost unlimited set of lifestyle, career, hobby, and other options. Without a clear foundation of values or ideologies to guide us, this array of choice is paralyzing.

We face this pressure often in our lives. Without a firm sense of purpose, what career can we choose that will satisfy our desire for identity and meaning? Without a firm moral compass, how can we view lifestyle alternatives, such as drug use or respect for the environment, in the right way? Without a clear sense of responsibility, how can we deal with the dozens of requests for charitable contributions and voluntarism we confront?

The sociologist Emile Durkheim argued at the turn of the twentieth century that "only if all members of a society were anchored" to common sets of values and assumptions "could moral unity be preserved." Without such common beliefs, "any society, whether primitive or modern, was bound to degenerate and decay," producing anomie—a condition in which "individual desires are no longer regulated by common norms and where, as a consequence, individuals are left without moral guidance in the pursuit of their goals."[3] There can be little question that, by the 1960s, the modern age was swimming in anomie. Marshall McLuhan referred to the result as an "Age of Anxiety."[4]

THE EXISTENTIALIST DIAGNOSIS

The term "existentialism" is an intimidating word for a set of ideas that, when boiled down to their essence, are fairly straightforward. (See table 18.1.) Existentialists are concerned with a vision of a vulnerable human consciousness confronting a universe that is cold, alien, and without objective values or meaning. Religious faith traditionally has filled that gap in meaning, and it was Friedrich Nietzsche who in many ways inaugurated modern existentialist analysis with his claim that the skeptical modern world had killed God and left only "nihilism" in His place. Meanwhile the human desire for meaning, for spirituality, for some form of religious expression has been partly undermined.[5] The existentialist diagnosis is nothing more than a portrait of human psychology turned loose in the world of weakened authority.

Individual human beings, cut off from the social and natural "objects" that surround them, shorn of their faith but possessing freedom, confront a multitude of complex, fragmented roles and choices. "This," Rollo May observes, "is why anxiety is so profoundly connected with the problem of freedom. If the individual did not have some freedom, no matter how minute, to fulfill some new potentiality, he would not experience anxiety. The existentialist philosopher Sören Kierkegaard described anxiety as 'the dizziness of freedom.'"[6] In the kind of world described by Trend Two—one in which freedom of all kinds, political as well as economic, is on the rise—this dizziness seems certain to become more profound and widespread than ever before.

ANXIETY AND "THE LAST MAN"

We find an echo of these themes in a book largely known for its history. As Francis Fukuyama has explained, citizens of his end-of-history nations—democratic, free-market, prosperous—may lose their sense of values, of direction, of life energy. The knowledge-era person is also "the creature who reportedly emerges at the end of history"—the "last man."[7]

Fukuyama's notion that history had ended has been widely discussed and debated, but not much attention has been paid to perhaps the most important implication of the thesis: the need to attend to the psychology of what he calls the "last man"—the bored, apathetic, disaffected characters, without idealism or clear values, who populate the end of history.[8] Fukuyama is describing the same problem of anxiety, the reaction to our apparently useless possession of complete freedom in a mechanistic and meaningless world. The desire for recognition was always there, but history has created a new problem for us: How do human beings achieve it in a time when wars and heroes are in short supply?

Here we find a fascinating thread that builds on our themes of process and paradox and that connects Trends Two, Five, and Six. Human beings are inherently progressive and future-oriented—the natural character of self-reflective beings. But as we have seen, change causes stress and instability. Thus a central paradox of human nature is that our character brings psychological stress on itself—another way, perhaps, of phrasing the insight of existentialism. (Figure 18.1 summarizes reported levels of stress in the United States.)

The philosopher José Ortega y Gasset reflected on this point in the 1940s. "Man, a pure and continual do-ing, a constant activity, is total movement, drawn forward to a goal," he argued. And yet man in the modern era, as we have been suggesting, "has the spiritual dynamics of a released arrow that has lost sight of its target." The result is that "the entity *man,* whose sole reality consists in moving toward a target, is now suddenly without one; nevertheless he must still move forward. To what end? Where does one go when one doesn't have a place in mind? In what direction do the lost turn?"[9]

Short of warfare and a new assault on democracy, the major implication of the psychology of the last man is a comprehensive relativism of values. Many people go looking for values to believe in but are stopped in their tracks by the pluralism of the age. "The very variety of choices is bewildering, and those who decide on one path or another do so with an awareness of the myriad other paths not taken."[10] The result can be anxiety and a resulting decadence, a lack of energy for

TABLE 18.1

Existentialism's Diagnosis of Modern Psychology

The philosophy of existentialism as well as related fields such as postmodern sociology focus on a few specific elements of the "modern mind." These include:

- *Abstraction.* William Barrett, existentialism's greatest interpreter, has written that it could be called a "critique of abstractions," that it represents "an endless effort to drag the balloon of the mind back to the earth of actual experience."[11] In the knowledge era, examples of abstraction include concepts such as "the global community," virtual realities, and the fact of dealing in information rather than goods.
- *Mass Society.* As Barrett explains, the feeling of "homelessness" caused by the decline of religion is "intensified in the midst of a bureaucratized, impersonal mass society."[12] Mass conformism was a hallmark of the modern, bureaucratic, industrial era. The knowledge era is working to overturn it, but will only do so partially.
- *Finitude,* "a sense of the basic fragility and contingency of human life; the impotence of reason confronted with the depths of existence,"[13] both hallmarks of the postmodern era.
- *The Subject/Object Distinction.* Existentialist writers have attempted to break down the strict line in Western thought between "subjects"—human beings—and "objects," the world around them. The ecology movement reminds us that we are creatures *of* nature, not *outside* it—an insight that also forms the basis for the social construction theory discussed in Trend Two.
- *Compartmentalization.* The chief characteristic of modernity, writes Rollo May, is "the breaking up of personality into fragments."[14] This problem has its roots in the immense fragmentation and pluralism of the modern world.
- *Relativism.* The unspoken "uneasiness" with the state of modern culture, wrote Leo Strauss, "can be expressed by a single word: relativism. Existentialism admits the truth of relativism, but it realizes that relativism . . . is deadly. Existentialism is the reaction of serious men to their own relativism."[15] Trend Four described this phenomenon and how the knowledge era exacerbates it.

positive change. Apart from a return to warfare, the great risk facing the last man is indifference—the self-conscious fatigue of an era that has seen through its own myths.[16]

This problem of inaction and jadedness reinforces the idea that the crisis of authority described in Trend Five need not manifest itself in open rebellion. Authorities in the industrialized world are not so much attacked today as they are merely ignored. If mutiny against authority characterized the modern world, apathy toward those authorities is a hallmark of postmodern life. "The hallmark of our age is not revolt, which has happened often enough in the past, but sheer indifference," writes philosopher Roger Holmes. "In this sense, the society of use really has gone further than ever before. *Authority is no longer even attacked;* this is the crucial development, this is the qualitative jump of recent times." The current phenomenon "is not that of the revolt against the Establishment: it is the disappearance of the Establishment into irrelevance and absurdity."[17]

Apathy would not, at first, seem to hold the same dangers as violent insolence. Yet indifference could be the greater long-term menace: In a world populated by the kind of intense social, economic, and environmental challenges that characterize the knowledge era, apathy could be disastrous. Our problems will worsen from inattention, and by the time crises emerge to focus our energies, it may be too late to avoid societal or ecological catastrophe.

ANXIETY: CURES AND TREATMENTS

For Nietzsche, the solution to the problem of anxiety was straightforward: the exercise of will, the choice of action and engagement over indifference. Nietzsche may have got a lot of things wrong, and his philosophy may have contributed to some hateful political movements, but he was right about this much: in the modern (and now postmodern) worlds, individuals must become empowered to deal with their world in a constructive way.

The idea of self-actualization, of course, is a well-known one, both in professional psychology and its pop-culture variants. Abraham Maslow writes of "self-actualizing people," for example, who fulfill their needs this way: "These most mature of all people were also strongly

FIGURE 18.1

Stress Levels in the Postmodern Era

(Percentage of adults reporting high or moderate levels of stress
in the preceding two weeks, 1985–1993)

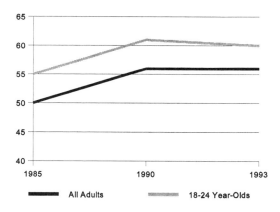

Source: American Demographics (June 1996): 44.

childlike. These same people, the strongest egos ever described and the most definitely individual, were also precisely the ones who could be most easily ego-less, self-transcending, and problem centered."[18] The philosopher Martin Heidegger placed his curative emphasis on a slightly different tactic: nurturing the reality of every human being "in the world," rather than apart from it; and, broadly, relaxing our obsession with beings—things, objects, possessions—and giving more thought to the *process* of being (note again one of our core themes), the continuous involvement in life.[19]

The knowledge era may encourage us to undertake these cures for anxiety—including the idea of "flow" outlined in the issue feature. It does so by enhancing the level of meaning and self-control available in the lives of individuals—in short, by *empowering* people.

It is no accident that the phrase "will to power" and the word "empowering" contain the same root. Workplace democracy gives employees a larger share in decision making; decentralization and

ISSUE FEATURE: "FLOW"

The psychologist Mihaly Csikszentmihalyi has proposed one of the most promising avenues to mental health in the knowledge era—his notion of "flow." By this he means something like the experience of drowning in each moment, of being totally absorbed in an activity in which we are skilled and gaining the satisfaction that comes from doing it well. There is an important element of unselfconsciousness in true flow—clearing one's head while one does woodwork, or losing oneself in the ebb and flow of a basketball game.

Csikszentmihalyi reassures us that there is something in human nature that loves complexity and seeks it out, that is only satisfied when we are stretching our potential, an enjoyment "that comes from surpassing ourselves, from mastering new obstacles"—in other words, the "joy of creativity." He writes, "Such feelings—which include concentration, absorption, deep involvement, joy, a sense of accomplishment—are what people describe as the

> "The quality of life depends on" flow experiences.
> —Mihaly Csikszentmihalyi

best moments in their lives. They can occur almost anywhere, at any time, provided one is using psychic energy in a harmonious pattern. . . . I have called these feelings *flow* experiences, because many respondents in our studies have said that during these memorable moments they were acting spontaneously, as if carried away by the tides of a current."[20]

Csikszentmihalyi emphasizes that true flow generally requires a solid foundation of skill and training. This is partly the notion, which many athletes, musicians and others have mentioned, of being so skilled in the rudiments of the activity that you can forget about all the little cues that keep you doing the thing right and "let things flow." Flow also depends on a set of clear goals and an opportunity for achieving them; it's not necessarily about mediating without any end. Flow is very much about making things happen and progressing. And it isn't blind to quality; a continuous feedback loop is in place in flow processes, telling the person how well they are doing—without which satisfaction would be harder to attain.

informatization makes the expression of political preferences easier; a host of choice-based reforms, from school vouchers to medical savings accounts, will expand the control of individuals over social institutions. The result will be a freedom not merely to observe in frozen anxiety but to *participate* and build meaning in our own lives.

At base, the issue is transcendence—the human ability for reflection, self-criticism, and self-improvement. The same human faculty that lies at the basis of anxiety—self-awareness—can, if properly mobilized, also become its cure through the recognition of the potential of freedom. The knowledge era offers extraordinary opportunities for transcendence, perhaps the greatest in human history. Through its accumulation of information, its self-conscious criticism, and its global media, this age demands that we transcend our day-to-day concerns. It offers both traditional religious institutions and an enormous variety of pluralistic faiths. It presents us with an unprecedented range of career choices, educational opportunities, and lifestyle options.

Yet this marvelous urge to transcendence can also become a mischief-maker; it is a source of the human desires for identity, dignity, and recognition that have led to so much misery in history. The challenge is to focus the transcendence urge in positive direction—a challenge that points once again to those central leitmotifs of this volume, *ethical values* and *responsibility.*

A Habit of Alienation

On the road to transcendence and empowerment, a second major psychological challenge of the knowledge era crops up, a natural complement to anxiety: alienation. Stripped of familiar moral, social, and political landmarks, caught up in the swift current of the knowledge era or left stumbling in its wake, people all over the globe are experiencing new kinds and intensities of personal and group alienation.

Alienation is closely related to the phenomenon of anxiety. The latter involves the psychological pressure of freedom in a world without absolute values, which is a form of alienation. But alienation's reach is broader; it is a wide-ranging sense of loneliness and apartness from society and others. Anxiety, as the dictionary puts it, is "a state of uneasiness and distress about future uncertainties"; alienation is "estrangement between the self and the objective world."[1]

The crisis of authority is perhaps paramount, although it is hardly alone, in sparking alienation. The advent of the crowded technopolis, the economic pressures of the knowledge economy, and the contradictory impulses of globalism and tribalism—in short, all the major trends of the next ten years—contribute to the same result. Samuel Huntington wrote in the 1960s that the "disruptive effects of social and economic modernization" produce "alienation and anomie, normlessness generated by the conflict of old values and new,"[2] and the knowledge era's turbulence and uncertainty have much in common with modernization's impacts on developing nations. By now the idea of alienation has become so common, and is believed to be so inevitable, that its presence is no longer deemed surprising. Alienation has become ordinary, trite. We are in the habit of being alienated.

In the last half of the eighteenth century and the first half of the nineteenth, the mass society of the industrial or modern era became the frequent target of social critics who pointed to the crushing uniformity of industrial, technological, urban, and bureaucratic societies. This vein of thought came to include the most famous social criticism produced in the last 100 years,[3] from such authors as Karl Polanyi, William Whyte (and his dispiriting portrait of the 1950s "organization man"), John Kenneth Galbraith, Herbert Marcuse, and Jacques Ellul.

Now the postmodern, postindustrial knowledge era has arrived—and it has brought some characteristics of modernity to fruition while turning others on their head. Decentralization, rather than a centralized conformism, is now the order of the day; noncompliance is valued rather than condemned; the social focus has returned from organizations to individuals. Yet none of this means that the problem of alienation has been solved; it has merely taken on new guises—some of which build on certain elements of modernism, such as diverse societies, and some of which represent modernism turned on its head. Plenty of books are still published on the broad theme of the depersonalized mass culture of our era—Neil Postman's 1992 volume *Technopoly,* which describes the "surrender of culture to technology," is one recent example.[4] Compared to its modern predecessor, the knowledge era is one of both increased and reduced alienation.

REASONS AND CAUSES

A moment's reflection should suggest why a fragmented society of relative values, the kind of world described in Trends Four and Five, is an alienated one. These trends have arguably long been under way in the United States, where cultural tradition is weakest of almost any country in the world and where the speed of history is the most rapid. But they are increasingly hitting home throughout the world, in nations and cultures commonly thought to be family-oriented and tradition-bound. No region of the world is immune to the alienating effects of modernization, globalization, and the transition from one historical era to another.

The death of ideologies has put an end to many of the unifying themes we use to combat estrangement. Many observers have commented on the decline of the sacred, of national and religious myth, even of the socialist ideal as ideas that stand against the void. "A postindustrial society," the famed sociologist Daniel Bell admits, "cannot provide a transcendent ethic. . . . The lack of a rooted moral belief system is the cultural contradiction of the society, the deepest challenge to its survival."[5] The crisis of authority exacerbates this trend, depriving people of credible social institutions to establish order and predictability in life.

A second cause of alienation has to do with the challenge of coping with a knowledge-rich age—information overload and the lack of context for the information we can process. People feel alone and helpless in the midst of a bewildering array of information. Issues such as personal finance and career choices become maddeningly complex. An astounding array of information vies for our attention—dozens of cable television channels, at least several major newspapers, a clutch of glossy newsmagazines, thousands of Internet sites, tens of thousands of new books every year, radio stations, books on tape, fact-packed CD-ROMs, nonprofit think tanks, and more. Culling this information, separating the wheat from the chaff and finding what's most useful and interesting, is a daunting task. It is also one that will create important new business opportunities in the years ahead as people look more and more for "information middlemen"—services that help them organize, manage, and make sense of the glut of information surrounding them.

One specific result of this surfeit of information is to imbue the knowledge era with an unprecedented degree of social complexity—a third route to alienation. Social issues, their characteristics as well as causes and cures, seem more complicated than ever before. This perhaps helps explain the appeal of Forrest Gump—the simpleminded character played by Tom Hanks in the film of the same name—as someone who can approach life simply, directly, without the paralyzing complications of our age.

A fourth engine of alienation is the speed and degree of change. In an economic sense, people are increasingly alienated from the lifelong careers and the expectations of a sound retirement that sustained our parents and grandparents. The rapidly changing, diverse global economy has created the need for serial careers and rapid changes of career direction. Writer David Hitchcock's interviews in East Asia produced strikingly similar reactions. In China, one scholar told him, "rapid change has made people feel sort of lost and requires decisions in multiple fields of society" that are difficult and confusing. In South Korea, novelists have taken up the country's "sense of rootlessness" and "depression" as central themes. A Japanese university professor worries that students today "have no faith, no particular ideals and, with some exceptions, no ambitions."[6]

Fifth, a global media age also alienates individuals from perhaps the most important measure of psychological stability and grounding: a firm sense of *place,* physical as well as social. Joshua Meyrowitz discussed this phenomenon in his insightful 1985 book *No Sense of Place.* "At one time," he wrote, "physical presence was a prerequisite for first-hand experience. To see and hear a President speak in his office, for example, you had to be with him in his office." This, of course, is no longer the case. "The evolution of media has decreased the significance of physical presence in the experience of people and events."[7] Our ability to locate ourselves in the world may be weakened by electronic media's constant assault on any location at all. Other features of modern life contribute to the same result: the impersonal and massive nature of modern architecture, for example,[8] or the distancing of urban people from nature.

Sixth and finally, alienation is exacerbated by another, related phenomenon—the pervasiveness of abstract realities. An era in which society and economy revolve around knowledge is bound to become more abstract, in a host of ways: in relationships sustained over great distances (or "relationships" with television or movie characters); in the emphasis on intangible stocks, bonds, and other financial instruments over land and buildings; in the breaking down of certainties about the physical world and their replacement with complicated and abstract new theories like quantum mechanics and complexity theory.[9]

"Today, from the moment they wake up to the morning news until the moment they turn off their TV at night," writer Larry Letich explains, "Americans must constantly process information about things they can't see, touch or really even imagine." Merely to "function as halfway competent adults," Americans "must exercise a kind of abstract thinking that until recently had been the domain of a small minority."[10] Everything, wrote Erich Fromm in 1955, "including ourselves, is being abstractified; the concrete reality of people and things to which we can relate with the reality of our own person, is replaced by abstractions, by ghosts."[11]

THE PRICE OF ALIENATION

This thorough sense of alienation, a product of myriad aspects of the knowledge era, carries real costs. It encourages movements able to feed off its effects, such as militia groups and cults. It gives an angry and partisan tinge to debates over such issues as back-to-basics education and national identity. Perhaps most worrisome of all, it underpins the antigovernment feeling so prevalent throughout the world: People increasingly view government officials as out for their own good, not the common good. More and more younger people are unwilling to believe that bloated bureaucracies can change things for the better. This attitude discredits society's primary institution for addressing its ills.

Both brute psychological facts and the insightful analysis of a number mental health professionals reinforce a feeling we all have to some degree or another: the postmodern world is launching an assault on our psychological resources.

One especially frightening indication that something may be amiss in human psychology at the turn of the millennium is the increase in clinical depression around the world. Depression is now essentially, in terms of victims and economic impact, the world's second most insidious illness, behind heart disease. The numbers astonish: 330 million people worldwide suffer from depression; through absenteeism, lost productivity, and other causes it costs the world more than any illness save heart disease—$44 billion a year in the United States alone, according to one estimate; the number of Americans encountering major depression sometime in their lives has skyrocketed from under 10 percent for Baby Boomers and their parents to as much as 25 percent for the post-Baby Boom generation.[12]

Depression is far from a U.S., or even developed world, phenomenon. Rates appear to be growing rapidly from China to Russia, from South Africa to Sweden. Much remains unknown about its causes, and it would of course be foolish to chalk up such a complex and misunderstood family of illnesses to the speed and complexity of the

SURPRISE SCENARIO:
AN ALIENATION-BASED DEMAGOGUE

Among the dangers posed by the knowledge era, one of the most disturbing is its potential to generate new kinds of demagogues who take advantage of the flow of information and the disenchantment produced by globalization, rapid change, economic uncertainty, risk, and general alienation to promote agendas of hatred, scapegoating, and coercion.

This scenario posits the emergence of a knowledge-era demagogue in the West. Knowledge-era provocateurs could break the bounds of industrial-era demagogues: They could appeal to a regional or global rather than local or national audience; represent a high-tech rather than backward constituency and ideology; make sophisticated use of Twenty-First century propaganda techniques; and take advantage of the pluralism of views and relativism of modern societies to legitimize his ideas.

Much of the dissatisfaction to which a new demagogue would appeal already fuels pseudodemagogues on national stages, such as Pat Buchanan, Jean-Marie Le Pen, and Vladimir Zhirinovsky, and thoroughgoing local demagogues. What is missing is a trigger—a precipitating spark for the spread of such views. The most likely trigger is the emergence of serious and persistent bad economic times. A severe recession might expand the demagogues' base of support and produce a number of chilling results.

- *Discrimination against and persecution of minority and immigrant groups* as scapegoats for economic decline.
- Resulting *ethnic wars within states* that have become far more plural, and within which power has decentralized to a greater degree, than the demagogues assume.
- A return to *wide-ranging state economic planning, protectionism, and mercantilism* as demagogues amass power and seek answers to economic problems.
- *International conflict* as competitive states headed by demagogues turn their scapegoating beyond their own borders.

knowledge era. But those factors—combined with such things as the media Pessimism Syndrome (which I'll discuss in a moment), the decline of social authorities like family and church, and all the abstraction and relativism of the new era—could surely have something to do with the lengthening shadow cast by depression on the postmodern world.

One expert who believes there is a definite connection between the character of our age and mental illness is the psychologist Richard DeGrandpre. In the 1999 book *Ritalin Nation*, DeGrandpre launched a broadside attack on knowledge era culture. All of its hallmarks—incredible media saturation, personal and professional mobility, the decay of social institutions, and the crushing emphasis on progress and profits—have spawned a "hurried" generation that is addicted to stimulation, DeGrandpre worries.

By 1992, he observes, studies found that one in three Americans "always" felt rushed as "rapid-fire culture" gave rise to "rapid-fire consciousness" and a refusal to appreciate the value of slowness, of patience, and of ease. The result is not merely that human life is accelerating, but that people crave the acceleration—a phenomenon especially noticeable in today's children, whose entire lifetimes have been saturated with stimuli. DeGrandpre traces the explosion of attention deficit disorder—and its accompanying drug treatment, Ritalin—to children's need for constant stimulation. Already, two million U.S. children take the drug, and some estimates suggest that the number will reach 8 million, 15 percent of all school-aged kids, early in the next century. For adults and children alike, he contends, our rapid-fire culture produces an "experience of unsettledness, characterized by feelings of restlessness, anxiety, and impulsivity."[13]

The Swarthmore psychologist Kenneth Gergen has diagnosed similar maladies in the knowledge era mind. Gergen focuses on the idea of "social saturation," in which we're overwhelmed by a deluge of relationships, contacts, pieces of information, distractions, and entertainments. Contemporary life, he writes, "is a swirling sea of social relations. Words thunder in by radio, television, newspaper, mail, radio, telephone, fax, wire service, electronic mail, billboards, Federal Express, and more." New faces, new people we encounter, "are everywhere—in town for a day, visiting for the weekend, at the Rotary lunch, at the church social—and incessantly and incandescently on television." We travel "casually across town, into the countryside, to neighboring towns, cities, states; one might go thirty miles for coffee and conversation."[14]

One result, for Gergen, is the onset of what he calls a "*multiphrenic* condition, in which one begins to experience the vertigo of unlimited multiplicity"—our minds no longer have to cope merely with being one fairly easily defined person ("the town blacksmith"), but with dozens of

ISSUE FEATURE:
AN EMERGING GLOBAL MENTAL CRISIS

A number of recent studies have documented an uncomfortable trend in human psychology: it appears to be under growing strain, and not just in the United States.

Harvard social medicine experts Arthur Kleinman and Alex Cohen helped to run a major mid-1990s study on world mental health by the World Health Organization, and its results were disquieting. The stunning progress of economic growth and measures of physical well-being like life spans and general health in the developing world, they wrote, "has been accompanied by a deterioration in mental health. In many areas outside North America and western Europe, schizophrenia, dementia and other forms of mental illness are on the rise." Their study estimated, for example, that schizophrenia alone would afflict nearly 25 million people in the developing world by the year 2000, almost half again as many as suffered from the illness fifteen years earlier.[15]

Apart from the obvious human toll, mental illness can be a crushing economic burden for developing nations that barely have the resources to provide a minimal level of physical, let alone mental, well-being for their people. And as I explain in the text, recent estimates of the economic costs of depression and depression-related illness are daunting.

There seems to be little question that the world's accelerating rush into the knowledge era, and all the associated psychological strains (some of them documented in this Trend), has something to do with the worsening global psychological picture. The "link between suicide rates and social upheaval," for example, has been documented by psychologists since the nineteenth century, Kleinman and Cohen explain—a fact that makes it somewhat less surprising, though no less amazing, that fully 40 percent of the world's suicides occur in China.

We're accustomed to being deluged with the pressing need for basic necessities like food or medicine, or improved general medical care, in developing nations. What most Americans, and most governments throughout the world, have yet to appreciate is the psychological burden of our rapid social transformation, a burden that will become ever more apparent in the decade to come.

"multiple and disparate potentials for being"—husband, researcher, martial artist, novelist, counselor, teacher, mentor; and in the dim future, psychologist, commentator, congressman, bureaucrat, comedian. "We are not one, or a few," Gergen contends, "but like Walt

Whitman, we 'contain multitudes.' . . . All the selves lie latent, and under the right conditions may spring to life." We feel, as a result, a kind of vertigo of roles and identities, less sure than our ancestors of who, precisely, we are.[16]

And the worrisome thing is that, with imbedded wireless systems, cheaper global communications, 500-channel cable systems and a passel of other innovations on the horizon, "The process of social saturation is far from complete"[17]—indeed, I'd say it has just begun.

As the last issue feature suggests, these trends are hardly unique to the United States. France has become another of the developed world's primary symbols of postmodern alienation. Columnist Jim Hoagland recently pointed to the rise and entrenchment of an "anti-immigration, anti-Semitic right-wing party along France's border regions," much of it oriented around Jean-Marie Le Pen's National Front. In an April 1995 presidential runoff election, Le Pen captured 15 percent of the vote. The reason: Economic globalization is creating unemployment and other tensions, especially in border regions. "French alienation is becoming quagmire deep," Hoagland warns, and this has disturbing implications "for other industrial democracies buffeted by the economic and social disturbances of globalization."[18]

The same could be said of dozens of countries. In Mexico and Colombia, cynicism about corruption is aiding rebel movements and threatening social fragmentation. In South Korea and Japan, government/business ties provoke opposition and scandal. In Africa, state collapse is almost universal.

The dissident Liu Binyan worries that "spiritual deterioration and moral degradation are eroding China's cultural foundation. Forty-seven years of communist rule have destroyed religion, education, the rule of law, and morality. Today this dehumanization caused by the despotism, absolute poverty and asceticism of the Mao era is evident in the rampant lust for power, money and carnal pleasures among many Chinese." As he concludes, "Coping with this moral and spiritual vacuum is a problem not just for China but for all civilizations."[19]

Yet as I have said, the knowledge era is double-edged. It offers not merely the risk of an alienation at least as profound as that of the industrial era but at the same time the prospect of an *escape* from alienation to a degree unprecedented in the modern world. Previous trends have held out the hope that the knowledge era will help reconcile

ISSUE FEATURE:
MEDIA AND "SOCIALIZATION SPHERES"

The term "socialization spheres" refers to the social surroundings in which we grow and mature as human beings. The family is one; the education system is another. And as Joshua Meyrowitz recognized over a decade ago, the new media environment of the knowledge era revolutionizes them all.

It used to be that a child's age was a "prime determinant of what he or she knew. Very different types of children were exposed to similar information because they were in the same age *group*. Now, children of every age are presented with 'all-age' social information through electronic media." Much more than in a "print culture," when parents and teachers could monitor the information flow, children today are "thrust back on their *individual* cognitive and social development as a means of attaining their social status. Strict age-grading of activities and roles and knowledge no longer seems as appropriate or necessary." In a broad sense, media's "homogenized information networks . . . lead to a less selective diet of information and therefore to less distinct sets of knowledge and perspective at different life stages."[20] The results:

> Modern media "blur the differences between people at different stages of socialization and between people in different socialization processes."
> —Joshua Meyrowitz

- A *"blurring of childhood and adulthood,"* in which our society becomes full of "adultlike children and childlike adults"—a phenomenon described by other social observers (such as Neil Postman, in *The Disappearance of Childhood*).[21] Marshall McLuhan put the issue in slightly different terms—children in primitive cultures always grew up quickly, he contended, a habit lost in some premodern or modern cultures to which we are now returning. But the impact is the same: "My children had lived several lifetimes compared to their grandparents," McLuhan quotes an IBM official as remarking, "when they began grade one."[22]
- A *"merging of masculinity and femininity,"* in which traditional male-female distinctions give way to a media-inspired "homogenization of gender roles." This has been one by-product of the women's rights movement, but it also stems from the decline of tradition noted in Trend Five and the march of workplace reform.

economic growth and ecology, impel the further spread of economic and political freedom throughout the world, and provide individuals with stunning educational and entertainment options; in sum, through its effect on the workplace and other social institutions, the knowledge era can and should be about the empowerment of individual human beings. In the process, human alienation—from nature, from society, from self—would give way to new levels of connectedness and satisfaction. The ultimate human need for dignity and identity outlined in Trend Two would be met: Each member of a sustainable society would possess the tools to master his or her world and prosper.

Some of the advantages of a human resources economy, for example, become evident in the psychologist Erich Fromm's "roads to freedom," his roadmap for social health and stability, outlined in 1955. Fromm's research uncovered evidence for the "enlivening and stimulating effect of the active and responsible participation of the worker in his job." It was not so much monotonous, technical tasks that caused alienation, psychologists had discovered; it was an alienation from the overall work context—the big picture. The first requirement for an answer to workplace alienation was therefore that the worker "is well informed not only about his own work, but about the performance of the whole enterprise." But such knowledge is not enough on its own, Fromm argued: "The worker can become an active, interested and responsible participant only if he can have influence on the decisions which bear upon his individual work situation and the whole enterprise. . . . The principal point here is not *ownership of the means of production,* but *participation in management and decision making.*"[23]

The parallel between Fromm's advice and knowledge-era management theories is astonishing. The general principles of empowerment and decentralization for which Fromm called, in politics as well as business, find a mirror in the knowledge era. But these hopeful outcomes are not inevitable—they must be molded, created, manufactured—and the nature of an information-rich age will complicate this task.

As we try to meet these challenges, we can't expect help from heroes, political or otherwise. Heroes are the first casualty of a cynical, jaded, media-saturated world. Creating great leaders requires some level of myth-making, and television tends to bring politicians down to our level; even if we continue to respect them, we know too much about them to idolize them in the manner of a true hero. The dearth of wars deprives us of military heroes, and a combination of media saturation and callous behavior robs us of heroes from the world of sports (with a few notable exceptions). And a number of recent people who flirted with hero status—Colin Powell comes to mind—seem to have been scared away from political leadership by our society's tendency to ruin its heroes so quickly after elevating them.

The passing of heroes can have its advantages: It forms a natural bulwark against demagogues, who frequently attempt to assume the most "heroic" poses of political leaders. But it complicates our social challenges by removing from the scene the people who could inspire us to rise to another level; people who could lead us, through the force of their character, to a better future. It is up to us, the citizens of the knowledge era, to meet the challenges to our society; no one, any more, is going to do it for us. And the psychological burden of this fact is immense.

This burden requires nothing less than a conscious effort to attend to "mentalities" or "ecologies of mind," as Geoff Mulgan puts it. The notion of government trying to tinker with human psychology sounds pretty terrifying, but it is equally undeniable that, as Mulgan says, "no state or society can honestly remain neutral about the mentalities it produces."[24] Businesses and militaries know this very well, but the knowledge era's bracing roster of psychological challenges seems to me to demand much more universal training in the skills of mental health and self discipline. This means cultivating self-esteem, teamwork and communication skills, moral sensibilities, "emotional intelligence," and a calm thoughtful, meditative approach to knowledge era life and it's challenges. We should foster an attitude that will urge us, whatever our religious beliefs, to append to them the insights of such meditative and individualistic spiritual traditions as Zen Buddhism.

The "Pessimism Syndrome"

There is an odd paradox of modern life in the United States and in many other nations in the developed and developing worlds alike: Things have never been so good, yet people have rarely been so negative about their country's situation and so pessimistic about the future. Political commentators during the 1994 election, write Clifford Cobb, Ted Halstead, and Jonathan Rowe, "were perplexed by a stubborn fact. The economy was performing splendidly, at least according to the standard measurements," but the "applause never came. Voters didn't *feel* better." Federal Reserve Chairman Alan Greenspan referred to the "seemingly inexplicable" conundrum that, even in promising economic times, there "remains an extraordinarily deep-rooted foreboding about the [economic] outlook."[1]

This same paradox manifests itself in other ways. In January 1995 *American Demographics* magazine published results from a recent poll about Americans' sense of satisfaction, which found that people saw events *in general* in far more negative terms than in *their own situation*. On the issue of crime, for example, almost 90 percent said it was rising in general—but just over half said it was rising in their area. On education, 21 percent gave U.S. education as a whole a grade of A or B; almost three-quarters awarded such grades to schools in their own towns. Only 35 percent thought Congress did a good job, while over 60 percent thought highly of their own representative.[2] In a 1997 poll of young people ages 18 to 29, almost 90 percent expressed satisfaction with the direction of events in their personal life, while less than half were as sanguine about the direction of the country.[3] These polls reflect a gap—a growing and dangerous gap—between perception and reality, a gap that is a product of a profit- and publicity-seeking media with natural incentives to exaggerate the negative and downplay the positive. Most of the information individuals get to counteract this portrait comes from their experience—which is why, in survey after survey, people consistently think their own lives are going far better than society as a whole.

Yet our own personal observation seems to count for little against the vast wave of information sweeping over us each day in a dozen forms, swamping our perceptions and washing away the familiar landmarks of our experience. Together, these phenomena produce the *pessimism syndrome:* the pervasive tendency to think things are getting precipitously worse when they are not. This tendency substantially complicates the psychological challenges of the knowledge era by skewing our perceptions in unhelpful ways.

One recent poll by Harvard University, the *Washington Post,* and the Henry Kaiser Family Foundation shows the syndrome at work. Their survey found that the average American thought that the unemployment rate was four times higher than it actually was; indeed a quarter of those polled said the jobless rate was more than 25 percent, the same rate as the Great Depression. Americans at that time thought inflation and the deficit were much bigger than was the case, and three-quarters of them thought that the number of jobs in the U.S. economy had actually declined during the previous five years, when the economy actually added 9 million jobs in that period.[4]

The problem, as one might expect, is not restricted to the United States. As former French prime minister Edouard Balladur explains, when the French are asked whether their children will live a better life, "the majority now reply in the negative. In that balance between 'fear of falling' and 'hope of rising,' which Tocqueville saw as the driving force of free societies, fear of falling is now carrying the day—and is paralyzing French society."[5] Liberal journalists in Russia, writes author and editor David Remnick, "after years of talking about ideas and ideals," have grown "cynical, intent only on discussing economic interests; the worst sin is to seem naive or woolly or bookish—or hopeful."[6] Former Pakistani president Benazir Bhutto worries that the media "follows stories which interest it; not all stories are considered interesting, and usually those stories are considered interesting which are scandalous or which are not good." As a result, offering young people positive role models—heroes, admired historical figures—has been replaced by attempts "to scrutinize and analyze to such an extent that one is not looking for the good qualities in a person; that's not news, good news is not news. But scandal is."[7]

This idea is similar to, but distinct from, the thesis of Robert Samuelson's 1996 book, *The Good Life and Its Discontents.* Samuelson sees the same gap between reality and perception, but chalks it up to a different cause: an entitlement mentality. Having experienced, in the postwar era, one of the most astounding increases in national growth and wealth in modern history, Americans came to assume that things would always be that way. As things now return to a more typical state of affairs, they mistake normalcy for collapse, slow and steady growth for no growth, the need to work hard for a lack of opportunity. "What upsets us, in short," Samuelson writes, "is that we have inherited a country and world different from those that we felt were our due."[8]

Samuelson is absolutely right, and his analysis is superb. But the profound effect of information in skewing people's perceptions is at least as important in nurturing our depressed state of affairs than the entitlement mentality. As Samuelson himself phrases it, "The modern press gives the worst side of us much more exposure and respectability than ever before. We are constantly immersed in our imperfections and failings, and the effect is to convince us that we are worse off than we actually are."[9]

A MEDIA AGE—AND A PESSIMISTIC ONE

People have always sought to understand the world around them; today that understanding comes primarily from news outlets, whether print or broadcast. And if you listen to the press, you almost undoubtedly think that the world is disintegrating. "Television is now, indisputably, the primary source of news for most Americans," argued David Shaw in a recent series in the *Los Angeles Times.* "It may also be the primary source of the cynicism that increasingly pervades the news media and society at large." Shaw continued with a neat summary of the hypothesis: "Just as studies have shown that viewers who see crime-dominated local TV news shows are likely to think that crime is much more prevalent than it really is, so viewers who watch national news shows, magazine shows, and the weekend political talk shows are likely to think that the world in general, and politicians in particular, are much worse than they really are."[10]

The reasons are not hard to find. Bad news gets good ratings; good news doesn't—or so the media presumes. Reality, writes Jay Bryan in the *Montreal Gazette,* "is too annoyingly complicated to make a snappy news story. Doom and disaster, on the other hand, are dramatic, attention getting and easy to understand. . . . Few people think it is very newsworthy when a plane doesn't crash, and the same is true with the economy" or any other issue.[11] Columnist William Raspberry has been among the most eloquent critics of media cynicism, and he chalks it up in part to an "institutional mind-set"—reporters are trained to be cynical and skeptical to get the story. "Our training, the news values we inculcated, the feedback we get from our editors," Raspberry writes, "all encourage us to look for trouble: for failure, for scandal and, above all, for conflict."[12]

Marshall McLuhan recognized this fact a quarter of a century ago. "Both book and newspaper are confessional in character, creating the effect of inside story by their mere form," he wrote. "It is for this reason that the press seems to be performing its function most when revealing the seamy side. Real news is bad news—bad news about somebody, or bad news for somebody." This media pessimism would spur intense and shocking advertising, McLuhan presciently suggested, because, as essentially "good" news, ads "have to shrill their happy message loud and clear in order to match the penetrating power of bad news."[13]

The Center for Media and Public Affairs in Washington, D.C., does yeoman's work each year chronicling the persistently negative bias of the press. Their figures are stunning. Take crime: The three major network television news shows saturated Americans with 2,574 news stories about crime in 1995—exceeding by about 100, amazingly, the number of stories devoted to the Persian Gulf War in 1991. Some 800 of those crime stories were about the O.J. Simpson trial, which artificially inflated the figures for crime reports, but not decisively. In 1991 the three networks broadcast only 632 crime stories, so the non-O.J. increase was still phenomenal. And this at a time when crime rates were in the middle of a several-year decline.[14]

In 1991 the center did an exhaustive analysis of network news and *New York Times* stories on the rapidly recovering U.S. economy. An astounding 96 percent of stories about the general economy were negative in tone; pessimism occupied 87 percent of the stories on real estate, 88 percent of the features on the auto industry, and a perfect 100 percent of stories on manufacturing. Almost 60 percent of reports painted a dim picture of America's economic future; one economist told ABC News that the economy "almost looks as if it is sliding off a cliff"[15]—a forecast that, now that the intervening years have produced one of the longest economic expansions of the postwar era, looks positively foolish.

The environment receives equally pessimistic treatment. An April 1995 Center for Media and Public Affairs study of children's shows found that over 90 percent of environmental themes focused on doom rather than hope.[16] On the issue of global warming, media coverage during the latter half of the 1980s was frequently alarmist: More than 90 percent of television, newsmagazine, and newspaper reports on the issue carried a core theme that global warming would be "cataclysmic" in its effects.[17]

Social relations in the United States provide more convenient fodder for the pessimism syndrome. As the *Washington Post*'s Richard Morin explains, hundreds of news stories describe America as a country wracked by "culture wars." Yet there is "one problem: America hasn't become more polarized over social issues in recent years. Just the contrary. On most issues, we're closer to consensus today than we were two decades ago." One major Princeton University study of two decades' worth of public opinion data, for example, found no support for the notion that public opinion on major social issues in the United States had polarized since the 1970s.[18] One would never know this from the U.S. media, addicted as it is to portrayals of a country coming apart at the seams.

Another example of the influence of social pessimism can be found in public attitudes toward time. Americans today feel as if they have less time to spend on themselves; pessimistic social commentators argue that people are working longer hours for less pay. In 1995, echoing psychological studies described above, 83 percent of American adults judged themselves "always" or "sometimes" rushed, up 10 points from 1971.[19] Yet people have more free and leisure time than ever before. By using surveys of detailed "time diaries," University of Maryland professor of sociology John Robinson and Penn State professor of leisure studies Geoffrey Godbey found that working hours have shrunk over the last 30 years and free time has expanded by as much as a full hour per day. Yet the pessimism syndrome is alive and well here, too, for Americans who do not keep specific time diaries *believe* that they are working longer hours even when that is not the case.[20]

Confronted with such an overwhelming diet of pessimism, it is no wonder that Americans as well as the citizens of many other industrialized and developing nations, become depressed at both the state of their societies and their future prospects, even as they see little evidence of such unrelieved catastrophe in their personal lives. The broad message delivered to most Americans is simple: Things are bad, disasters await us at every turn, the future holds enormous peril. This trend cannot help but reinforce our habits of anxiety and alienation.

The negative media bias is especially pronounced in the coverage of politics. An analysis by Thomas Patterson of Syracuse University concluded that "the press nearly always magnifies the bad and underplays the good" when covering the White House.[21] During the 1960 presidential campaign, references in major weekly U.S. newsmagazines to substantive policy issues outnumbered stories about "campaign controversies" by 2 to 1; by 1988 controversies outnumbered issues by 25 percent. Favorable references to the two major presidential candidates in *Time* and *Newsweek* declined from 75 percent in 1960 to 40 percent in 1992. During the 1994 to 1996 congressional term, Patterson found coverage to be negative 70 percent of the time.[22]

The situation has become dire enough that leading media figures themselves point to the need for change. James Fallows, editor of *U.S. News & World Report,* devoted a major portion of his first 1997 issue to the presentation of *hopeful* news—reporters writing on 20 ways to make society a better place. "Ask a group of reporters about journalism's greatest achievements," Fallows wrote in the section's lead essay, "and the answers are likely to sound like those the police would give. We found a problem, and we brought the culprit in." Such an "inspector-general" function of the press is essential to democracy, Fallows argues, but it is—or ought to be—only half the story. People want a helping of good news to go with the bad, but reporters do not see such "feel-good" news as part of their brief. They "will toil around the clock . . . when it comes to explaining a corporate or political failure. But when they have good news to serve up, they often feel compelled to do so in a condescending and cutesy way, as if this were not 'real' journalism."[23]

EVERYTHING STINKS; I'M OKAY

Broad social and economic trends are demonstrably not as bad as people assume. In fact, they may not be very bad at all: When an American looks at demography, or the environment, or violent crime, or the economy, or the risk of war, most broad global trends are running in directions that could be called positive. And the paradoxical truth is that most people appreciate this fact when asked about their own lives. "When surveyed, about four-fifths of us say we are satisfied with our own lives," explains Robert Samuelson. "But when asked about the country—whether it's 'moving in the right direction'—Americans are routinely glum."[24]

Take one 1995 worldwide Gallup poll (taken from www.gallup.com). "People Throughout the World Largely Satisfied with Personal Lives," the lead headline trumpets. In five countries—including the United States—an astonishing 80 percent or more of people surveyed expressed general satisfaction with their lives. In most countries, the percent dissatisfied barely reached into the 20s. But glance down half a page, and it looks like a different survey: "Pessimism About Future Blankets Most Countries Surveyed," the report exclaims. "Citizens in the 18 countries surveyed tend to be pessimistic about the future, expecting it to be worse than the present." Not surprisingly, "The United States is among the most pessimistic, with 60 percent saying the future will be worse, and just 23 percent saying it will be better." And all of this, the Gallup report wryly concludes, "despite the fact that, for many people, today's world is much better than the world in which their parents grew up."

Similar results emerge in a December 1994 poll of Americans by Republican pollster Frank Luntz. Almost three-quarters of Americans believed that they have already achieved or are "closing in on" the "American dream"—yet nearly 80 percent believed that dream would be harder to attain in the future. Only 26 percent of Americans "strongly" agreed with the statement "I am optimistic about America's future," and only 64 percent agreed with it at all.

FIGURE 20.1

Trends Are Disastrous; My Life Is Good

Percentage believing things are headed in the "right direction"
or the "wrong track" at different levels

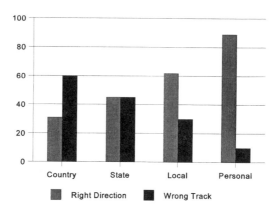

Source: "The American Dream—Renewing the Promise," A Survey Analysis for the Hudson Institute by Dr. Frank I. Luntz, December 8, 1994, p. 20.

The perceptual gap emerges most stunningly in one chart in Luntz's study, entitled "Right Direction/Wrong Track." (See figure 20.1.) Asked to rate five levels of society—the country, their state, their local community, and their personal lives—in terms of which direction they are headed, the question elicited a perfect visual summary of the pessimism syndrome. The numbers for "headed in the right direction" started at 30 percent for the country as a whole and marched steadily upward to reach an astounding nearly 90 percent for personal lives. Meanwhile, the percentage of those who said things were "on the wrong track" began at 60 percent for the country and fell steadily to hit just 10 percent for the respondents' personal lives. The closer to their own personal lives they focus, the more optimistic people are; the more they think about society, the more depressed they become.

THE DANGERS OF UNFULFILLED EXPECTATIONS

The pessimism syndrome could work to destabilize knowledge-era societies in a number of ways. In the most general terms, an incessant

FIGURE 20.2

Americans' Perception of Broad Social Trends

Percentage of Americans saying their are satisfied or dissatisfied with
"way things are going in the country"

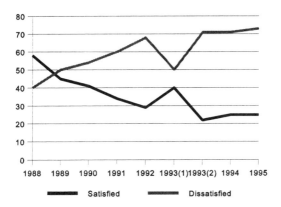

Satisfied   Dissatisfied

Source: "The American Dream—Renewing the Promise," A Survey Analysis for the Hudson Institute by Dr.
Frank I. Luntz, December 8, 1994, p. 3.

pessimism syndrome will produce substantial amounts of personal
depression. Its resolutely negative portrayal of trends encourages
people to believe that the world is falling apart and is beyond their
control. Figure 20.2 offers disturbing trends in Americans' general
sense of satisfaction with the "way things are going in the country."
The absence of positive social anchors—trends moving in the right
direction with which people can identify—could, in the long run,
increase the instance of psychological illness by magnifying the
alienation and rootlessness already produced by the fast-moving,
virtual, telecommuting knowledge era.

The pessimism syndrome also could stifle entrepreneurship and
progress. In a world of broad-based pessimism, it is no surprise that
confidence in problem-solving institutions declines. If the world is
going badly wrong—as most Americans believe—then obviously
those traditional institutions of power that influence social trends
must be doing a bad job. This assumption, a natural by-product of
the pessimism syndrome, manifests itself in the rock-bottom level of

faith Americans have in their institutions today. In the Frank Luntz poll mentioned earlier, just 38 percent of Americans had "a lot of confidence" in the ability of religious institutions "to promote morals and values in our society"—and the church was the big winner. Just 17 percent were very confident of schools' ability to "teach children what they need to know," 8 percent had faith in the news media "to give you the full and unbiased truth," and a shocking 6 percent strongly agreed with "the government's ability to solve a problem." Just 16 percent of those polled trusted government to "do what was right" all or even most of the time. It is therefore hardly surprising that voter turnout has fallen to perilously low levels.[25] In this manner, the pessimism syndrome may dampen momentum for policy reform and change. As William Raspberry writes, it "discourages those who might be tempted to try to make a difference."[26]

People who are worried about their economic security and pessimistic about the future are also more likely to look for scapegoats for these problems. "Americans who believe the economy is performing badly," concluded the *Washington Post,* are angry about it, and many "want to punish those they think are responsible"—such as welfare recipients, nations that receive U.S. foreign aid, and immigrants.[27] The pessimism syndrome thus opens the door for demagogues to marshal public sentiment against minority groups.

All of this may bring home to highly industrialized countries a source of instability heretofore largely confined to newly modernizing ones: a revolution of rising expectations. Samuel Huntington described the phenomenon in his classic 1968 text *Political Order in Changing Societies.* By "rising expectations," he meant "enhanced aspirations and expectations that, if unsatisfied, galvanize individuals and groups into politics."[28] The key is the disparity between wants and progress, a gap "between aspiration and expectation, want formation and want satisfaction," a gap that largely explains political instability in modernizing countries.[29] There is little question that this gap is alive and well in America, although the gap between reasonable expectations and objective reality is not very great. The real aspirations/expectations gap today is a perceptual one, and it is the product of the pessimism syndrome (as well as the entitlement mentality Samuelson has documented). The question is how far this process will go. Could it produce real social instability, on the model of developing nations? Will the gap become so pronounced that people turn to nationalists or autocrats in a hopeless effort to close it?

At a minimum, a persistent cynicism and pessimism could produce national policies that impair future economic performance. Some of these might be state interventions designed to "protect" workers from the "decline of work"—a series of new and stifling regulations, taxes, ill-designed job training programs, and other steps that impair innovation and growth. Much more worrisome, however, is the impact of the pessimism syndrome on trade policy: It already is creating a new strain of nationalist protectionism in many countries, which, if it spreads, could impair the functioning of the emergent world trade system. This helps to explain why President Clinton's recent call for fast-track trade authority fared so badly even amid promising economic times: People just didn't believe the good news they were hearing.

A perceptual revolution of rising expectations also might exacerbate ethnic tensions in the United States and other diverse nations. Minority groups whose objective standard of living is increasing—perhaps even relative to the majority—might come to believe the opposite under a barrage of media focus on failures rather than success stories. These groups would press for additional benefits against strengthening resistance from a majority that saw no need for them.

Internationally, a phenomenon of rising expectations and dashed hopes could serve to undermine U.S. power. Much of American influence comes from the example of optimism, dynamism, and energy we set for the rest of the world. It imbues American foreign policy with things like the attraction of American ideals, which magnify and in some cases replace the exercise of traditional military force. The American idea is indeed conquering much of the world, a fact that is of utmost importance to our national security—not to mention the freedom of literally billions of people in reforming countries trying to attain political and economic liberty. But how effective will our example be if Americans become increasingly cynical, pessimistic, and angry? Will a culture thoroughly infected with the pessimism syndrome still be one capable of spreading its example abroad? And will this loss of faith and example undermine the energy, vision, responsibility, and persistence the world will require to make the transition to the knowledge era?

SOLUTIONS—IF WE WANT THEM

What, then, is there to do? Quite a bit—if we recognize the danger posed by the pessimism syndrome and work toward solutions.

The first element of the solution involves a demand for more objectivity on the part of the news media. It would be wrong, and simplistic, simply to ask network news broadcasters or weekly newsmagazines to report "happy news"; ignoring problems is no alternative to exacerbating them, and one of the media's most important roles is to uncover social ills and direct public attention to their remediation. But if that noble purpose is not balanced with a careful effort to portray the good along with the bad—as James Fallows, for example, was trying to do during his tenure as editor of *U.S. News*—then the pessimism syndrome will spread.

Thus, as the columnist William Raspberry has suggested, editors and broadcasters should ask themselves if they can find ways to offer hopeful messages along with perilous ones. The idea that only bad news sells is largely untested; sensationalistic shows often grab headlines, but it should be equally possible to offer sensational stories of community heroes or amazing new technological breakthroughs. Dozens of examples already exist—the newsmagazine *Nightline* perhaps chief among them—of extraordinary (and very consistent) ratings achieved by shows that deal with controversial issues, but in a balanced, not cynical or pessimistic, fashion.

More fundamentally, the real solution to the pessimism syndrome is education. Citizens of developed and developing nations alike need a context to understand information they receive, a basis of objective facts that help moderate the news and critical or reflective reasoning skills necessary to think problems through rather than merely react to information.

These observations lead to a more hopeful conclusion—and, in a sense, a secondary hypothesis besides the pessimism syndrome. Democratic, free-market, knowledge-era societies may well be *self-correcting,* not self-defeating. A knowledge-era democracy may turn out to be the one form of social system truly capable of self-analysis and correction; it is constantly in the process of assessing its condition and reflecting on needed improvements. This has always been true of democracies, and it is truer than ever in a knowledge era that has dramatically accelerated this process of self-correction.

The mechanism is simple and well known. A problem exists: say, water pollution caused by industrial waste dumping, or the plight of children in the inner city. The media in its broadest sense—including television and radio, print journalism, documentary filmmakers, writers, commentators, and others—highlights the issue and makes people aware of it. Politicians take it up, for reasons of personal fame as well as real concern, and this redoubles the media focus. Pressure builds to find meaningful solutions, with the media helping to shoot down half-baked ideas and ideological rhetoric. Once new policies are adopted, media sources and government agencies follow its progress and press for midcourse corrections. This process is hardly perfect: Filtered through the quirks of human nature at all levels—the media, politics, the public at large—it is delayed, twisted to fit personal agendas, sidetracked. But it continues inexorably, constantly reassessing what is being done and whether it could be done better, what problems exist and what can be done to solve them.

The genius of the mechanism is precisely the same aspect of the knowledge era that lies at the heart of the pessimism syndrome—the broken distinction between personal and social. When we are bombarded daily with the news of the world beyond us, this contrast blurs and frays and becomes more tenuous. When people tend to think things are going badly, their own personal experience is corrupted by the broader social context. But this same process works in reverse, focusing attention on problems that before would have been dismissed as someone else's business. One or two centuries ago, if your land was not being polluted by industrial runoff, you might not have seen the need to curb it. People could insulate themselves from the plight of the urban poor and safely ignore them. Now, often anyone's problem becomes everyone's problem.

This is not to say that people respond automatically to distant suffering. Many Americans can still dismiss the plight of inner-city youth; most wondered just why the United States was trying to bring peace to Somalia, a small country so far away. And some issues—such as urban poverty—are so complex that they defy easy solution even when the mechanism just described has lurched into motion. Nonetheless, social awareness is evolving and growing. The fact that the United States was drawn into Somalia in the first place is evidence of the power of the knowledge era to demand solutions to severe social problems, solutions supported (even requested) by people who have no direct experience of those problems.

We might call this process the *self-correction mechanism* of knowledge-era democracies. Like the pessimism syndrome, it isn't a new idea; the notion that democracy can correct for its own flaws is a venerable one. But the mechanism was imperfect before the knowledge era, which has bridged the personal-social gap. It is a powerful source of progress—and an important reason for optimism. And in the end, it will help to correct for the pessimism syndrome: The fact that things are better than people think will become news; the effect of negative press bias on popular opinion will be debated and discussed, and media practices will change; stories of success and hope will become more prevalent once again.

One wonders, however, whether this hopeful mechanism will spring into action before the pessimism syndrome has done serious damage. Fast track trade authority for the president may have been its most recent casualty and a harbinger of worrisome things to come. The point is not to become a nation, or a world, of Pollyannas. Many social, economic, and environmental challenges await our attention. But we will not be able to meet them effectively if we are too depressed and cynical to think our efforts will come to anything.

A RADICAL ADVANCE IN HUMAN EVOLUTION

In retrospect, it is hardly surprising that the kind of the wrenching transition to a new socioeconomic age should turn out to have immense implications for individual human psychology. Those implications, as we have seen, are seldom simple or linear; more often they are complex, paradoxical, and full of surprises. The complexity and speed of this age constitute perhaps its most fundamental challenge to our ability to cope.

Yet it is possible to identify some of the most important psychological challenges facing humankind as it approaches a new millennium. I have tried to lay out a few in the preceding pages: the various engines of alienation of the knowledge era; the distorting effects of an information culture biased toward pessimism; the psychological ramifications of an increasingly virtual, computer- and Internet-based modern culture; and the challenge of preserving cultural identities and values in a manner that does not spark conflict.

POLICY RECOMMENDATIONS: *TREND SIX*

1. For the media, *encourage presentations of positive and hopeful news* alongside reports of scandal and disaster, and do so on a regular basis.
2. *Redouble efforts to expand educational achievement and reform,* including courses designed to provide holistic overviews of social trends.
3. *Support the emergence of new social values and a renewal of community ties* as partial responses to alienation.
4. For business, *offer new forms of "information frameworks"* designed to help people manage and make sense of their complex knowledge-era lives.

In broader terms, virtually every trend I have examined in this volume points to an increasing emphasis on *individual responsibility*—the expectation that every person will be increasingly able to navigate his or her own independent way through the complex maze of risks and opportunities that comprises the knowledge era. I suggested in the last trend that the social instincts and needs of the human animal may be much older and more firmly grounded that the individualistic ones. This fact is a source of hope, but it also poses a relentless challenge: to recalibrate our thinking, more fundamentally than ever before, in the direction of individual rather than social responsibilities.

In order to fulfill this expectation, human beings in the knowledge era must be equipped—and their societies must make the decision to *ensure* that they are equipped—with the requisite tools and skills (and the policy recommendations text box offers a few ideas of how to make that happen). Through this process, knowledge era societies can fashion their cultural evolution in a humanistic, civilizing, prosperous, and ultimately hopeful direction. Today the most important tool of all is knowledge itself, the most important skill the employment of knowledge—and therefore the dominant social activity is *education,* a theme to which I return in the conclusion. And more than simply general education, which is critical enough, is the tricky subject of *moral* education. Public schools often are considered unsuitable avenues for conveying values, but various trends under way point to a growing role for moral education in public schools.

ISSUE FEATURE:
HUNTER-GATHERERS OF INFORMATION

The images of nomadism and gathering are powerful metaphors for understanding our psychological predicament. Joshua Meyrowitz refers to our situation as "hunters and gatherers in an information age": nomadic peoples "have no loyal relationship to territory. They, too, have little 'sense of place'; specific activities and behaviors are not tightly fixed to specific physical settings." Meyrowitz notes fascinating parallels between knowledge-era societies and those of hunter-gatherer bands. Both tend to be highly egalitarian; boundaries between "careers" or roles, between play and work, between peace and "war" are blurred; authority cannot be maintained by a distant "aura" and must be won by persuasion and performance; and in their children both foster "self-reliance rather than obedience to adults."

But the truth is more complicated than a simple parallel. For we are obviously different from pre-modern hunter-gatherer bands in as many ways as we are like them. We are "spiraling forward rather than circling backward" to some imagined, nomadic past; we "regain some features of the pre-modern world as we advance into a new frontier"[30]—precisely the same combination of past and future that characterizes the meeting-point between the modern and postmodern worlds, and the kind of complex mixing of eras that is so rife with paradox and blurred boundaries.

Ultimately, the psychological opportunities of our unfolding age can outweigh its costs, because the knowledge era has everything to do with empowerment and self-realization. Marshall McLuhan put it this way: "Men are suddenly nomadic gatherers of knowledge, nomadic as never before, informed as never before, free from fragmentary specialism as never before—but also involved in the total social process as never before." The patterns of this age "are those of self-employment and artistic autonomy"—self-navigation, in other words. This is the ultimate answer to the danger of an Orwellian future of totalitarian states; for "Panic about automation as a threat of uniformity on a world scale is the projection into the future of mechanical standardization and specialism, which are now past."[31]

The basic message of this trend has been that the knowledge era imposes immense psychological pressures and costs on individual human beings, who are the fundamental social actors of this decentralized age. The question of whether our limited human consciousness can respond to the demands of our time remains open. But we can find hope in one fact: It is none other than we who shall answer it because, in the end, we are the engines of our own history. That simple fact is one of the most important lessons of the knowledge era, and it is the theme to which I now turn.

Toward a New Society

How confusing,
there is no end to it all!

Tao Te Ching

"The past thirty or forty years have been the most revolutionary era in recorded history," the famed historian Eric Hobsbawm wrote in the 1980s. "Never before has the world, that is to say the lives of the men and women who live on earth, been so profoundly, dramatically . . . transformed within such a brief period."[1]

More than anything else, the message of this book has been that the coming decades represent a social tranformation that will overshadow the changes of the past 40 years—and perhaps the past 400. The next 10 to 50 years will sieze the title of the most profound transition in human history. It embodies unprecedented risk and opportunity for our societies.

As long ago as 1933, Carl Jung offered some discreet thoughts at the end of a characteristically brilliant essay. "In coming to a close after so many bold assertions," Jung wrote, "I would like to return to the promise made at the outset to be mindful of the need for moderation and caution. Indeed, I do not forget that my voice is but one voice, my experience a mere drop in the sea, my knowledge no greater than the visual field of my microscope, my mind's eye a mirror that reflects a small corner of the world, and my ideas—a subjective confession."[2] So it is with this project. I have had the temerity to offer thoughts and forecasts in a dozen fields of endeavor. I hope the result has in some modest way confirmed the importance of holistic thinking about the interrelated trends reshaping the world.

I began this book, if you will recall, from a position of "cautious optimism"; and although it has been sorely tested over the last few trends, I remain wedded to it. I believe that the dominant threads of the knowledge era are hopeful—empowering, democratizing, egalitarian, environmentally healthy. "There is a strong, deeply held sense among those at the forefront of business," the editors of *Fast Company,* the preeminent chronicle of knowledge-era business thinking, have observed, "that purpose, community, and sustainability are lasting values that inform the work we all do—and the future that we are all working toward," a future "that is enormously hopeful, powerfully energizing, and absolutely achievable."[3] The new organizational models and work-place habits discussed in Trends Three and Five match almost precisely the recommendations of at least some psychologists and sociologists of the optimal way to organize human experience.

But the dangers inherent in the knowledge era, the reactions to change and by-products of the age's hopeful trends, mandate a cautious version of optimism. The key, as I have stressed throughout this book, is not fate but choice: the choices we make over the next decade to shape the future. Fate has provided us with the raw material of a new renaissance in human society, but it is up to us to make that renaissance a reality.

A major reason for my optimism is that the knowledge era has conclusively upset the forecasts of the last half century of mass hierarchical conformism as a result of the industrial era. The naturalist Robert Ardrey worried as late as the 1970s that "the organization of modern life devours the individual. . . . A workingman, he will be denied the right of excellence by his union. An organization man, he will be required to deposit his most secret riches in the company safe." From an "anonymous house in an anonymous suburb," Ardrey continued, "he will take his anonymous seat in an anonymous train to reach an anonymous office where he will perform the tasks he performed yesterday, suppress the resentments he suppressed yesterday, return to his . . . anonymous home where he will have the martinis he had yesterday, renew the quarrels he had yesterday, watch lights and shadows on a television screen indistinguishable from the lights and shadows he watched the night before."[4] How quaint that account now seems, as the knowledge era's tidal waves of decentralization, empowerment, and individualism wash over the globe.

Yet we will not realize this hopeful promise without effort, which is why the theme of responsibility has played such a powerful role in my analysis. The connection between knowledge and responsibility is obvious: Each relies on the other to realize its full potential. The corollary of this fact is that the knowledge era is correspondingly an "era of responsibility," for individuals and societies alike.

We are, as never before, aware of the way our world works. We have an unprecedented ability to shape that world. And this power bequeaths an extraordinary obligation to use our newfound knowledge and power wisely.

A New Kind of Society

Our era's transitional character helps to account for another theme underlying many of the trends: the dialectical character of change. Each trend produces reactions and countertrends, with the interaction then producing a new synthesis. This simple paradigm helps to explain a great deal: why countries in transition to democracy are the most warlike of all; why modernizing states are most unstable; why globalization produces countertrends of tribalism and some level of cultural tension.

Previous chapters have gone into some detail about the precise form of this new society, the knowledge era. It represents not a reversal but a further development and modification of the industrial or modern era. ("The moments which [History] seems to have left behind," wrote the philosopher Georg Hegel, "it still possesses in the depth of its present."[1]) And it embodies greater challenges and opportunities than any previous era in human history. In the sections that follow, I outline three of the most important lessons suggested by this transition: the decisive role of education, the primacy of moral values, and the need for a re(new)ed capitalism.

THE DECISIVE ROLE OF EDUCATION

As I have pointed out repeatedly in previous chapters, in a knowledge society education determines the fates of individuals and nations. Never before has learning been so important to the fate of humankind as it is

ISSUE FEATURE: THE NEW SYNTHESIS

If history indeed moves dialectically—one age or set of social characteristics (the "thesis") challenged by an alternative (the "antithesis")—the product of their interaction, the new era I have argued is in the process of emerging, will be a new "synthesis." It will, for one thing, incorporate elements of both the new and the old, which is why fresh social ages always build on rather than exterminate their predecessors. In a more practical sense, however, this "new synthesis" might manifest itself in a host of public policy issues, encouraging us to transcend today's sharply drawn partisan divisions.

The debate, for example, between proponents of *responsibility* and *charity* on issues such as welfare reform will give way to new models that emphasize both—welfare laws that are unflinchingly tough on those who merely don't want to work, and at the same time lavishly generous with those who do.

Arguments about the *size of government*, while continuing at the margin (especially in places such as Europe), may recede before a much-expanded discussion of ways to make sure government works effectively, through means such as "reinventing government." The age-old war between the prophets of free markets and the evangelists of government intervention could well die down amid a new consensus that splits the difference: liberal economics tempered by the social and economic values that capitalism cannot itself guarantee.

The intense U.S. *dialogue on race* may leave behind the controversy over preferences and quotas in favor of a more sophisticated approach to racial harmony emphasizing iron-clad enforcement of laws prohibiting discrimination against minorities, expanded efforts to encourage discussion and mutual understanding among young people of differing races, and a broad-based social commitment to increasing minority and women's representation in the centers of power.

Bitter quarrels about *environmental protection* might finally be superseded by an exploding recognition of the financial and public relations value to business of sound ecological practices and the immense promise of new technologies in such areas as renewable energy.

today. This fact argues not only for much expanded education but also for improved forms of it: The industrial-era learning processes that prevail throughout the world will not meet the needs of the knowledge era.

Partly due to the decline of military threats in the world, education, and the knowledge and intelligence it provides, offers defenses against much more common threats to security than foreign enemies—the threats of creative destruction inherent in our transitional era.

As important as education is, it is not done very well today. "The education industry everywhere is using the same techniques that were common 150 years ago: students in groups of ten to forty being taught by a single teacher," writes futurist and author Hamish McRae. "The subjects taught have changed, but the teaching method has not. Education has only just begun to think of ways of increasing its output."[2] The recognition of the need for educational reform is strong even in that region of the world famed for its extensive, disciplined school systems: East Asia. Scholars and officials interviewed by writer David Hitchcock "were almost unanimous in the criticism of their own educational institutions." One Thai businessman complained that "our education does not develop the critical mind." Korean scholars said much the same thing: "Our curriculum has been far too rigid," argued one; another explained that some Korean teachers are "trying to break away from rote learning." "Our kids come back from the United States and find the Japanese system stuck," worries one prominent Japanese academic. A Chinese scholar admitted that "There is too much emphasis on discipline and collective thinking as a way to solve problems, and too little emphasis on the individual and on creativeness."[3]

Thus dramatic reform of education is one of the clear requirements of the next decade. Knowledge-era learning must display a number of clear advances from the sort we know today: It must become more *holistic,* showing the relationships between disciplines and issues; it must become more *high-tech,* using software games, virtual reality, and the like; it must emphasize *creativity and participation* to a degree seldom seen; it must come to be characterized by more *choice and competition* at all levels, including charter schools and voucher plans of some kind; and more than ever before, it must become *egalitarian.* Of all the social responsibilities we face in the knowledge era, none is more profound than the requirement for serious educational reform.

A variety of teachers, education experts and public-policy analysts have proposed specific avenues to achieve such reform. Over the coming decade, different countries and school districts within countries are likely to try every one of these alternatives to some degree. No single model of education reform will be dominant, even within the United States; as we would expect in a thoroughly pluralistic era, the next decade will witness a diverse quilt of new ideas and reforms. New information technologies, for example, will allow schools to increase students' interest in learning without sacrificing content while helping to develop the skills necessary to thrive in a high-tech, virtual world. One child learning specialist reports that children who use computer games "develop hypertext minds. They leap around. It's as though their cognitive strategies were parallel, not sequential."[4] Famed movie director George Lucas has created an educational branch of his company, Lucasfilm, called Lucas Learning Ltd., to promote high-technology, interactive educational alternatives. The director of his new company, Susan Schilling, explains that the new technologies will bring education into the virtual era—and in so doing, enhance access. Teaching in the electronic realm "allows equal access to a high-quality presentation that enhances learning," Schilling says. "That learning can be done in the schools, in the homes, in the centers that serve the more disadvantaged populations."[5]

The next decade will also inject much greater elements of parental and student choice into primary and secondary education in the United States (and, to some extent, throughout the developed world). Competition always improves quality in the long run; no monopoly institution has the same incentive to improve as do organizations competing for resources and, in this case, students.

The specific forms of educational choice will be as diverse as the schools they represent. The purest form of choice is a straightforward "voucher" program that allows parents to send their student to any school in the region they choose, using their voucher—representing the taxes they pay to support the system—to gain admission to some mixture of public and/or private schools. In theory, schools that cannot attract enough students will "go out of business," and this process of natural selection will improve quality over time. Opponents raise powerful objections to full-fledged voucher schemes; some argue that most voucher experiments have produced at best minor enhancements in test scores and other measures of academic quality, and others point to the very real risk that schools in the process of being selected out of the system—schools of poor quality in the midst of failure—could limp along for several years, trapping students in an even worse learning environment than they suffer today.

A less dramatic form of choice is provided by "charter schools," publicly funded but independently managed schools freed from many of the bureaucratic constraints of traditional public institutions but required to accept a random selection of students from the district or state pool. The results to date are promising. In Boston, for example, charter schools such as City on a Hill and Boston Renaissance take the usual challenging urban mix of students and achieve impressive advances in test scores, while offering a useful combination of tough discipline and cutting-edge exercises in creative thinking and empowerment like town-hall meetings and dance classes conducted in French. Nationwide in the United States, the number of charter schools has jumped from almost none in 1992 to nearly 1,000 by early 1999, and President Clinton called for a further increase to 3,000 early in the next century.[6]

In higher education, too, choice will revolutionize learning. Today the American system of higher education embodies some of the very worst business values in the world: At some exclusive schools, students pay $30,000 tuitions for frequently mediocre instruction from teachers who clamor to spend more of their time on research and writing than on teaching itself, and whose promotion and tenure often are based on success at endeavors other than actual instruction. No one can deny the necessity of a college degree, or the earnings value it represents; but the actual value of the physical service offered by the most expensive universities is often exceedingly poor.

Several avenues are available to reform higher education. One would be the creation of new, bare-bones colleges specializing in high-quality, highly respected instruction at a fraction of the cost of today's top-rank schools. The *Atlantic Monthly*'s Nicholas Lemann has proposed a "Fantasy College": an institution begun from scratch whose role would be "to offer a top-flight undergraduate liberal arts education at a reasonable price, say $15,000 a year." His school would eliminate research faculty and expensive "Club Med" campus facilities, and attract students with gold-plated postgraduation placement offices that would, provided their academic work allowed, nearly guarantee them a job in their field upon graduation.[7]

The idea is a brilliant one, and the price could be far less than Lemann proposes. If the new university combined dedicated, teaching-oriented faculty, inexpensive facilities on cheap land, liberal use of virtual classrooms to reduce further overhead costs, and other cost-saving measures, there is no reason it could not run at a level of between $6,000 and $7,500 per student, just above the average cost of public universities.

Another likely evolution in U.S. and global higher education is toward greater use of the virtual classroom. Especially at the university level, students are independent and generally technology-savvy enough to make profitable use of the Internet, videoconferencing, classes held as "chat rooms," and other forms of electronic teaching. Again, at first this will only supplement existing methods of classroom instruction on most campuses, even at the end of the coming decade. In the long run, however, there is no reason why large numbers of students could not be exposed to the best teachers in the country through nationwide virtual classes, perhaps supplemented by local discussion sessions and testing moderated by younger teachers or teaching assistants.

The result of all this reform may be a growth of a more pluralistic education industry. It will, for example, involve private companies as much as public schools, a trend that is already well established.[8] James K. Glassman of the *Washington Post* has written that "My candidate for the hottest industry in 2005 is education"; he expects a much larger proportion of the $400 billion now spent by government in the area to flow into the private sector. Glassman cites a Lehman Brothers analyst who notes that "The education market today reminds us of what the health care business looked like 10 to 15 years ago."[9]

THE PRIMACY OF MORAL VALUES

A second fundamental lesson of the preceding chapters is the absolute necessity for strong, or stronger, moral and ethical standards to guide human conduct over the next decade. Faced with the immense responsibilities of the knowledge era, we will need values other than greed, a desire for personal security, and the search for profits. The most important step in this process is to remove the question of values from the highly partisan and confrontational context in which it is viewed today. Properly conceived, a strong moral foundation is an entirely universal and nonpartisan attribute of a healthy society.

Because it magnifies the human ability to shape our own future and that of our world, because it poses so many difficult moral choices, the knowledge era demands that we work to find common ground on the values that unite us. Too much time is wasted arguing about *means* rather than first principles, as if a debate about how best to solve the problem of poverty is actually a debate about whether we should try to do so at all.

Jim Wallis, the social activist and writer whom Cornel West has called "the major prophetic evangelical Christian voice" in the United States, has written eloquently and movingly about the urgent requirement for values in politics. Although he is more pessimistic about the character of a globalized and capitalistic age than this book, his emphasis on spiritual values rings true. "Our intuition tells us that the depth of the crisis we face demands more than politics as usual," Wallis contends. "The fundamental character of the social, economic, and cultural renewal we urgently need will require a change of both our hearts and our minds. But that change will demand a new kind of politics—a politics with spiritual values."[10]

Wallis is writing as a liberal and a Christian, but his argument has been echoed by dozens of other prominent intellectuals and politicians from all sides of the political spectrum and from a stunning range of religious and secular humanist perspectives. Jeffrey Klein, publisher and editor of the ultra-liberal magazine *Mother Jones,* has argued that "the realm of the soul—real or imagined—is where most of us make our most important moral decisions"; spirituality, "if approached with integrity and intelligence, is an effective force for the public good."[11] William Raspberry of the *Washington Post* has been an eloquent spokesman for the role of spiritual values in public policy; our "societal failure to address" the longing for spiritual connectedness, Raspberry writes, "tempts us into the nonspiritual excesses that threaten to bring us ruin."[12] Internationally, too, as outlined in Trend Four and in the work of researchers such as David Hitchcock, there is an intense and growing recognition that many of the challenges of modernization, globalization, and social transition are spiritual and moral in nature. Despite this emerging consensus, the effort to forge a clear and consistent set of human values for the knowledge era will be arduous. This is partly because the fragmenting, relativistic trends of our time mitigate against a unified set of values, and partly because moral values are controversial and prone to firestorm debates rather than sober and mature dialogue.

The scope of the challenge, however, does not render it any less necessary. Those who would promote moral values of any sort must begin to see others doing the same as kindred spirits—even if the political tinge of their efforts appears to represent the opposite end of

ISSUE FEATURE:
A MEETING OF WESTERN AND EASTERN VALUES

Political leaders and academics today frequently speak about the differences between "Western" and "Asian" values. The next decade, however, may well bring the "Asian values debate" to a crashing halt, by making clear that a mutual infiltration and movement in the direction of a melding of the two value systems are under way.

The grandfather of cultural studies, Arnold Toynbee, conceived of "the progressive erection, by Western hands, of a scaffolding within which all the once separate societies have built themselves into one."[13] But this scaffolding would not be composed merely of Western values; it would instead represent an amalgamation of world cultures, at the end of which "the distinction—which looms large today—between the Western civilization" and other cultures "will probably seem unimportant."[14] Toynbee spoke in terms of millennia to finish this process, but developments since his time have accelerated it dramatically.

Two years before Toynbee made this case, in 1946, the philosopher F. S. C. Northrop—in a now little-known book called *The Meeting of East and West*—laid out much the same argument. East and West "can meet," Northtrop contended, "not because they are saying the same thing, but because they are expressing different yet complementary things, both of which are required for an adequate and true conception of man's self and his universe." Northrop predicted the rise of a new system of thought "in which the unique achievements of both the East and the West are united."[15]

Recent events show in powerful terms the need for values held dear in the West and the East—the freedom and accountability of Western society alongside the community solidarity and social order of the East, for example. It is thus perhaps little surprise that, after conducting over 100 interviews with key officials and scholars in seven Asian countries, David Hitchcock concluded that "although differences over values [between East and West] do indeed exist, they are being exaggerated." As Hitchcock points out, Toynbee's search "for a synthesis—the best of the East and of the West—is under way"; he cites one Chinese scholar who has proposed a "mutual infiltration" in which "Chinese culture and Western culture should mutually absorb each other's merits and make up for each one's shortcomings."[16] Such a process opens the way to a truly global value system.

the spectrum from one's own views. When moral leaders begin working together, they might learn that their value systems are actually not much different at all: The moral values of many hardworking single mothers in the inner city match very closely those of conservative political leaders trying to reform welfare; the love of the natural environment learned by a Republican hunter from Colorado parallels to some degree the feelings of a pony-tailed environmentalist in San Francisco. And if thoughtful people of various political views could come to agree on a set of measures to address a moral issue (for example, welfare reform) that reflects one or more moral values (in this case, helping the less fortunate as well as promoting self-respect and personal responsibility), then the tinge of controversy will have been removed from the issue to some degree—the sort of process I have in mind in my description of the "new synthesis" on public policy.

The issues of moral values and community are in fact closely linked, because it is often from the community that values emerge and through the community that they are enforced. Stronger values therefore imply stronger communities, an equally essential precondition for meeting the challenges of the next decade—and one that, through the decentralizing and empowering aspects of the knowledge era, we stand a good chance of meeting. In the process, we can reap the benefits of "social capital"— the "intricate web of relationships, norms of behavior, values, obligations, and information channels"[17] that bind human societies together. Scholars the world over have begun to demonstrate the value, in economic and other terms, of robust social capital: Vibrant nongovernmental groups help solve social ills, trust among members of a society makes for smoother economic transactions, values of thrift and hard work underpin strong economic fundamentals such as high savings and productivity rates.

A number of intersecting trends—the increasingly bipartisan character of discussions of spirituality, ethics, and morality in the United States, for example, alongside greater emphasis on so-called Asian values in the West—may, in the long term, point to the need for a new political party (at least in the United States) that more fully reflects this emerging set of values. This new party might marry the Republican emphasis on personal responsibility, self-discipline, and limited government to the Democratic commitment to charity, compassion, and government that works in the public interest. It would be global in outlook, activist and yet multilateralist in its foreign policy; interested in free trade broadly defined but not ignorant of environmental or human rights issues; and in favor of a robust but smaller and more modern and revolutionary military. This is, in fact, almost precisely the direction in which moderate Democrats and Republicans in the United States (and their counterparts in Europe) are trying to haul their reluctant parties.

TOWARD A RE(NEW)ED CAPITALISM

Finally, this analysis has suggested that the triumphant social-ideological system of our time—capitalism—must reinvent itself in profound ways if it is to meet the needs of the coming era in human affairs.

This does not mean, as I have said, abandoning capitalism. Its broad outlines remain the most successful socioeconomic system we have yet known. It just means making capitalism responsive to the human values that we must create if we are to make the knowledge era into a liberating and empowering, rather than divisive and alienating, age of human history. The reform may occur slowly enough that it is barely noticed, so that no social activists trumpet the "decline" of capitalism in favor of something else. But it will be reform, and fundamental reform, all the same.

Some of the specific reforms required include an effort to expand considerations of income disparity and poverty in the definition of an economic system's success; a broader definition of costs, to include environmental damage caused by economic activities as well as other factors; new roles for businesses with goals other than mere profit-making; and a continued and expanded trend of workplace democracy and employee ownership. These and other measures will help to humanize a system that has already proven itself to be a force for progress and prosperity. Each of them is under way already, in trends as diverse as open-book management and industrial ecology and the expanding social responsibilities of business. Together they will revolutionize what we know as capitalism. "Unbridled capitalism is a problem," William Bennett has said. "It may not be a problem for production, but it's a problem for human beings. It's a problem for that whole dimension of things we call the realm of values and human relationships."[18]

One eloquent—and surprising—exponent of this view is the financier George Soros. "I now fear," he wrote in a 1997 essay, "that the untrammeled intensification of laissez-faire capitalism and the spread of market values into all areas of life is endangering our open and democratic society."[19] Soros directs particular fire at the classical economic assumption that free markets produce equilibrium of supply and demand. Because they do not, he argues, "the contention that free markets lead to the optimum allocation of resources loses its justification." And without corrective mechanisms to give content to the idea of an "open society," Soros worries, pure free-market doctrines will lead only to moral and social degeneration. "We have now had 200 years of experience with the Age of Reason, and as reasonable people we ought to recognize that reason has its limitations. The time is ripe for developing a conceptual framework based on our fallibility."[20] Capitalism, Soros points out, depends for its success on a robust and effective set of moral and ethical values and on the foundation of a healthy society and community that it cannot itself provide.

One very practical way in which capitalism is being renewed even now is the growing emphasis, described in Trend Five, on corporate responsibility and social activism. As companies realize the value, both moral and profitwise, of investing in their employees, of respecting the natural environment, of working for social order and stability in the developing world, a handful of progressive ones are already marching in the vanguard of the movement for a capitalism that treats human beings and natural ecology as something more than goods.

Such simple observations hold true for the environment, for social equality, for mutual respect and adherence to the law, to expressions of cultural creativity and genius—in short, dozens of areas in which moral standards are critical for regulating human conduct. To be clear: Capitalism is not inherently *opposed* to such values; indeed, its successful operation in a manner that does not bring down a civilization depends on them. The fact is merely that some form of capitalist economics, while it may now be generally accepted as a *necessary* element of a socioeconomic system that will bring the greatest good to the greatest number, is far from a *sufficient* condition for such a society. This is why the connection between moral values and a reformed capitalism is so strong, and it is the basic justification for rethinking capitalism in the first place. Kazuo Inamori, chairman of the Japanese conglomerate Kyocera and a leader in Japan's corporate responsibility movement, agrees. "Capitalism is based on the principle of free competition," Inamori writes, "but in order for this principle to work, it is incumbent on economic entities—particularly the strongest and richest—to exercise self-control."[21]

The Authors of Our Own Destiny

I am hopeful about this new era in human affairs primarily because humanity is in control—not completely, to be sure, but to a sufficient degree to allow us to fashion the knowledge era into the brightest flowering of human potential yet known. The problem is that there is no guarantee we will have the values or cleverness to accomplish this immense task. As René Dubos points out, "Creating a desirable future demands more than foresight; it requires vision."[1]

José Ortega y Gasset laid out our challenge in striking terms half a century ago. The "only way to combat a lack of clarity" in human affairs, as in the kind created by transitional eras, "is by doing as man has always done in times of crisis, that is, by making life authentic again, by reconstructing its foundations—by beginning all over again to clarify fundamental themes, by adjusting and updating our basic repertoire of ideas so it accords with the present level of our historical experience, in short, by an intellectual rebirth. With man, who is always an inheritor and who has always a past, every historical birth is a renaissance."[2] A hopeful comparison, this idea of a *new renaissance* in human affairs, a flowering of new ideas and values that will someday come to be seen as events as decisive and influential as those of the first Renaissance. Whether it occurs, as Dubos suggests, is up to us; and whether we are capable of creating such a world will depend on our values.

One unique aspect of the knowledge era is its intriguing opportunity to reconcile some of the best elements of preindustrial and industrial civilization. Some historians and philosophers have the habit of pointing to a utopian, preindustrial (indeed, mostly preagricultural) past that combined small village community life with moral values, strong families, and respect for the environment. This is, like all utopian visions, inaccurate in at least some important ways; small village life can be as stifling as it is supportive, and recent scholarship has cast doubt on the ecological discretion of our distant forebears. But the mass, impersonal, fast-moving, environmentally destructive industrial era has its own problems. In its paradoxical combination of global awareness and local identity, of simultaneously accelerating economic growth and environmental protection, of greater tolerance and stricter values, the knowledge era could perhaps split the difference between ancient and postmodern human society quite nicely, establishing the most supportive context for human existence and psychology yet known.

The great Julian Huxley, one of the most eminent scientists of the century, described the human context in similar terms. "In the human phase of evolution," he wrote in 1953, "the struggle for existence has largely been superseded, as an operative force, by the struggle for fulfillment," at least in the advanced societies. "And fulfillment seems to describe better than any other single word the positive side of human development and human evolution—the realization of inherent capacities by the individual and of new possibilities by the race; the satisfaction of needs, spiritual as well as material; the emergence of new qualities of experience to be enjoyed; the building of personalities."[3]

And so it is with us, and our time, and our challenges. The astonishing transformation of human life under way today offers us the potential to fulfill ourselves in ways our ancestors could not have imagined—even as it bears the risk of rushing farther away from fulfillment than we have ever been. More than anything, I think, we need a new calmness of mind, a renewed patience, an urgent focus on integrity and compassion in all human affairs, values that will enrich our experience of life even as they furnish the perspective we need to meet our pressing challenges. I conclude, then, as I began, in the spirit of the *Tao*.

Pure and still,
one can put things right everywhere under heaven.

NOTES

INTRODUCTION NOTES

1. Peter F. Drucker, *Post-Capitalist Society* (New York: HarperBusiness, 1993), p. 1.
2. Cited in *The National Interest*, no. 41 (Fall 1995): 18.
3. Alvin Toffler, *The Third Wave* (New York: Bantam Books, 1981), p. 351.
4. Daniel Bell, *The Coming of Post-Industrial Society* (New York: Basic Books), p. 20.
5. International Labour Organization, *World Employment 1995* (Geneva: ILO, 1995), p. 27.
6. Vaclav Havel, "The Need for Transcendence in the Postmodern World," *The Futurist* (July–August 1995): 46.
7. The quotes come from Margaret Wheatley, *Leadership and the New Science* (San Francisco: Berrett-Koehler Publishers, 1994), pp. 6, 9, 38, 144.
8. John Peterson, head of the Arlington Institute and a prominent futurist, has spoken of the value of this methodology, which he calls "wild cards." Such "low-probability, high-impact events," he says, can have fundamental impacts on the human condition or individual businesses—and they will come faster and wilder in the next decade. See "Report from the Futurist," *Fast Company* (February–March 1998): 30.
9. Charles Handy, *The Age of Paradox* (Boston: Harvard Business School Press, 1994), pp. x, 12.
10. Zygmunt Bauman, "A Sociological Theory of Postmodernity," in Peter Beilharz et al., eds., *Between Totalitarianism and Postmodernity* (Cambridge, MA: The MIT Press, 1992), p. 149.
11. William Green, "Zen and the Art of Managerial Maintenance," *Fast Company* (June–July 1996): 50-54. See also Low's book, *Zen and Creative Management* (Rutland, VT: Charles E. Tuttle Company, 1992).
12. Handy, *The Age of Paradox*, pp. 12-13.
13. See Ian Somerville and John Edwin Mroz, "New Competencies for a New World," in Frances Hesselbein, Marshall Goldsmith, and Richard Beckhard, eds., *The Organization of the Future* (New York: The Drucker Foundation and Jossey-Bass Publishers, 1997), pp. 65-78.
14. Peter Coveney and Roger Highfield, *Frontiers of Complexity* (New York: Fawcett Columbine, 1995), pp. 7-8, 345.
15. Manuel Castells, *The Rise of the Network Society* (Oxford: Blackwell, 1996), p. 469.
16. Stephanie Pace Marshall, "Creating Sustainable Learning Communities for the 21st Century," in Hesselbein et al., *The Organization of the Future*, p. 181.

17. Walter Wriston, *The Twilight of Sovereignty* (New York: Scribner's, 1992), p. 25.

18. Postmodern writers have employed a similar theme of substituting the process of human relationships for the hard matter of social institutions. "If there is a common key to this postmodern habit of thought," writes the philosopher Jerome Klinkowitz, "it is the lesson learned from language: that the authentic phenomenon in any event is not *fact*, but *relationship*." An increased emphasis on human relationships, and the trust and values and compassion which govern them, thus becomes an important unifying message of many of the trends which follow. See Jerome Klinkowitz, *Rosenberg, Barthes, Hassan: The Postmodern Habit of Thought* (Athens: University of Georgia Press, 1988), p. 8.

19. Paul H. Ray, "The Emerging Culture," *American Demographics* 19, no. 2 (February 1997): 29-34, 56.

20. Ken Dychtwald, *Age Wave: How the Most Important Trend of Our Time Will Change Your Future* (New York: Bantam Books, 1990), p. 286.

21. B. Joseph Pine II and James H. Gilmore, "Welcome to the Experience Economy," *Harvard Business Review* (July–August 1998): 97-105.

22. Handy, *The Age of Paradox*, pp. 50-51. Watts Wacker and Jim Taylor use the sigmoid curve in a related sense to explain the history of product sales; see Wacker and Taylor, *The 500 Year Delta: What Happens After What Comes Next* (New York: HarperBusiness, 1997), pp. 55-60.

23. Stan Davis and Bill Davidson, *2020 Vision* (New York: Fireside Books, 1991), p. 22.

24. Handy, *The Age of Paradox*, p. 54.

25. Ibid., p. 55; the quote is from p. 53.

26. Wacker and Taylor stress the importance of values such as authenticity and a "new civility" in *The 500 Year Delta*, pp. 65-73.

27. Tom Peters, *Thriving on Chaos* (New York: HarperPerennial, 1991), p. 506.

28. Wacker and Taylor, *The 500 Year Delta*, pp. 112-114.

29. Peters, *Thriving on Chaos*, p. 506.

30. Bill Gross, "The New Math of Ownership," *Harvard Business Review* (November–December 1998): 70.

31. Marshall McLuhan and Quentin Fiore, *The Medium Is the Message: An Inventory of Effects* (New York: Bantam Books, 1967), p. 25.

TREND ONE

1. Information in the Issue Feature comes from Donald G. McNeil, Jr., "AIDS Stalking Africa's Struggling Economies," *New York Times*, November 15, 1998, p. 1; "AIDS in the Third World," *Economist*, January 2, 1999, pp. 42-43; and Murray Feshbach, "Dead Souls," *The Atlantic Monthly*, January 1999, p. 27. Both the World Bank (www.worldbank.org) and the World Health Organization (www.who.org) websites have excellent resources, including complete global and country-by-country reports, on the spread of AIDS.

2. Jesse Ausubel, "The Liberation of the Environment," *Daedalus* 125, no. 3 (Summer 1996): 15.

CHAPTER 1

1. George D. Moffett, "Global Population Growth: 21st Century Challenges," Foreign Policy Association *Headline Series,* no. 302 (New York: Foreign Policy Association, 1994), 6.

2. Joel E. Cohen, *How Many People Can the Earth Support?* (New York: W. W. Norton, 1995), p. 367.

3. U.S. Department of State, *Population Trends Over the Coming Decade— Global Impacts* (Washington, D.C.: U.S. Department of State, August 1994), p. 1; and World Resources Institute, U.N. Environment Program, U.N. Development Program, and the World Bank, *World Resources 1996–1997: A Guide to the Global Environment* (New York: Oxford University Press, 1996), pp. 174-75 (hereafter cited as *World Resources 1996–1997*).

4. Carl Haub, "World Growth Rate Slows, But Numbers Build Up," *Population Today* 22, no. 11 (November 1994): 1.

5. United Nations, *World Economic and Social Survey* (New York: United Nations, 1995), pp. 145-46.

6. Gregg Easterbrook, *A Moment on the Earth: The Coming Age of Environmental Optimism* (New York: Viking, 1995), p. 486.

7. U.S. Department of State, *Population Trends,* p. 1.

8. U.N., *World Economic and Social Survey 1995,* p. 147.

9. *World Resources 1996–1997,* pp. 174-75.

10. Paul Kennedy, *Preparing for the 21st Century* (New York: Random House, 1993), p. 25.

11. U.S. Department of State, *Population Trends,* p. 1.

12. Easterbrook, *A Moment on the Earth,* p. 477.

13. *World Resources 1996–1997,* p. 227.

14. Cohen, *How Many People Can the Earth Support?* pp. 100-101.

15. U.S. Department of State, *Population Trends,* p. 2.

16. Eugene Linden, "The Exploding Cities of the Developing World," *Foreign Affairs* 75, no. 1 (January–February 1996): p. 53. See also Chauncey Starr, "Sustaining the Human Environment," *Daedalus* 125, no. 3 (Summer 1996): p. 248.

17. *World Resources 1996-1997,* pp. 3-8, and Linden, "Exploding Cities," p. 53.

18. *World Resources 1996-1997,* p.1.

19. Linden, "Exploding Cities," pp. 54-55.

20. *World Resources 1996-1997,* p. 9.

21. Ibid., pp. 1, 10, 174. On the natural advantages of cities as knowledge-era economic units, see Christopher Farrell et al., "Brighter Lights for Big Cities," *Business Week,* May 4, 1998, pp. 88-95.

22. *World Resources 1996-1997,* pp. 1, 11-12, 23, 62.

23. U.S. Department of State, *Population Trends,* pp. 4-5.

24. Numbers are drawn from Anthony H. Cordesman, "World Population Trends, Regional Issues, and the Middle East as a Case Study," CSIS Middle East Dynamic Net Assessment Project (Washington, D.C.: Center for Strategic and International Studies, February 1996).

25. U.N., *World Economic and Social Survey 1995,* p. 271; see generally pp. 263-82.

26. Census Brief, "Warmer, Older, More Diverse: State-by-State Population Changes to 2025," U.S. Department of the Census (December 1996).

27. Richard Disney, *Can We Afford to Grow Older? A Perspective on the Economics of Aging* (Cambridge, MA: The MIT Press, 1996), pp. 7-10.

28. Milton Ezrati, "Japan's Aging Economics," *Foreign Affairs* 76, no. 3 (May–June 1997): 96-104.

29. These implications are drawn from Hamish McRae, *The World in 2020: Power, Culture and Prosperity* (Boston: Harvard Business School Press, 1994), p. 107; and Ken Dychtwald, *Age Wave: How the Most Important Trend of Our Time Will Change Your Future* (New York: Bantam Books, 1990), pp. 299, 115-45, 286, and 311-40.

30. The World Bank, *Averting the Old Age Crisis* (Oxford: Oxford University Press, 1994), pp. 1, 349-53.

31. These statistics are drawn from Victoria Benning and Todd Shields, "Wave of Students Could Swamp Universities," *Washington Post,* August 22, 1996, pp. A1, A19; "U.S. School Enrollment to Hit Record This Year," *Washington Post,* August 22, 1997, p. A3; and Dale Russakoff, "The Millennium Generation is Making Its Mark," *Washington Post,* June 29, 1998, pp. A1, A9.

32. *World Resources 1996-1997,* p. 316.

33. U.S. Department of Energy, Energy Information Administration, *Annual Energy Outlook 1996* (Washington: DoE/EIA, January 1996), pp. 1-3.

34. See The World Bank, *Monitoring Environmental Progress* (Washington, D.C.: The World Bank, 1995), pp. 30-32, 40-42, 50, and 11.

35. Easterbrook, *A Moment on the Earth,* pp. 15, 258-59. Easterbrook's volume has become controversial, with environmentalists pointing out what they consider to be numerous errors of fact and hotly disputing his basic notion of environmental optimism. While I cannot judge the scientific accuracy of many of his claims, I continue to cite the book because my own research convinces me that a carefully hedged version of his basic thesis—that the technologies of the knowledge-era point in a promising environmental direction—remains valid. The reader should compare more pessimistic works, including Mark Hertzgaard's fascinating *Earth Odyssey* (New York: Broadway Books, 1998).

36. Paul Hawken, *The Ecology of Commerce: A Declaration of Sustainability* (New York: HarperBusiness, 1993), pp. 13, 75-76. See also Paul Roberts, "Ecotrust Stirs Up a New Shade of Green," *Fast Company* (April–May 1997): 56.

37. Frosch and 3M example cited in Kevin Kelly, *Out of Control: The New Biology of Machines, Social Systems and the Economic World* (Reading, MA: Addison-Wesley, 1994), pp. 178-79.

38. Catherine Arnst et al., "When Green Begets Green," *Business Week,* November 10, 1997, pp. 98-106.

39. Amory B. Lovins, "Save Energy, Make Piles of Money," *Washington Post,* January 5, 1998, p. A19.

40. Emily Thornton, "Only God and Toyota Can Make a Tree," *Business Week,* March 30, 1998, p. 58.

41. Ann Goodman, "Rooms with a View," *Fast Company* (June–July 1997): 52-54.
42. "Economists Urge Reduced U.S. Emissions," *Washington Post*, February 14, 1997, p. A3.
43. "International Watchdog Agency Sees Rise in Energy Use, Global Warming," *Washington Post*, April 25, 1995, p. A3.
44. Easterbrook, *A Moment on the Earth*, p. 313.
45. Note my use of the qualifier "almost." One lesson of chaos theory is the potential for discontinuous change—sudden, rapid movements in new directions emerging out of a rapid confluence of factors. "The complexity of the global climate," write Peter Coveney and Roger Highfield, "is such that a gradual increase in levels of greenhouse gases does not always result in a gradual shift in climate: it can trigger a sudden climate flip within a single lifetime." Coveney and Highfield, *Frontiers of Complexity* (New York: Fawcett Columbine, 1995), p. 330. Such a rapid flip is not out of the question even during the next decade, although it remains highly unlikely.
46. *World Resources 1996–1997*, p. 317.
47. Ibid., p. 247.

CHAPTER 2

1. These statistics are drawn from Dennis Avery, "The World's Rising Food Productivity," in Julian L. Simon, ed., *The State of Humanity* (Oxford: Blackwell Publishers, 1995), pp. 376-91.
2. Steven Mufson, "China's Global Grain of Difference," *Washington Post*, February 9, 1996, pp. A1, A31.
3. For the paradigmatic pessimist's case on China and food, see Lester R. Brown, *Who Will Feed China?* (New York: W. W. Norton, 1995).
4. Robert L. Paarlberg, "Rice Bowls and Dust Bowls," *Foreign Affairs* 75, no. 3 (May–June 1996): 129.
5. "Chinese Grist to the Malthusian Mills," *The Economist*, May 4, 1996, p. 33.
6. This case is made in Roy L. Prosterman, Tim Hanstad, and Li Ping, "Can China Feed Itself?" *Scientific American* 275, no. 5 (November 1996): 90-96.
7. *India Abroad*, New York ed., 27, no. 4 (October 25, 1996), p. 36. Khush adds: "Just to give you an example, the average yield per hectare (2.47 acres) is three tons. In China it is six tons and in Egypt it is eight tons. So we have a lot of scope for closing that gap in terms of production."
8. Paul E. Waggoner, "How Much Land Can Be Spared for Nature?" *Daedalus* 125, no. 3 (Summer 1996): p. 87; and Jesse Ausubel, "The Liberation of the Environment," *Daedalus* 125, no. 3 (Summer 1996): 15.
9. Robert J. Samuelson, "A Coming Food Crisis? Unlikely," *Washington Post*, August 22, 1996, p. A31.
10. "The New Economics of Food," *Business Week*, May 20, 1996, p. 78.
11. Dennis T. Avery and Alex Avery, "Farming to Sustain the Environment" (Indianapolis: The Hudson Institute, Hudson Briefing Paper No. 190, May 1996), pp. 2-3, 6-7.
12. See Donella H. Meadows, Dennis L. Meadows, and Jørgen Randers, *Beyond the Limits* (Post Mills, VT: Chelsea Green Publishing Company, 1992), pp. 52-53.

13. "Will the World Starve?" *The Economist*, November 16, 1996, pp. 21, 23.

14. This information comes from Ausubel, "The Liberation of the Environment," p. 6, and Waggoner, "How Much Land Can Be Spared," p. 77.

15. World Resource Institute, U.N. Environment Program, U.N. Development Program, and the World Bank, *World Resources 1996-1997: A Guide to the Global Environment* (New York: Oxford University Press, 1996), pp. 228-29, 235 (hereafter cited as *World Resources 1996–1997).*

16. Ibid., p. 301.

17. Robert Engelman and Pamela LeRoy, *Sustaining Water: Population and the Future of Renewable Water Supplies* (Washington, D.C.: Population Action International, 1993), p. 11.

18. These figures are drawn from Peter H. Gleick, "Water and Conflict: Fresh Water Resources and International Security," *International Security* 18, no. 1 (Summer 1993): 100-101.

19. Cited in *World Press Review* (November 1995): pp. 8-9.

20. Cited in Ibid., p. 9.

21. Kenneth L. Whiting, "Water, Water Everywhere, But Not for Long," *Washington Post*, January 8, 1997, p. A20.

22. These figures are cited in "Turning Off the Tap," *Economist*, November 14, 1998, p. 29.

23. Gregg Easterbrook, *A Moment on the Earth: The Coming Age of Environmental Optimism* (New York: Viking, 1995), p. 349.

24. Jesse Ausubel, "The Liberation of the Environment," *Daedalus* 125, no. 3 (Summer 1996): 5.

25. Hamish McRae comes to this conclusion in *The World in 2020: Power, Culture and Prosperity* (Boston: Harvard Business School Press, 1994), p. 127.

26. Office of Integrated Analysis and Forecasting, Energy Information Administration, U.S. Department of Energy (hereafter EIA), *International Energy Outlook 1995* (Washington, D.C.: U.S. Government Printing Office, May 1995), p. 1.

27. *World Resources 1996–1997*, p. 278.

28. EIA, *International Energy Outlook 1995*, pp. 2-3, 23.

29. Rick Wartzman and Anne Riefenberg, "Big Energy Imports Are Less of a Threat Than They Appear," *Wall Street Journal*, August 17, 1995, p. 1. See also Paul Blustein, "An Unstable Middle East Won't Put the U.S. Over a Barrel," *Washington Post*, September 18, 1996, p. F1.

30. Of all the additions to worldwide crude oil reserves discovered from 1960 to 1990, almost 80 percent were in OPEC member countries. EIA, *International Energy Outlook 1995*, p. 26. Already 14 million barrels of crude pass through the critical Strait of Hormuz every day; see the information at www.eia.doc.gov, the Energy Department's Energy Information Administration Web site.

31. Joseph J. Romm and Charles B. Curtis, "Mideast Oil Forever?" *The Atlantic Monthly* 277, no. 4 (April 1996): 57.

32. Kent E. Calder, "Asia's Empty Tank," *Foreign Affairs* 75, no. 2 (March–April 1996): 58.

33. Cited in Romm and Curtis, "Mideast Oil Forever?" p. 60.

34. Calder, "Asia's Empty Tank," pp. 59-60.

35. Ibid., p. 61.
36. Cited in Romm and Curtis, "Mideast Oil Forever?" p. 64.
37. *World Resources 1996–1997*, pp. 276-77. See also the careful review in James Mackenzie, "Oil as a Finite Resource," World Resources Institute, 1996; available on the Internet at http://www.wri.org.
38. EIA, *Annual Energy Outlook 1996* (Washington, D.C.: U.S. Department of Energy, January 1996), p. 50.
39. EIA, *International Energy Outlook 1995*, p. 35. Information in the issue feature on nuclear energy is drawn from ibid., pp. 49-51.
40. Ibid., pp. 1, 11.
41. Ibid., pp. 5, 10.
42. Wartzman and Reifenberg, "Big Energy Imports," p. A6.
43. Because of the small driving ranges and severe smog problems of cities, for example, "the future of urban driving belongs to electric vehicles," concludes one recent *American Demographics* analysis (December 1996, p. 15). See also Frank Field and Joel Clark, "A Practical Road to Lightweight Cars," *Technology Review* 100, no. 1 (January 1997): 28-36; Daniel Sperling, "The Case for Electric Vehicles," *Scientific American* 275, no. 5 (November 1996): 57; and Paul Ray, "The Emerging Culture," *American Demographics* 19, no. 2 (February 1997): 32.
44. Sperling, "The Case for Electric Vehicles," p. 59.
45. James F. Moore, *The Death of Competition: Leadership and Strategy in the Age of Business Ecosystems* (New York: HarperBusiness, 1996), pp. 101-2.
46. William J. Cook, "Nothing But Blue Skies Over Jakarta?" *U.S. News & World Report*, December 30, 1996–January 6, 1997, pp. 68-69.
47. Many of these ideas and numbers, and the quotation are drawn from Amory B. Lovins and L. Hunter Lovins, "Reinventing the Wheels," *Atlantic Monthly* (January 1995): 75-93.
48. Sperling, "The Case for Electric Vehicles," p. 59.
49. Gary McWilliams and Wendy Zellner, "Making Sense of a Topsy-Turvy Energy Market," *Business Week*, October 14, 1996, p. 39.

CHAPTER 3

1. Lawrence E. Harrison, *Who Prospers? How Cultural Values Shape Economic and Political Success* (New York: Basic Books, 1992), p. 1.
2. Thomas Sowell, *Race and Culture: A World View* (New York: Basic Books, 1994), p. 1.
3. Harrison, *Who Prospers?* p. 15.
4. Sowell, *Race and Culture*, p. 25.
5. Peter L. Berger, *Invitation to Sociology: A Humanistic Perspective* (Garden City, N.Y.: Anchor Books, 1963), pp. 106, 121.
6. Samuel Huntington, "The Clash of Civilizations?" *Foreign Affairs* 72, no. 3 (Summer 1993): 22.
7. Robert S. Chase, Emily B. Hill, and Paul Kennedy, "Pivotal States and U.S. Strategy," *Foreign Affairs* 75, no. 1 (January–February 1996): 33-51.

CHAPTER 4

1. Gregory Benford, "Biology 2001: Understanding Culture, Technology, and Politics in 'The Biological Century,'" *Reason* 27, no. 6 (November 1995): 29.
2. Rick Weiss, "Scottish Scientists Clone Adult Sheep," *Washington Post,* February 24, 1997, p. A1.
3. The quote and the 750 meg fact come from Charles Platt, "Evolution Revolution," *Wired* 5.01 (January 1997): 160.
4. William H. Allen, "Farming for Spare Body Parts," *Bioscience* (February 1995): 73-75.
5. Brad Wieners and David Pescovitz, *Reality Check* (San Francisco: Hard Wired Press, 1996), p. 19.
6. John Henkel, "A New Tomato," *FDA Consumer,* April 8, 1995, p. 8.
7. John Henkel, "Genetic Engineering: Fast Forwarding to Future Foods," *FDA Consumer,* April 8, 1995, p. 6.
8. Wieners and Pescovitz, *Reality Check,* p. 49.
9. Platt, "Evolution Revolution," pp. 201-2.
10. Benford, "Biology 2001," p. 27.
11. Gregg Easterbrook, *A Moment on the Earth* (New York: Viking, 1995), p. 357.
12. Michael G. Zey, *Seizing the Future* (New York: Simon and Schuster, 1994), p. 68.
13. William Hoagland, "Solar Energy," *Scientific American* (September 1995): 170, 172.
14. Ibid., pp. 172-73.
15. Ibid., p. 171.
16. Robert Righter, *Wind Energy in America: A History* (Norman: University of Oklahoma Press, 1996), chapter 12.
17. Hoagland, "Solar Energy," pp. 171-72.
18. Easterbrook, *A Moment on the Earth,* p. 361.
19. Richard G. Lugar and R. James Woolsey, "The New Petroleum," *Foreign Affairs* 78, no. 1 (January-February 1999): 88-102
20. The quotes and facts here come from "At Last, the Fuel Cell," *Economist,* October 25, 1997, pp. 89-92; and Jacques Leslie, "Dawn of the Hydrogen Age," *Wired* 5.10 (October 1997): 138-48 and 191.
21. Stan Davis and Bill Davidson, *2020 Vision* (New York: Simon and Schuster, 1991), p. 34.
22. Robert H. Reid, "Real Revolution," *Wired* 5.10 (October 1997): 125.
23. Eric Schine et al., "The Satellite Biz Blasts Off," *Business Week,* January 27, 1997, pp. 62-63; and Mike Mills, "Orbit Wars," *Washington Post Magazine,* August 3, 1997, pp. 8-13, 24-26.
24. Neil Gross and Otis Port, "The Next Wave," *Business Week,* August 31, 1998, pp. 80-83.
25. Ralph C. Merkle, "It's a Small, Small, Small, Small World," *Technology Review,* February–March 1997, available at www.techreview.com/articles/fm97/merkle.html.
26. Figures are from *Economist,* September 12, 1998, p. 75.
27. Geoffrey Smith, "Silicon Eyes," *Business Week,* October 12, 1998, pp.94-100.
28. Geoffrey Cowley, Susan Miller, Rebecca Crandall, and Mary Hager, "RoboDocs and Mousecalls," *Newsweek,* February 27, 1995, pp. 66-67.

CHAPTER 5

1. Francis Fukuyama, *The End of History and the Last Man* (New York: The Free Press, 1992), p. xiv. See also Ernest Gellner, *Nations and Nationalism* (Ithaca, NY: Cornell University Press, 1983), pp. 35, 116, 118-19, 121-22.
2. Arnold J. Toynbee, *A Study of History* (New York: Oxford University Press, 1934).
3. Arnold J. Toynbee, *Civilization on Trial* (New York: Oxford University Press, 1948), pp. 71, 91.
4. Ibid., pp. 214-15.
5. Vaclav Havel, "The Need for Transcendence in the Postmodern World," *The Futurist* (July–August 1995): 47.
6. Fouad Ajami, "The Summoning," *Foreign Affairs* 72, no. 4 (September–October 1993): 6.
7. Laura Sessions Stepp, "Global Truths: Sharing Like Values, Beliefs and Goals," *Washington Post,* June 27, 1996, p. C5.
8. See Abraham H. Maslow, "A Theory of Human Motivation," *Psychological Review* 50 (1943): 370-96.
9. Matt Ridley, *The Origins of Virtue* (New York: Penguin Viking, 1997), pp. 5-6, 249.

CHAPTER 6

1. Mitchell Waldrop, *Complexity: The Emerging Science at the Edge of Order and Chaos* (New York: Simon and Schuster, 1992), p. 11.
2. Kevin Kelly, *Out of Control: The New Biology of Machines, Social Systems and the Economic World* (Reading, MA: Addison-Wesley, 1994), pp. 22-23.
3. Waldrop, *Complexity,* p. 11.
4. Max Boisot, *Information Space* (London: Routledge, 1995), p. 19.
5. Cited in *Fast Company* (February–March 1998): 64.
6. Waldrop, *Complexity,* p. 330.
7. Murray Gell-Mann, "The Simple and the Complex," in David S. Alberts and Thomas J. Czerwinski, eds., *Complexity, Global Politics, and National Security* (Washington, DC: National Defense University Press, 1997), pp. 27-28.
8. Waldrop, *Complexity,* p. 102.

CHAPTER 7

1. Ronald Inglehart, *Culture Shift in Advanced Industrial Society* (Princeton, NJ: Princeton University Press, 1990), p. 3.
2. Ibid., p. 13.
3. See, for example, "Liberalism Lives," *Economist,* January 2, 1999, pp. 59-61.
4. Thomas Friedman, "Turkey Wings It," *New York Times,* July 17, 1996, p. A23.
5. Walter Wriston, *The Twilight of Sovereignty* (New York: Scribner's, 1992), p. 45.
6. Paul W. Schroeder, "The New World Order: A Historical Perspective," *Washington Quarterly* 17, no. 2 (Spring 1994): 33, 35.
7. Chris Patten, "Beyond the Myths," *The Economist,* January 4, 1997, p. 20.

8. Henry S. Rowen, "The Short March: China's Road to Democracy," *The National Interest* (Fall 1996): 29, 36.

9. Adam Przeworski and Fernando Limongi, "Modernization: Theories and Facts," *World Politics* 49, no. 2 (January 1997): 156-57, 159.

10. Francis Fukuyama, *The End of History and the Last Man* (New York: The Free Press, 1992), pp. 90, 125.

11. Ibid., pp. 146-47.

12. Ibid., pp. 202, 206-7.

13. The information in this issue feature is drawn from "China's Grassroots Democracy," *Economist,* November 2, 1996, pp. 33-35. See also Daniel Kelliher, "The Chinese Debate Over Village Self-Government," *The China Journal,* no. 37 (January 1997): 63-86.

14. Rowen, "The Short March"; see also Rowen, "With Growth, China Could Get Democracy Soon," *International Herald-Tribune,* October 11, 1996.

15. For evidence that these ideas have indeed begun to infect Beijing, see Steven Mufson, "China Tolerates Talk of Reform," *Washington Post,* August 10, 1997, p. A1.

16. Przeworski and Limongi, "Modernization," p. 165. The text box quote is from p. 166.

17. "The Bloodhounds of History," *The Economist,* April 12, 1997, p. 21.

18. For the Microsoft story, see Fred Moody, "Wonder Women in the Rude Boys' Paradise," *Fast Company* (June–July 1996): 85ff.

19. Fukuyama, *The End of History,* p. xx.

20. Alexander Wendt, "Anarchy Is What States Make of It: The Social Construction of Power Politics," *International Organization* 46, no. 2 (Spring, 1992): 415.

21. Stuart Kauffman, *At Home in the Universe: The Search for the Laws of Self-Organization and Complexity* (New York: Oxford University Press, 1995), pp. 275, 299.

22. Geoff Mulgan, *Connexity: How to Live in a Connected World* (Boston: Harvard Business School Press, 1998), pp. 35, 1.

TREND THREE

1. Walter Wriston, *The Twilight of Sovereignty* (New York: Scribner's, 1992), p. 5.

2. Max Boisot, *Information Space* (London: Routledge, 1995), p. 20.

3. Marshall McLuhan, *Understanding Media: Extensions of Man* (New York: McGraw-Hill, 1964), p. 207.

CHAPTER 8

1. James R. Beniger, for example, suggests that the information sector grew from 0.2 percent of the labor force in 1800 to 4.2 percent in 1850, 12.8 percent in 1900, 30.8 percent in 1950, and 46.6 percent in 1980. "The Information Society," Beniger contends, has roots in the industrial era, in developments "that began more than a century ago." Beniger, "The Control Revolution," in Albert H. Teich, ed., *Technology and the Future,* 6th ed. (New York: St. Martin's Press, 1993), pp. 56, 58, 62.

2. Michael Mandel, "Innovation: You Ain't Seen Nothing Yet," *Business Week,* August 31, 1998, p. 60.
3. Blinder and Krugman are quoted in Clay Chandler and Steven Pearlstein, "Debating Myth or Miracle Behind a 'New Economy,'" *Washington Post,* October 11, 1997, p. D2.
4. Max Boisot, *Information Space* (London: Routledge, 1995), pp. 20-21.
5. Some of these categories are drawn from Charles Handy, *The Age of Unreason* (Boston: Harvard Business School Press, 1990), pp. 15-16.
6. Peter F. Drucker, *Post-Capitalist Society* (New York: HarperBusiness, 1993), p. 40.
7. Peter F. Drucker, "The Changed World Economy," *Foreign Affairs* 64, no. 4 (Spring 1986): 770, 773-74.
8. William Knoke, *Bold New World: The Essential Road Map to the Twenty-First Century* (New York: Kodansha International, 1996), p. 119.
9. Hamish McRae, *The World in 2020* (Boston: Harvard Business School Press, 1994), p. 16.

CHAPTER 9

1. These citations are drawn from Richard D'Aveni, *Hypercompetition: Managing the Dynamics of Strategic Maneuvering* (New York: The Free Press, 1994), pages xiii-xiv, 4-11, 18, 99-100, 225-28, 341-42, 349; his analysis of antitrust is on pp. 357-90.
2. Cited in Jeremy Rifkin, *The End of Work* (New York: G. P. Putnam's Sons, 1995), pp. 190-91.
3. Joan O'C. Hamilton, Stephen Baker, and Bill Vlasic, "The New Workplace," *Business Week,* April 29, 1996, pp. 112-117; and Amy Dunkin, "Saying Adios to the Office," *Business Week,* October 12, 1998, p. 152.
4. Brad Wieners and David Pescovitz, *Reality Check* (San Francisco: Hard Wired Press, 1996), p. 37.
5. Peter Kilborn, "In New Work World, Employers Call All the Shots," *New York Times,* July 5, 1995, pp. 1, 7.
6. Don Tapscott, *The Digital Economy* (New York: McGraw-Hill, 1996), p. 198.
7. Charles Handy, "Trust and the Virtual Organization," *Harvard Business Review* 73, no. 3 (May–June 1995).
8. Ibid., p. 42.
9. William Knoke, *Bold New World: The Essential Road Map to the Twenty-First Century* (New York: Kodansha International, 1996), pp. 156-82.
10. Wieners and Pescovitz, *Reality Check,* p. 23.
11. Tom Peters, *Thriving on Chaos* (New York: HarperPerennial, 1987).
12. The information and quotes in this issue feature are drawn from Bill Gross, "The New Math of Ownership," *Harvard Business Review,* November–December 1998, pp. 68-74.
13. See Stan Crock et al., "They Snoop to Conquer," *Business Week,* October 28, 1996, pp. 172-76.
14. Anthony Giddens, *The Consequences of Modernity* (Stanford, CA: Stanford University Press, 1990), pp. 18, 21.
15. Joel Kotkin, "A Chinese Century?" *The American Enterprise* (July–August 1998): 26-32.
16. Ibid., pp. 26, 83.

17. Gerald Segal, "Asians in Cyberia," *Washington Quarterly* 18 (Summer 1995): 11. See also the literature review by Michael J. Mazarr, "Culture and International Relations," *Washington Quarterly* 19 (Spring 1996): 177-97.

18. Anne Swardson, "Best Minds Bidding France Adieu," *Washington Post,* March 21, 1998, p. A1.

19. Peter F. Drucker, "The Changed World Economy," *Foreign Affairs* 64, no. 4 (Spring 1986): p. 775.

20. Ibid., p. 778.

21. Peter F. Drucker, *Post-Capitalist Society* (New York: Harper Business, 1993), p. 69.

22. Rolf Anderson, *Atlas of the American Economy* (Washington, D.C.: Congressional Quarterly Press, 1994), p. 14; and World Bank, *Global Economic Prospects and the Developing Countries* (Washington, D.C.: The World Bank, 1995), p. 44.

23. Holman W. Jenkins, Jr., "The Problem with 'Us' vs. 'Them,'" *Wall Street Journal,* February 27, 1996.

24. Figures from *Business Week,* March 11, 1996, pp. 52-53, 56.

25. Manuel Castells, *The Rise of the Network Society* (Cambridge, MA: Blackwell Publishers, 1996), pp. 259-60 (note 78) and 265.

CHAPTER 10

1. Manuel Castells, *The Rise of the Network Society* (Cambridge, MA: Blackwell Publishers, 1996) pp. 164-66. See also Kevin Kelly, *Out of Control: The New Biology of Machines, Social Systems and the Economic World* (Reading, MA: Addison-Wesley, 1994), pp. 186-87.

2. James F. Moore, *The Death of Competition: Leadership and Strategy in the Age of Business Ecosystems* (New York: HarperBusiness, 1996), pp. 3, 11-12, 13.

3. Erik R. Peterson, "Surrendering to Markets," *Washington Quarterly* 18, no. 4 (Autumn 1995): 104-5.

4. See Kevin Phillips, *Boiling Point: Democrats, Republicans, and the Decline of Middle-Class Prosperity* (New York: Random House, 1993).

5. Thomas A. Bass, "The Phynancier," *Wired* 5.01 (January 1997): 152, 154; emphasis added.

6. See Richard B. Freeman, "Toward an Apartheid Economy," *Harvard Business Review* 74, no. 5 (September–October 1996): 114-21.

7. Charles Handy, *The Age of Paradox* (Boston: Harvard Business School Press, 1995), p. 20.

8. Robert Reich, *The Work of Nations* (New York: Vintage, 1992), pp. 302-3.

9. For recent information on this subject, see Sheldon Danziger and Peter Gottschaulk, *America Unequal* (Cambridge, MA: Harvard University Press, 1995), chapter 3.

10. Daniel H. Weinberg, "A Brief Look at Postwar U.S. Income Inequality," Census Current Population Reports P60-191, June 1996; available at www.census.gov. Both of the figures in this section are drawn from this report.

11. By contrast, Japanese and German chief executive officers average 20 to 35 times the pay of an average worker. The numbers are drawn from Jeremy

Rifkin, *The End of Work* (New York: Putnam's, 1995), pp. 169, 172-73, and 177.

12. Robert Kuttner, "Soaring Stocks: Are Only the Rich Getting Richer?" *Business Week,* April 22, 1996, p. 28.

13. Clay Chandler, "Boom Is Fine—If You Own Stock," *Washington Post,* April 7, 1998, pp. A1, A12.

14. Amy Harmon, "Racial Divide Found on Information Highway," *New York Times,* April 17, 1998, p. 1.

15. Spencer Rich, "Study Finds Nest Eggs Vary Greatly," *Washington Post,* July 25, 1995, p. A11.

16. Scott McCartney and Jonathan Friedland, "Computer Sales Sizzle as Developing Nations Try to Shrink PC Gap," *Wall Street Journal,* June 29, 1995, p. A1.

17. David I. Hitchcock, "Factors Affecting East Asian View of the United States" (Washington, D.C.: Center for Strategic and International Studies, 1997), draft ms.; cite from p. 19.

18. "The Backlash in Latin America," *The Economist,* November 30, 1996, p. 20, and Steven Mufson, "China's Growing Inequality," *Washington Post,* January 1, 1997, pp. A1, A26-27.

19. "The Distribution of Wealth: Increasing Inequality?" American Enterprise Institute *Conference Summary,* August 1996.

20. Christopher Farrell et al., "A Rising Tide," *Business Week,* August 31, 1998, pp. 72-75.

21. Robert I. Lerman, "Is Earnings Inequality Really Increasing?" Urban Institute, Reports on Economic Restructuring and the Job Market, no. 1 (March 1997).

22. Robert I. Lerman, "Meritocracy without Rising Inequality?" Urban Institute, Reports on Economic Restructuring and the Job Market, no. 2 (September 1997).

23. Andrew Wyckoff, "Imagining the Impact of Electronic Commerce," *The OECD Observer,* no. 208 (October–November 1997): 5-8.

24. World Bank, *Global Economic Prospects and the Developing Countries* (Washington, DC: The World Bank, 1995), p. 47.

25. Michael Mandel, "The Digital Juggernaut," *Business Week: The Information Revolution 1994,* p. 26.

26. Robert Gilpin, "APEC in a New International Order," National Bureau of Asian Research *Analysis* 6, no. 5 (December 1995): 11.

27. McCartney and Friedland, "Computer Sales Sizzle," pp. A1, A8.

28. World Bank, *Global Economic Prospects,* p. 63.

29. Bernard Wysocki, Jr., "Imports Are Surging in Developing Nations," *Wall Street Journal,* July 8, 1996, p. 1.

30. Paul Krugman, "Dutch Tulips and Emerging Markets," *Foreign Affairs* 74, no. 4 (July–August 1995): 35, 43.

31. United Nations, *World Investment Report 1995* (New York: United Nations, 1995) p. 157.

32. Hitchcock, "Factors Affecting East Asian Views," 13, 75.

33. Boisot, *Information Space,* p. 5. See also David M. Kreps, "Economics—The Current Position," *Daedalus* 126, no. 1 (Winter 1997): 73-77.

34. W. Brian Arthur, "Increasing Returns and the New World of Business," *Harvard Business Review* 74, no. 4 (July–August 1996): 100, 103.
35. See Bernard Wysocki, Jr., "For This Economist, Long-Term Prosperity Hangs on Good Ideas," *Wall Street Journal,* January 21, 1997, p. A1.
36. Arthur, "Increasing Returns," pp. 100, 104.
37. Boisot, *Information Space,* p. 5.
38. Arthur, "Increasing Returns," p. 105.
39. Ibid., p. 107.

CHAPTER 11

1. Walter Laqueur, "Postmodern Terrorism," *Foreign Affairs* 75, no. 5 (September–October 1996): 35.
2. Many of the examples here are drawn from Douglas Waller, "Onward Cyber Soldiers," *Time,* August 21, 1995, pp. 38-46.
3. Eric R. Sterner, "Digital Pearl Harbor: National Security in the Information Age," *National Security Studies Quarterly* 2, no. 3 (Summer 1996): 43-44.
4. These quotes are taken from Arie de Geus, "The Living Company," *Harvard Business Review* 75, no. 2 (March–April 1997): 51-59. De Geus has also published a book by the same name with the Harvard Business School Press, 1997.
5. Kenichi Ohmae, *The Borderless World* (New York: HarperBusiness, 1990), pp. 12, 103.

TREND FOUR

1. I am not the first to use this specific term. See, for example, William Knoke, *Bold New World: The Essential Road Map to the Twenty-First Century* (New York: Kodansha International, 1996), pp. 185-205.
2. Benjamin Barber, *Jihad vs. McWorld* (New York: Random House Times Books, 1995), pp. 3-4.

CHAPTER 12

1. Peter F. Drucker, "The Changed World Economy," *Foreign Affairs* 64, no. 4 (Spring 1986): p. 791.
2. Paul Krugman, "Competitiveness: A Dangerous Obsession," *Foreign Affairs* 73, no. 2 (March–April 1994): 34.
3. Robert J. Samuelson, "Spooked by the 'Global Economy,'" *Washington Post,* May 3, 1995, p. A21.
4. Vincent Cable, "The Diminished Nation-State: A Study in the Loss of Economic Power," *Daedalus* 124, no. 2 (Fall 1995): 24, 51.
5. Ernest H. Preeg, *Trade Policy Ahead: Three Tracks and One Question* (Washington, D.C.: Center for Strategic and International Studies, 1995), p. 6.
6. The World Bank, *Global Economic Prospects and the Developing Countries* (Washington, D.C.: The International Bank for Reconstruction and Development/The World Bank, 1995), p. 7; and World Bank, *World Development Indicators 1998* (Washington, D.C.: World Bank, 1998), p. 171.
7. United Nations Conference on Trade and Development, *World Investment Report 1994: Transnational Corporations, Employment and the Workforce* (New

York: United Nations, 1994), pp. 12, 19; and United Nations, *World Investment Report 1998* (New York: United Nations, 1998), p. 2.

8. See, for example, "One World?" *Economist,* October 18, 1997, p. 79.
9. United Nations, *World Investment Report,* pp. 120-21.
10. Preeg, *Trade Policy Ahead,* p. 16. In the Japanese case, those imports and exports from within the region grew from 24 percent of exports and 23 percent of imports in 1985 to 36 and 32 percent, respectively, in 1993.
11. Klaus Schwab and Claude Smadja, "Power and Policy: The New Economic World Order," *Harvard Business Review* (November–December 1994): 44.
12. Preeg, *Trade Policy Ahead,* pp. 13-14. On this general point see also Michael Moynihan, *The Coming American Renaissance* (New York: Simon and Schuster, 1996), pp. 120-23.
13. Paul Krugman, "The Localization of the World Economy," chapter 13 of Krugman, *Pop Internationalism* (Cambridge: MIT Press, 1996).
14. United Nations, *World Investment Report,* pp. 123, 127. The quote comes from ibid., p. 129.
15. Ibid., p. 127.
16. Ibid.
17. Ernst B. Haas, "Why Collaborate? Issue-Linkage and International Regimes," *World Politics* 32, no. 3 (April 1980): 367-69.
18. Watts Wacker and Jim Taylor, *The 500 Year Delta* (New York: HarperBusiness, 1997), p. 187.
19. Anthony Giddens, *The Consequences of Modernity* (Stanford, CA: Stanford University Press, 1990), pp. 63-64.
20. Ibid., pp. 65, 123, 178.
21. Vaclav Havel, "The Need for Transcendence in the Postmodern World," speech given in Philadelphia on July 4, 1994; available at www.worldtrans.org/whole/havelspeech.html.
22. *Economist* Survey, "The Death of Distance: A Survey of Telecommunications," *The Economist,* September 30, 1995, p. 27.
23. Information on the "death of distance" comes from "The Revolution Begins, At Last" and "The Death of Distance," *The Economist,* September 30, 1995, pp. 5, 15; and from "Try Beating These Long-Distance Rates," *Business Week,* April 22, 1996, p. 131.
24. Moynihan, *The Coming American Renaissance,* p. 95; see also p. 45.
25. Mike Mills, "In the Modern World, White-Collar Jobs Go Overseas," *Washington Post,* September 17, 1996, p. A1.
26. United Nations, *World Investment Report,* p. 129.
27. Ibid.
28. Samuelson, "Spooked by the 'Global Economy.'"
29. William Knoke, *Bold New World* (New York: Kodansha, 1996), pp. 75-76.
30. Kelly Holland and Amy Cortese, "The Future of Money," *Business Week,* June 12, 1995, p. 68.
31. United Nations, *World Investment Report,* p. xxii.
32. United Nations, *World Investment Report 1998* (New York: United Nations, 1998), pp. 39-40.

33. Marina Whitman, "Foreign Direct Investment and the Internationalization of Business," in Dick Clark, ed., "International Trade and the U.S. Economy," Aspen Institute *Congressional Program* 10, no. 3 (1995): 25.
34. Cable, "The Diminished Nation-State," p. 30.
35. "The World Isn't Their Oyster Yet," *Business Week,* October 14, 1996, p. 30.
36. Cable, "The Diminished Nation-State," p. 31.

CHAPTER 13

1. *The American Heritage Dictionary,* 2nd college ed. (Boston: Houghton Mifflin Company, 1985), p. 955.
2. Robert J. Samuelson, *The Good Life and Its Discontents* (New York: Times Books, 1995), pp. 57, 210-11.
3. Gianni Vattimo, *The Transparent Society* (Baltimore: Johns Hopkins University Press, 1992), pp. 8-9.
4. "The New America," *U.S. News & World Report,* July 10, 1995, pp. 18-32; quotes are drawn from pp. 19-20.
5. "The Keenest Recruits to the Dream," *Economist,* April 25, 1998, pp. 25-27.
6. Don Tapscott, *The Digital Economy: Promise and Peril in the Age of Networked Intelligence* (New York: McGraw Hill, 1996), p. 51.
7. Albert Borgmann, *Crossing the Postmodern Divide* (Chicago: University of Chicago Press, 1992), p. 73. See also Hamish McRae, *The World in 2020: Power, Culture and Prosperity* (Boston: Harvard Business School Press, 1994), p. 13. Max Boisot has also discussed a similar idea in his analysis of "fief and clan" business organizations; see Boisot, *Information Space* (London: Routledge, 1995), p. 443.
8. Eric Schine and Linda Himelstein, "The Explosion in Private Justice," *Business Week,* June 12, 1995, p. 88.
9. Marshall McLuhan, *Understanding Media: Extensions of Man* (New York: McGraw-Hill, 1964).
10. Françoise Sabbah, cited by Manuel Castells, *The Rise of the Network Society* (Cambridge, MA: Blackwell Publishers, 1996), p. 339.
11. William Dawkins, "Spiritual Uplift and Poison Gas," *Financial Times* Survey: Japan, July 10, 1995, p. 6.
12. Richard John Neuhaus, "The Religious Century Nears," *Wall Street Journal,* July 6, 1995, p. A8.
13. Joel Garreau, *The Nine Nations of North America* (Boston: Houghton Mifflin Company, 1981).
14. Zygmunt Bauman, *Modernity and Ambivalence* (Ithaca: Cornell University Press, 1991), p. 249.
15. Robert L. Heilbroner, *The Worldly Philosophers,* 6th ed. (New York: Simon and Schuster, 1992), p. 165.
16. Drucker, "The Changed World Economy," *Foreign Affairs* 73, no. 2 (March–April 1994): 778-779.
17. Udayan Gupta, "New Business Incorporations Reached Record in 1994," *Wall Street Journal,* June 6, 1995, p. B2.
18. Rolf Anderson, *Atlas of the American Economy* (Washington, D.C.: Congressional Quarterly Publications, 1994), p. 24.

19. "The Death of Distance: A Survey of Telecommunications," *The Economist,* September 30, 1995, p. 26.

20. Tony Porter, "Capital Mobility and Currency Markets: Can They Be Tamed?" *International Journal* 51, no. 4 (Autumn 1996): 683. See also William Knoke, *Bold New World* (New York: Kodansha, 1996), p. 79.

21. John Naisbitt, *Global Paradox* (New York: Morrow, 1994), pp. 13-15. In "The 'Big' Organization of the Future," Ric Duques and Paul Gaske give the following advice: "Act like a small company," in such terms as flexibility, responsiveness, and personal attention. "'Acting small' means behaving like a small company that needs to satisfy its clients and retain them in order to survive." In Frances Hesselbein, Marshall Goldsmith, and Richard Beckhard, eds., *The Organization of the Future* (San Francisco: Jossey-Bass Publishers, 1997), pp. 35-36.

22. Patrick Glynn, "The Age of Balkanization," *Commentary* (July 1993): 22-23.

23. Peter L. Berger, *Invitation to Sociology: A Humanistic Perspective* (Garden City, NY: Anchor Books, 1963), pp. 49-50.

24. Bauman, *Modernity and Ambivalence,* p. 274.

CHAPTER 14

1. Benjamin Barber, *Jihad vs. McWorld* (New York: Random House Time Books, 1995), pp. 155, 157.

2. Philip G. Cerny, "Globalization and Other Stories: The Search for a New Paradigm for International Relations," *International Journal* 51, no. 4 (Autumn 1996): 617, 619, and 637.

3. Patrick Glynn, "The Age of Balkanization," *Commentary* (July 1993): 21.

4. Kim Byung-ik, "Universalism versus Tribalism," translated and reprinted in *Korea Focus* 2, no. 6 (November–December 1994): 79, 83.

5. These quotes are drawn from Evan I. Schwartz, "The Father of the Web," and Lee Marshall, "The World According to Eco," both in *Wired* 5.03 (March 1997): 140 and 144.

6. David I. Hitchcock, "Factors Affecting East Asian Views of the United States" (Washington, D.C.: Center for Strategic and International Studies, 1997), draft ms., pp. 13, 23.

7. Lewis A. Coser, *Masters of Sociological Thought* (New York: Harcourt Brace Jovanovich, 1977), p. 91.

8. Ernest Gellner, *Conditions of Liberty* (New York: Viking Penguin, 1994), p. 75.

9. Peter Drucker, "The Age of Social Transformation," *The Atlantic,* November 1994, p. 68.

10. Richard John Neuhaus, "The Religious Century Nears," *Wall Street Journal,* July 6, 1995.

11. Zygmunt Bauman, "A Sociological Theory of Postmodernity," in Peter Beilharz, Gillian Robinson, and John Rundell, eds., *Between Totalitarianism and Postmodernity: A Thesis Eleven Reader* (Cambridge, MA: The MIT Press, 1992), p. 160.

12. Don Oldenburg, "Committed Corporations," *Washington Post,* June 27, 1995, p. E5.

13. "The Myth of the Powerless State," *The Economist,* October 7, 1995, pp. 15-16.
14. Claire Turenne Sjolander, "The Rhetoric of Globalization: What's in a Wor(l)d?" *International Journal* 51, no. 4 (Autumn 1996): 604.

TREND FIVE

1. Anthony Giddens, *The Consequences of Modernity* (Stanford, CA: Stanford University Press, 1990), p. 67.
2. Roger Holmes, "The Psychology of Authority," in Clifford Rhodes, ed., *Authority in a Changing Society* (London: Constable, 1969), p. 26.
3. James P. Pinkerton, *What Comes Next: The End of Big Government—and the New Paradigm Ahead* (New York: Hyperion, 1995), p. 9.

CHAPTER 15

1. Hannah Arendt, *Between Past and Future: Eight Exercises in Political Thought* (Middlesex, England: Penguin Books, 1985; originally published 1954), p. 91.
2. Marshall McLuhan, *Understanding Media: Extensions of Man* (New York: McGraw-Hill, 1964), p. 272.
3. Peter F. Drucker, *Post-Capitalist Society* (New York: HarperBusiness, 1993), p. 65.
4. Albert Borgmann, *Crossing the Postmodern Divide* (Chicago: University of Chicago Press, 1992), p. 76.
5. Thomas Frank, "Just Break the Rules: Business and Bad Values," *Washington Post,* June 11, 1995, pp. C1-C2.
6. Joshua Meyrowitz, *No Sense of Place* (New York: Oxford University Press, 1985), pp. 160, 64, and 161.
7. Roxanne Roberts, "The Remote Controllers," *Washington Post,* June 10, 1995, p. B5.
8. Charles Handy, *The Age of Unreason* (Cambridge, MA: Harvard Business School Press, 1989), pp. 9-10.
9. Richard Sennett, *Authority* (New York: W. W. Norton, 1980), p. 19.
10. James N. Rosenau, *Turbulence in World Politics: A Theory of Change and Continuity* (Princeton, NJ: Princeton University Press, 1990), pp. 394-95; the author cited is R. B. Harris, in *Authority: A Philosophical Analysis* (University: University of Alabama Press, 1976).
11. Anthony Giddens, *The Consequences of Modernity* (Stanford, CA: Stanford University Press, 1990), pp. 101-5.
12. U.S. Census Bureau, *Statistical Abstract of the United States, 1997* (Washington, D.C.: U.S. Department of Commerce, 1997), pp. 59, 67, 79.
13. Tamar Lewin, "Family Decay Global, Study Says," *New York Times,* May 30, 1995, p. A5.
14. David I. Hitchcock, "Factors Affecting East Asian Views of the United States" (Washington, D.C.: Center for Strategic and International Studies, 1997), draft ms., pp. 13-15.
15. Barbara Dafoe Whitehead, "Dan Quayle Was Right," *Atlantic Monthly* (April 1993); available in full at www.theatlantic.com.

16. These quotes, and the information in the issue feature, are drawn from Hitchcock, "Factors Affecting East Asian Views," pp. 23-24, 31-32, 35-36.

17. These figures are drawn from the following news releases and fact sheets, all available at the National Center for Health Statistics Web page, www.cdc.gov/nchswww: "Teen Sex Down, new Study Shows," May 1, 1997; Stephenie J. Ventura et al., "Teenage Births in the United States: National and State Trends, 1990-1996," April 30, 1998; "Teenage Births in the United States," June 30, 1998; and "Teens Less Likely to Have Second Baby," December 17, 1998. See also the fascinating section on social trends, "Is America Turning a Corner?," in *The American Enterprise,* January–February 1999, 36-51.

18. Robert J. Samuelson, "George Soros, Don't Give Up Your Day Job," *Washington Post,* March 5, 1997, p. A21.

19. Robert D. Putnam, "Bowling Alone: America's Declining Social Capital," *Journal of Democracy* (January 1995): 65-78.

20. Statistics in this section are drawn from Cheryl Russell, "True Crime," *American Demographics* (August 1995): 22-31.

21. The quote is from ibid., p. 30.

22. Ibid., pp. 27-28.

23. "FBI Data Show 12 Percent Decline in Murder, Biggest Drop in Decades" *Washington Post,* December 18, 1995, p. A4; and "Violent Crime Survey Shows Steep Decline," *Washington Post,* April 14, 1997, p. A7.

24. Pierre Thomas, "Arrests Soar for Violent Crime by Juveniles," *Washington Post,* September 8, 1995, pp. A1, A14.

25. Cited in Adam Walinsky, "The Crisis of Public Order," *Atlantic Monthly* 276, No. 1 (July 1995): 39-54; John J. DiIullio, "New Crime Policies for America," in LaMar Alexander and Chester E. Finn, eds., *The New Promise of American Life* (Indianapolis, IN: The Hudson Institute, 1995), pp. 261-84.

26. Russell, "True Crime," p. 29.

27. Walinsky, "The Crisis of Public Order."

28. Craig Torres, "Mexico City Crime Alarms Multinationals," *Wall Street Journal,* October 29, 1996, p. A18.

29. Edward Cody, "China's New Wealth Fuels Crime Wave," *Washington Post,* December 31, 1996, p. A11. Public perception of this epidemic is unmistakable: One poll found that 60 percent of Chinese believe that "China's social order has deteriorated in recent years." See also Michael Dutton, trans., "The Basic Character of Crime in Contemporary China," a 1989 report by the Ministry of Public Security Research Unit No. 5, *The China Quarterly,* no. 149 (March 1997): 160-77.

30. Hitchcock, "Factors Affecting East Asian Views," pp. 20-22. One good recent survey is "A Global War Against Bribery," *Economist,* January 16, 1999, pp. 22-24.

31. John Naisbitt and Patricia Aburdene, *Megatrends 2000* (New York: William Morrow and Company, 1990), p. 271. See also Richard John Neuhaus, "The Religious Century Nears," *Wall Street Journal,* July 6, 1995, p. A8.

32. Samuel Huntington, *The Clash of Civilizations and the Remaking of World Order* (New York: Simon and Schuster, 1996), p. 95. He lays out his evidence on pp. 95-101.

33. Robert W. Fogel, "The Fourth Great Awakening," *Wall Street Journal*, January 9, 1996, p. A14.

34. Naisbitt, *Megatrends 2000*, pp. 273, 275. See also the excellent discussion of this point in Watts Wacker and Jim Taylor, *The 500 Year Delta* (New York: HarperBusiness, 1997), p. 140; and Ronald Inglehart, *Modernization and Postmodernization* (Princeton, NJ: Princeton University Press, 1997), pp. 280-85.

35. Charles Trueheart, "The Next Church," *Atlantic Monthly* 278, no. 2 (August 1996): 47, 52-53.

36. Ibid.

37. Karl Jaspers, *Philosophy of Existence* (Philadelphia: University of Pennsylvania Press, 1971), p. 92.

38. Sennett, *Authority*, p. 45.

39. Geoff Mulgan, *Connexity: How to Live in a Connected World* (Boston: Harvard Business School Press, 1998), pp. 6-7.

CHAPTER 16

1. Samuel Huntington, *Political Order in Changing Societies* (New Haven: Yale University Press, 1966), pp. 10, 37.

2. Ibid., p. 41.

CHAPTER 17

1. Richard Sennett, *Authority* (New York: W.W. Norton, 1980), p. 129; emphasis added.

2. Margaret J. Wheatley, *Leadership and the New Science* (San Francisco: Berrett-Koehler Publishers, 1994), p. 143.

3. Richard Rosecrance, "The Rise of the Virtual State," *Foreign Affairs* 75, no. 4 (July–August 1996): p. 45.

4. Ibid., pp. 46-47.

5. The Chinese NGO figures come from Kathy Chen, "China's Alternative Voices Grow Louder," *Wall Street Journal*, August 29, 1995, p. A10.

6. James K. Glassman, "Tightfisted at the Top," *Washington Post*, December 17, 1996, p. A23.

7. David Kuo, "No More Excuses: Now, Conservatives Like Me Need to Do More for the Poor," *Washington Post*, February 9, 1997, p. C4.

8. Rene Sanchez, "Survey of College Freshmen Finds Rise in Volunteerism," *Washington Post*, January 13, 1997, p. A6.

9. Gary Hamel, "Strategy as Revolution," *Harvard Business Review* 74, no. 4 (July–August 1996): 69-71, 73, and 75-76.

10. Peter Coveney and Roger Highfield, *Frontiers of Complexity* (New York: Fawcett Columbine, 1995), p. 16; and David Ruelle, *Chance and Chaos* (Princeton, NJ: Princeton University Press, 1991), p. 36.

11. Joshua Meyrowitz, *No Sense of Place* (New York: Oxford University Press, 1985), p. 163.

12. John Case, "The Open-Book Revolution," *Inc.* (June 1995): 28-29.

13. *Business Week*, November 18, 1996, p. 10.

14. Frederick G. Harmon, "Future Present," in Frances Hesselbein et al., eds., *The Organization of the Future* (San Francisco: Jossey-Bass, 1997), p. 241.

15. Eric Ransdell, "IBM's Grassroots Revival," *Fast Company,* October–November 1997, p. 182.

16. This quote, and the Enos quote earlier, come from Steven Pearlstein, "Reinventing Xerox Corp.," *Washington Post,* June 29, 1998, p. A8.

17. Max Boisot, *Information Space* (London: Routledge, 1995) p. 20.

18. Daniel Bell, *The Coming of Post-Industrial Society* (Cambridge: Harvard University Press, 1976), p. 263.

19. Meyrowitz, *No Sense of Place,* pp. 171, 323.

20. Jane J. Mansbridge, *Beyond Adversary Democracy* (Chicago: University of Chicago Press, 1983), p. 7.

21. Mihalyi Csikszentmihalyi, *The Evolving Self* (New York: HarperCollins, 1993), pp. 272, 285-86.

22. Lawrence Grossman, *The Electronic Republic* (New York: Viking, 1995), p. 3.

23. *Economist* Survey, "Full Democracy," December 21, 1996, pp. 3, 14.

24. Grossman, *The Electronic Republic,* pp. 16, 28.

25. Norman Ornstein and Amy Schenkenberg, "The Promise and Perils of Cyberdemocracy," *American Enterprise* (March/April 1996): 53-54.

26. Richard Miniter, "Small Towns, Big Government," *American Enterprise* 8, no. 6 (November–December 1997), pp. 32-34.

27. Charles Handy, *The Age of Paradox* (Boston: Harvard Business School Press, 1994), pp. 153, 159; emphasis added. William McDonough of the Federal Reserve Bank of New York has been among the most eloquent spokespeople for a larger business role; see, for example, McDonough, "The Challenge to U.S. Business," *Harvard Business Review* 74, no. 5 (September–October 1996): p. 125.

28. This figure is from *Business Week,* March 11, 1996.

29. James F. Moore, *The Death of Competition: Leadership and Strategy in the Age of Business Ecosystems* (New York: HarperBusiness, 1996), pp. 272-73.

30. See "Balancing Work and Family," *Business Week,* September 16, 1996, pp. 74-80.

31. Ibid., p. 74.

32. Watts Wacker and Jim Taylor, *The 500 Year Delta* (New York: HarperPerrennial, 1997), pp. 144-49.

33. Kotler, "Competitiveness and Civic Character," in Hesselbein et al., eds., *The Organization of the Future,* p. 158.

34. Figures cited in *Business Week,* April 7, 1997, p. 8.

35. James Dale Davidson and Lord William Rees-Mogg, *The Sovereign Individual* (New York: Simon and Schuster, 1997).

36. Csikszentmihalyi, *The Evolving Self,* p. 79.

37. Zygmunt Bauman, *Modernity and Ambivalence* (Ithaca: Cornell University Press, 1991), p. 278.

38. James N. Rosenau, *Turbulence in World Politics: A Theory of Change and Continuity* (Princeton, NJ: Princeton University Press, 1990), p. 335.

39. Daniel H. Pink, "Free Agent Nation," *Fast Company* (December–January 1998): 131-160.

40. See Chip Walker and Elissa Moses, "The Age of Self-Navigation," *American Demographics* (September 1996): 36-42.

41. Stephen Scheinberg, "Conclusions," in Aurel Braun and Scheinberg, eds., *The Extreme Right: Freedom and Security at Risk* (Boulder, CO: Westview Press, 1997), p. 256.

42. José Ortega y Gasset, *Historical Reason* (New York: W. W. Norton and Company, 1984), pp. 177-78. The lecture in question was given in 1944.

43. Michels cited in Nicholas Kittrie, *The War Against Authority* (Baltimore: Johns Hopkins University Press, 1995), p. 258.

TREND SIX

1. Nathaniel Branden, "Self-Esteem in the Information Age," in Hesselbein et al., eds., *The Organization of the Future* (San Francisco: Jossey-Bass Publishers, 1997) p. 221.

2. Rollo May, *The Discovery of Being: Writings in Existential Psychology* (New York: W. W. Norton and Company, 1983), p. 57.

3. Sigmund Freud, *Civilization and Its Discontents* (New York: Doubleday, 1930), pp. 103-4. See also Carl Jung, *Modern Man in Search of a Soul* (San Diego: Harcourt, Brace and Company, 1933), p. 200.

CHAPTER 18

1. Merlin Donald, *Origins of the Modern Mind: Three Stages in the Evolution of Culture and Cognition* (Cambridge, MA: Harvard University Press, 1991), pp. 359-60.

2. Robert Kegan, *In Over Our Heads: The Mental Demands of Modern Life* (Cambridge, MA: Harvard University Press, 1994), p. 134. A similar argument is made by Jerald Hage in "Post-Industrial Lives: New Demands, New Prescriptions," in Ann Howard, ed., *The Changing Nature of Work* (San Francisco: Jossey-Bass Publishers, 1995), pp. 485-87.

3. Lewis A. Coser, *Masters of Sociological Thought: Ideas in Historical and Social Context* (Fort Worth: Harcourt Brace Jovanovich, 1977), pp. 132-33.

4. Marshall McLuhan, *Understanding Media: The Extensions of Man* (New York: McGraw-Hill, 1964), p. 5.

5. Jeffrey Satinover, "Science and the Fragile Self: The Rise of Narcissism, the Decline of God," in David Michael Levin, ed., *Pathologies of the Modern Self* (New York: New York University Press, 1987), pp. 85, 109.

6. May, *The Discovery of Being*, p. 112.

7. Francis Fukuyama, *The End of History and the Last Man* (New York: The Free Press, 1992), p. 300.

8. Fukuyama, *The End of History*, pp. 289, 312.

9. José Ortega y Gasset, *Historical Reason* (New York: W. W. Norton and Company, 1984), pp. 207, 15.

10. Fukuyama, *The End of History*, p. 307.

11. William Barrett, *Irrational Man: A Study in Existential Philosophy* (Garden City, NY: Doubleday Anchor Books, 1962), p. 18.

12. Ibid., p. 35.

13. Ibid., p. 36.

14. May, *The Discovery of Being*, p. 62.
15. Leo Strauss, "An Introduction to Heideggerian Existentialism," in Leo Strauss, *The Rebirth of Classical Political Rationalism*, selected and introduced by Thomas L. Pangle (Chicago: University of Chicago Press, 1989), p. 36.
16. See Alan Gran, "Who Cares?" *Washington Post*, November 22, 1996, p. A31.
17. Roger Holmes, "The Psychology of Authority," in Clifford Rhodes, ed., *Authority in a Changing Society* (London: Constable, 1969), p. 14.
18. Quoted in Daniel Schneider, *The Paradoxical Self* (San Francisco: Insight Books, 1990), p. 144.
19. Barrett, *Irrational Man*, pp. 212, 217-18.
20. Mihaly Csikszentmihalyi, *The Evolving Self* (New York: HarperCollins, 1993), pp. 175-77. See also his book *Flow: The Psychology of Optimal Experience* (New York: Harper and Row, 1990).

CHAPTER 19

1. Samuel P. Huntington, *Political Order in Changing Societies* (New Haven, CT: Yale University Press, 1968), pp. 36-37.
2. For a superb survey of this literature, beginning in the nineteenth century, see Erich Fromm, *The Sane Society* (Greenwich, CT: Fawcett, 1955), pp. 185-204.
3. Neil Postman, *Technopoly* (New York: Vintage Books, 1992).
4. Daniel Bell, *The Coming of the Post-Industrial Society: A Venture in Social Forecasting* (New York: Basic Books, 1973), p. 480.
5. David I. Hitchcock, "Factors Affecting East Asian Views of the United States" (Washington, D.C.: Center for Strategic and International Studies, 1997), draft ms., pp. 14, 34, 36.
6. Joshua Meyrowitz, *No Sense of Place: The Impact of Electronic Media on Social Behavior* (New York: Oxford University Press, 1985), p. vii.
7. See Tony Hiss, *The Experience of Place* (New York: Vintage Books, 1990).
8. Robert Nisbet, *The Present Age: Progress and Anarchy in Modern America* (New York: Harper and Row, 1988), p. 87.
9. Larry Letich, "Is Life Outsmarting Us?" *Washington Post*, April 2, 1995, p. C5.
10. Fromm, *The Sane Society*, p. 106.
11. Hannah Arendt, *The Origins of Totalitarianism* (San Diego: Harcourt Brace Jovanovich, 1951), p. 341.
12. This information is drawn from the superb essay on this subject, "Spirit of the Age," in *The Economist*, December 19, 1998, pp. 113-117.
13. Richard DeGrandpre, *Ritalin Nation: Rapid-Fire Culture and the Transformation of Human Consciousness* (New York: W. W. Norton, 1999), pp. 19, 23, 32.
14. Kenneth J. Gergen, *The Saturated Self: Dilemmas of Identity in Contemporary Life* (New York: Basic Books, 1991), p. 61.
15. The quotes in the Issue Feature are drawn from Arthur Kleinman and Alex Cohen, "Psychiatry's Global Challenge," *Scientific American*, March 1997, pp. 86-89.
16. Gergen, *The Saturated Self*, pp. 49, 69, 71.
17. Ibid., p. 61.

18. Jim Hoagland, "The French Fringe," *Washington Post,* April 27, 1995, p. A21.
19. Liu Binyan, "Civilization Grafting: No Culture Is an Island," *Foreign Affairs* 72, no. 4 (September–October 1993), p. 21.
20. Meyrowitz, *No Sense of Place,* p. 151; text box quote is from p. 157.
21. Meywrowitz's analysis of the childhood-adulthood merger is in ibid., pp. 226-267; the quote comes from p. 226. The Postman book is *The Disappearance of Childhood* (New York: Vintage, 1982).
22. Marshall McLuhan, *Understanding Media: The Extensions of Man* (New York: McGraw-Hill, 1964), p. vii, 324.
23. Fromm, *The Sane Society,* pp. 263, 265, 280, and 281. Emphasis in original.
24. Geoff Mulgan, *Connexity: How to Live in a Connected World* (Boston: Harvard Business School Press, 1998), pp. 110-111.

CHAPTER 20

1. Both quotes come from Clifford Cobb, Ted Halstead, and Jonathan Rowe, "If the GDP Is Up, Why Is America Down?" *Atlantic Monthly* (October 1995): 60. The answer they give is different from mine: Rather than pointing to a pessimism syndrome, they argue that economic trends are not in fact so promising and that people are reacting to objective evidence of economic decline.
2. Cheryl Russell, "Are We in the Dumps?" *American Demographics* (January 1995): 6.
3. August 1997 Gallup poll, cited in *American Enterprise* (January–February 1998): 91.
4. Richard Morin and John M. Berry, "A Nation That Poor–Mouths Its Good Times," *Washington Post,* October 13, 1996, p. A1.
5. Edouard Balladur, "At the Crossroads," *The Economist,* March 1, 1997, p. 55.
6. David Remnick, *Resurrection: The Struggle for a New Russia* (New York: Random House, 1997), p. 358.
7. Laura A. Liswood, *Women World Leaders: Fifteen Great Politicians Tell Their Stories* (New York: Pandora, 1995), p. 125.
8. Robert J. Samuelson, *The Good Life and Its Discontents: The American Dream in the Age of Entitlement, 1945–1995* (New York: Times Books, 1995), p. 6.
9. Ibid., p. 212.
10. David Shaw, "Beyond Skepticism: Have the Media Crossed the Line Into Cynicism?" *Los Angeles Times,* April 19, 1996, p. A1. This is a three-part series, and subsequent citations might therefore come from different days.
11. Jan Bryan, "Cynicism . . . ," *Montreal Gazette,* December 17, 1992, p. C1.
12. William Raspberry, "Time for the Media to Look at What Works," *Arizona Republic,* February 12, 1995, p. F1.
13. Marshall McLuhan, *Understanding Media: Extensions of Man* (New York: McGraw-Hill, 1965), pp. 205, 210.
14. *Media Monitor: 1995 Year in Review* 10, no. 1 (January–February 1996): 1-2.
15. "Reporting on Recession," *Media Monitor* 5, no. 5 (May 1991).
16. S. Robert Lichter, Linda S. Lichter, and Daniel P. Amundsen, "Doomsday Kids: Environmental Messages on Children's Television," mimeo, April 1995.
17. Daniel P. Amundsen, S. Robert Lichter, and Linda S. Lichter, "Media Coverage of Global Warming: 1985–1991," mimeo, no date.

18. Richard Morin, "Unconventional Wisdom," *Washington Post,* February 23, 1997, p. C5.
19. Robert J. Samuelson, "Virtual Anxiety," *Washington Post,* June 4, 1997, p. A23.
20. John P. Robinson and Geoffrey Godbey, *Time for Life: The Surprising Ways Americans Use Their Time* (University Park, PA: Penn State Press, 1997), p. 94.
21. William Glaberson, "The Nation: Raking Mud," *New York Times,* October 9, 1994, sec. 4, p. 1.
22. Shaw, "Beyond Skepticism."
23. James Fallows, "Outlook 1997," *U.S. News & World Report,* December 30, 1996–January 6, 1997, pp. 36-38.
24. Samuelson, *The Good Life,* pp. 3-4. Again, Samuelson concludes that "the reason for this paradox is entitlement," whereas I am suggesting that the fundamental cause lies in a bad news–oriented media.
25. "A Nation That Poor-Mouths Its Good Times," p. A38.
26. Raspberry, "Time for the Media," p. F1.
27. "A Nation That Poor-Mouths Its Good Times," p. A38.
28. Samuel Huntington, *Political Order in Changing Societies* (New Haven, CT: Yale University Press, 1968), p. 47.
29. Ibid., pp. 54, 56.
30. Joshua Meyrowitz, *No Sense of Place: The Impact of Electronic Media on Social Behavior* (New York: Oxford University Press, 1985), pp. 315-17.
31. McLuhan, *Understanding Media,* pp. 358-59.

CONCLUSION

1. Cited in *Washington Post Book World,* October 19, 1997, pp. 4-5.
2. Carl Jung, *Modern Man in Search of a Soul* (San Francisco: Harcourt Brace, 1933), p. 220.
3. "The Agenda," *Fast Company* (April–May 1998): 106.
4. Robert Ardrey, *The Social Contract* (New York: Atheneum, 1970), p. 197.

CHAPTER 21

1. Georg W. F. Hegel, *Reason in History* (New York: Liberal Arts Press, 1954), p. 95.
2. Hamish McRae, *The World in 2020* (Boston: Harvard Business School Press, 1994), p. 15.
3. David I. Hitchcock, "Factors Affecting East Asian Views of the United States" (Washington, D.C.: Center for Strategic and International Studies, 1997), draft ms., pp. 37-38. See also "The Struggle to Create Creativity," *The Economist,* June 28, 1997, p. 46.
4. "Zap! Splat! Smarts?" *Business Week,* December 23, 1996, pp. 64-68.
5. Paula Parisi, "The Teacher Who Designs Videogames," *Wired* 5.01 (January 1997): 98- 103.
6. "Schools at the Top of the Hill," *The Economist,* February 22, 1997, pp. 27-28; and James Glassman, "Class Acts," American Enterprise Institute *On the Issues* Series, June 1998.

7. Nicholas Lemann, "How Can We Cut the Costs of a College Degree?" *U.S. News & World Report,* December 30, 1996–January 6, 1997, p. 45.
8. "Reading, Writing, and Enrichment," *The Economist,* January 16, 1999 pp. 55-56.
9. James K. Glassman, "It's Elementary: Buy Education Stocks Now," *Washington Post,* July 2, 1995, p. H1.
10. Jim Wallis, *The Soul of Politics* (San Diego: Harcourt Brace and Co., 1995), p. xiii. See also the superb discussion of moral values in Geoff Mulgan, *Connexity: How to Live in a Connected World* (Boston: Harvard Business School Press, 1998), pp. 124-43.
11. Essay in the November/December 1997 issue of *Mother Jones,* cited in William Raspberry, "Spirituality: A Force for the Public Good," *Washington Post,* October 27, 1997, p. A25.
12. Ibid.
13. Arnold J. Toynbee, *Civilization on Trial* (New York: Oxford University Press, 1948), pp. 71, 86, 91.
14. Ibid., pp. 214-15.
15. F. S. C. Northrop, *The Meeting of East and West* (New York: Collier Books, 1946), pp. 454-55, 478.
16. David I. Hitchcock, *Asian Values and the United States: How Much Conflict?* (Washington, D.C.: Center for Strategic and International Studies, 1994), pp. xii, 28.
17. Karen Pennar, "The Ties That Lead to Prosperity," *Business Week,* December 15, 1997, pp. 153-55.
18. Quoted in Paul Starobin, "Rethinking Capitalism," *National Journal,* January 18, 1997, p. 106.
19. George Soros, "The Capitalist Threat," *Atlantic Monthly* (February 1997): 45.
20. Ibid., pp. 50, 58.
21. Kazuo Inamori, *For People and for Profit: A Business Philosophy for the 21st Century,* trans. by T. R. Reid (Tokyo: Kodansha International, 1997), p. 63.

CHAPTER 22

1. René Dubos, *So Human an Animal* (New York: Scribner's, 1968), p. 265.
2. José Ortega y Gasset, *Historical Reason* (New York: Norton, 1984), p. 80.
3. Julian Huxley, *Evolution in Action* (New York: Mentor, 1953), p. 125.

INDEX

Abstract realities, 14, 243, 252-253
Accelerated Strategic Computing Initiative, 80
Aetna Life and Casualty, 231
Africa, AIDS rate, 27; alienation, 257; corruption, 208; and democracy, 107; fertility rate, 33; food crisis, 52-53; population trends, 36; urbanization, 35; water crisis, 54, 55; youth population bulge, 36. *See also specific countries.*
African-Americans, homicide rate, 207; single-parent families, 199. *See also* Minority issues.
Age of Reason, retreat from, 4-6
Age Wave, 40
Aging populations, implications of, 37-42; policy recommendations, 68; and wealth accumulation, 140
Agriculture, and biotechnology, 68, 75-76; employment in, 4; food supply, 49-53; policy recommendations, 68; productivity, 121
AID. *See* U.S. Agency for International Development
AIDS, 27
Airlines, 64, 129
Algeria, population trends, 36; and U.S. interests, 68
Alienation, alienation-based demagogues, 254; causes, 213, 235-236, 238, 249-253, 266; communications and, 257; community and, 275; definition, 249; policy recommendations, 275; price of, 253-260. *See also* Pessimism syndrome.
Altruism, 89, 111. *See also* Charitable giving
American Demographics, 261
Anomie, 107, 213, 240-241
Antitrust laws, 124, 136
Anxiety, causes, 240-241, 266; cures and treatments, 244-247; definition, 249; and "the last man," 241-244; Architecture, 252. *See also* Alienation; Pessimism syndrome.
Arc of crisis, 28, 52-53, 54, 55, 68-69
Ardrey, Robert, 280-281
Argentina, disaffection with reform, 188; fertility rate, 33; pension privatization, 220; unused cropland, 49
Arizona, school enrollment, 41

Arthur, Brian, 95-96, 149
ASCI. *See* Accelerated Strategic Computing Initiative
Asia, alienation, 252; corruption, 208; decline of family, 201, 203; declining authority, 200; and democratization, 103, 104-105; economic growth, 145; economic reform, 103; education reform, 285; financial crisis, 20, 148, 171, 203; food crisis, 52-53; gender equity, 108; and global-local paradox, 188; income distribution, 140-141; instability and modernization, 148; nuclear power, 62; oil imports, 59; privatization, 220; urbanization, 35; view of corporate responsibility, 230; water supply, 54. *See also specific countries.*
Association of Southeast Asian Nations, 112
Atlantic Monthly, 199, 287
Ausubel, Jesse, 28, 51, 53
Authority, characteristics of knowledge-era authorities, 218; decline of hierarchical, 197-199; indexes of declining, 199-211; and indifference, 244; instability and decline of, 213-215, 235-236; as interpretive process, 199; policy recommendations, 236; rise of new authorities, 217-236; transformation of, 195-196
Automation, 116, 121, 129, 131, 146
Banking automation, 121, 129, 146
Barber, Benjamin, 157-158, 187
Bauman, Zygmunt, 180, 191
Bell, Daniel, 3, 227, 251
Benford, Gregory, 73, 77
Bennett, William, 292-293
Berger, Peter, 66, 185
Berners-Lee, Tim, 188
Bhutto, Benazir, 262-263
Biodiversity, 47-48
Biological weapons, 77
Biotechnology, 68, 73-77, 113
Boisot, Max, 95, 115-116, 117-119, 148, 149, 226
Borgmann, Albert, 198
Bosnia, 154
Boston Renaissance, 287
Botswana, AIDS rate, 27
Brain Waves group, 87, 234

Brazil, aging population, 40; disaffection with reform, 188; fertility rate, 33; technology and economic progress, 146; unused cropland, 49; and U.S. interests, 68;British Petroleum, 45, 80
Buddhism, 11, 15, 210
Budget deficits, 154
Business, executive compensation, 139; living companies, 153, 155, 231; mission statements, 236; new management styles, 224-226; new roles for, 229-232; new strategies, 222-224, 236; and pluralism, 178-179, 182-184; policy recommendations, 154, 193; responsibility, 100, 231-232, 293; slogans, 198; small business renaissance, 183; virtual corporations, 4, 13-14, 91, 126-127, 129, 130, 178
Business Week, 64, 82, 168
California, school enrollment, 41; wind power, 80
Canada, environmental issues, 47; evolutionary learning example, 92; independence of Quebec, 181
Capitalism, and collapse of boundaries, 12, 21; renewed, 292-294
Castells, Manuel, 13, 132, 133
Catholicism, 190. *See also* Religion.
Cellular phones, 83, 121, 203
Center for Media and Public Affairs, 264-265
Chaos theory, 93-97, 113, 124, 149, 182
Charitable giving, 220-222, 236
Charter schools, 233, 285, 286-287
Children, blurring of childhood and adulthood, 258; child-labor laws, 136; single-parent families, 199-201; teen births, 41, 202
Chile, disaffection with reform, 188; economic opportunities, 33; fertility rate, 33; pension privatization, 220
China, aging population, 40; AIDS rate, 27; alienation, 252, 257; communications, 83, 167; comparisons to GDP of, 173, 178; corruption, 208, 214; crime, 205, 208-209; culture and economic reform, 130; declining authority, 198, 200, 202, 214; democratization, 103, 104-105, 106, 113, 198, 202; depression, 253; education reform, 285; environmental issues, 43, 47; fertility rate, 33; food production, 50, 52; income, 147; income distribution, 141; individual rights, 196, 198; lack of confidence in government, 208, 214; nongovernmental organizations, 220; oil imports, 59; population migrations, 33; regionalism, 181; suicides, 256; water supply, 54; world pressure for economic reform, 102
Citibank, 101, 115
Civilization and Its Discontents, 238
Clinton, Bill, 271, 287

Cloning. *See* Biotechnology
Colombia, alienation, 257; fertility rate, 33
Communications, and alienation, 257; and economies of scale, 183; globalization, 167-169; and political participation, 228; wireless, 83-84, 146-147, 167, 257
Communitarian movement, 204
Community, and alienation, 275; decline of, 204-209; and values, 280, 291
Competition, global economic competition, 144-145; in human resources economy, 127-131; hypercompetition, 124, 129, 222; and minority and gender equity, 108-109; for workers, 231-232
Complexity theory, 5, 12, 15, 21, 91, 93-97, 112, 113, 133, 149, 182, 218, 223, 252
Computers, and conflict, 152; economies of scale, 183; information technology, 3-4, 80-84. *See also* Internet; Technology.
Confucianism, 200.
Conservatism, synthesis of a new political party, 291-292; values of, 19
Consumer culture, globalization of, 112, 166; postmaterialist values, 100, 103-104, 110
Cooperation, 89, 111, 112, 204
Corporations, executive compensation, 139; living companies, 153, 155, 231; mission statements, 236; new management styles, 224-226; new roles for, 229-232; new strategies, 222-224, 236; and pluralism, 178-179, 182-184; policy recommendations, 154, 193; and regionalism, 181; responsibility, 100, 231-232, 293; slogans, 198; small business renaissance, 183; virtual, 4, 13-14, 91, 126-127, 129, 130, 178
Corruption, 208, 209, 214, 236, 257
Counterglobalism, 102, 157-158, 175-185
Coveney, Peter, 12, 223-224
Crime, corruption, 208, 209, 214, 236, 257; and declining authority, 204-209; and media, 264; organized, 208-209; policy recommendations, 236; reporting of, 204-205; and U.S. population trends, 205
Csikszentmihalyi, Mihaly, 228, 232, 246
Cuba, individual rights, 196
"Cultural Creatives," 16
Culture, and conflict, 102, 185; as foundation of human perception, 65-67; and pluralism, 177; policy recommendations, 193; and reorganization of work, 130-131; shifts in cultural values, 100, 193
Currencies, 172
Dartmouth Business School, 124, 129
D'Aveni, Richard, 124, 129, 149, 222
The Death of Competition, 133
De Geus, Arie, 153, 155, 231
Demagogues, alienation-based, 254; and lack of heroes, 260; and pessimism syndrome, 270

Democracy, and decline of major war, 110; democratization, 103-108; direct, 227-229, 233, 236; self-correction, 272-274

Demography, aging in developed world, 37-42; developing world population growth, 31-37; world population growth, 29-31

Depression, increasing rates of, 253-254; and pessimism syndrome, 269; and unemployment, 134. *See also* Alienation.

Dialectic of change, 12, 283, 284

Dictatorships, 88-89, 107, 202, 215

Disaster relief, 34, 68

Divorce rates, 199, 201, 202, 203

Downsizing, 219

Drucker, Peter, 1, 114, 119, 120, 131, 160, 183, 189-190

Dychtwald, Ken, 15, 40

Easterbrook, Gregg, 42, 78

Eastern Europe, AIDS rate, 27; corruption, 214; crime, 208; lack of confidence in government, 214; privatization, 220

Economic intelligence, 129, 155

Economic trends, central role of finance and capital markets, 135-137; and decline of major war, 110; and democratization, 101-102, 103-108; global economic meltdown, 8; globalization, 159-165; human resources economy, 115-121; income distribution, 137-143; media coverage, 265; and minority and gender equity, 108-109; networks, 133-135; new economic theory, 148-150; New Economy, 118; policy recommendations, 154; price spike economy, 49-64; reform, 99-103; shift to developing world, 145-148; virtual economics, 136; world economy: 1913 *vs.* 1997, 164. *See also* Employment.

The Economist, 50, 52, 81, 106, 108, 168, 183, 228

Education, and equity, 142-143; and globalization, 167; importance of, 126, 132, 154, 155, 219, 230, 238, 239, 275, 283-288; and income distribution, 137; moral, 275; need for reform, 12-13, 236; and pessimism syndrome, 261, 272; pluralism, 179; policy recommendations, 154, 236; population trends and school enrollment, 41; and productivity, 117-119; and reorganization of work, 126; and virtual state, 219

Egypt, population trends, 36; and U.S. interests, 68; youth population bulge, 36

Elaborated services trend, 121, 149

Electric cars, 61, 63

Ellul, Jacques, 176, 250

Employment, and death of distance, 170; and family issues, 231; and pessimism syndrome, 262; reorganization of work, 123-132; women and minorities, 108-109, 230. *See also* Unemployment.

Empowerment, age of, 12, 21-22; of consumers, 12; of individuals, 196, 232-235, 245-247, 259, 276-277; of women and minorities, 183, 230; of workers, 12, 225-226, 245, 259

Energy, and developing world, 147; global warming, 46-47, 265; and Middle East instability, 32, 56, 60; nuclear, 62; policy recommendations, 68; renewable sources, 78-80; supply and demand issues, 56-64

Energy Information Administration, 59

Entertainment, globalization of, 167

Environmental issues, biodiversity, 47-48; challenges, 42-43; developed world trends, 43-44; emerging dangers, 46-48; and global capital markets, 136; global issues, 169-171; global warming, 46-47, 265; industrial ecology, 44-46, 230; media coverage, 265; new synthesis, 284; regional environmental disasters, 48; and urbanization, 36

Equity, Idealab focus, 128; and income distribution, 137-143, 230; minorities and women, 108-109, 230; and political correctness, 190

Ethical issues, biotechnology, 76-77, 113; dangers of transition, 235-236; need for standards, 235, 247, 288-292; relativism, 184-185; resurgence of moral values, 190-191; and void of modern life, 240-241, 251

Europe, cellular phone use, 83; economic reform, 103; government decentralization, 179; multinational corporations, 174; and regionalism, 181; right-wing politics, 189; unemployment, 134; view of corporate responsibility, 230

European Union, free-trade area, 112, 163, 164, 165; and regionalism, 181; and social construction, 92

Evangelical Protestantism, 190, 209-210. *See also* Religion.

Evolutionary learning, 90-92

Experience, 14-17

Fallows, James, 266-267, 272

Family issues, decline of the family, 199-202; and employment, 231

Fast Company, 11, 233, 280

Fast-track trade authority, 143, 271, 274

FDI. *See* Foreign direct investment

Federal Reserve Board, 261

Fertility rates, 30, 33

Financial markets, central role of, 135-137; globalization, 171-173

Finland, cellular phone use, 83

Florida, aging population, 37

Food, genetically engineered, 75-76; policy recommendations, 68; supply and demand issues, 49-53

Food and Drug Administration, 75

Forecasting, dangers of, 6-7

Foreign direct investment, 161-163

Foreign exchange, 134, 183-184
Foreign policy, and global information, 152, 154; and pessimism syndrome, 271
France, aging population, 38; alienation, 257; culture and reorganization of work, 130; economic reform, 103; government spending, 202; immigration, 33; nuclear energy, 62; and pessimism syndrome, 262
Free-market economies, and decline of major war, 110; and democratization, 103-108; and economic reform, 99-103; minority and gender equity, 108-109, 142, 230; self-correction, 272-274
Fromm, Erich, 252-253, 259
Fukuyama, Francis, 65, 85-86, 95, 105, 110, 241-242
Futurist extremism, 8-9
GATT. See General Agreement on Tariffs and Trade.
Gender issues, empowerment of women, 183, 230; equity, 108-109, 142; homogenization of gender roles, 258
General Agreement on Tariffs and Trade, 163-165
General Motors, 63, 173
Genetic engineering. See Biotechnology.
Germany, government spending, 202; immigration, 33; nuclear energy, 62
Giddens, Anthony, 129-130, 166, 195-196, 199
Globalization, communications, 167-169; death of distance, 167, 168, 170, 240; environmental issues, 169-171; financial markets, 171-173; global awareness, 165-167; and global social contract, 109-113; policy recommendations, 113, 193; production, 173-174; tribalism within, 187-194; world economy, 159-165; world economy: 1913 vs. 1997, 164
Global social contract, 109-113
Global tribes, 157-158
Global warming, 46-47, 265
Glynn, Patrick, 185, 187
Government, antigovernment feeling, 253, 261; decentralization and federalism, 179; direct democracy, 227-229; lack of confidence in, 214; media and involvement in world conflict, 152, 154, 273-274; new synthesis, 14, 284; participation, 218-219; privatization, 220-222; role in finance, 203; spending, 202; and unemployment, 134; U.S. government employees, 229; virtual state, 219. See also Authority.
Great Britain, intrafirm trade, 173
Greece, and democracy, 107; income, 147
Gross, Bill, 22, 128, 228
Hamel, Gary, 149, 222-223
Handy, Charles, 10, 11, 18, 126, 137, 198-199, 229-230
Havel, Vaclav, 4, 23, 87, 167

Health care, 167, 231
Henry Kaiser Family Foundation, 262
Heroes, lack of, 259-260, 263
Higher education, 41, 287-288
Highfield, Roger, 12, 223-224
Hispanic-Americans, economic clout, 178; population growth, 178. See also Minority issues.
Hitchcock, David, 148, 188, 200, 201, 203, 208, 252, 285, 289, 290
Holistic thinking, 13-14. See also Interdisciplinary perspective.
Homophyly, 166
Homosexual rights, 109
Hudson Institute, 104, 141
Human Genome Project, 74
Humanitarian relief, increasing need for, 34; media effects, 152-154, 273-274; policy recommendations, 68
Human nature, 87-89
Human needs theory, 88-89
Human resources economy, central role of finance and capital markets, 135-137; income distribution, 137-143; influence of culture, 66, 119; and networks, 133-135; new economic theory, 148-150; New Economy, 118; policy recommendations, 154; and reorganization of work, 123-132; shift to developing world, 145-148; and trade and investment, 144-145; transformation to, 115-121
Hunter-gatherers of information, 276
Huntington, Samuel, 20, 65, 67, 102, 185, 209, 213, 249, 270
Hypercompetition, 124, 129, 222
IBM, 125-126, 173, 184, 225
Idealab, 22, 128, 129, 228
Immigration, and aging populations, 40; and pessimism syndrome, 270; and population growth, 33, 36
Income distribution, 137-143
India, aging population, 40; AIDS rate, 27; communications, 83; and decline of authority, 215; economic reform, 103; environmental issues, 43; fertility rate, 33; GDP compared to multinationals, 173; income, 147; nuclear power, 62; poverty, 34; and U.S. interests, 69
Individualism, 12, 21-22, 196, 218, 232-235, 245-247, 259, 276-277. See also Psychology.
Indonesia, democratization, 103, 198, 215; economic opportunities, 33; fertility rate, 33; GDP compared to multinationals, 173; and globalization, 188; and U.S. interests, 68
Industrial ecology, 44-46, 230
Industrial espionage, 129, 155
Information age. See Knowledge era

Information technology, 3-4, 80-84. *See also* Internet.

Inglehart, Ronald, 100, 103-104

Innovation, 15, 149-150, 223-224, 226

Instability and change, 2, 18, 20-21, 88-89, 113, 143, 213-215

Interdependence, 189-190

Interdisciplinary perspective, 6, 11-13, 91, 285

Internet, 82, 83, 84, 121, 168, 170, 188, 229

Iran, individual rights, 196; population trends, 37; youth population bulge, 36

Iraq, population trends, 37; world requirements, 102; youth population bulge, 36

Islam, 32, 37, 190. *See also* Religion.

Israeli-occupied territories, population trends, 37

Italy, aging population, 38

Japan, aging population, 38, 39, 40; alienation, 252, 257; cellular phone use, 83; corruption, 208; culture, 66, 130; declining authority, 200, 215; economic reform, 99-101, 103; education reform, 285; environmental issues, 47; family issues, 203; food imports, 50; future challenges, 26; intrafirm trade, 173; Japan-bashing, 103; multinational corporations, 174; nuclear energy, 62; oil imports, 59; pension crisis, 39; population trends, 26, 37; religions, 180; tariff rates, 164; trade area, 165; unemployment, 134

Jordan, population trends, 37

Jung, Carl, 238, 240, 279-280

Justice system, crisis of enforcement, 207-208; pluralism, 179

Kauffman, Stuart, 96-97, 112

Kenya, AIDS rate, 27

Knoke, William, 127, 172

Knowledge era, 2-6

Krugman, Paul, 118, 147-148, 163

Labor unions, and direct democracy, 228; effects of global capital markets, 136

"Last man," 241-244

Latin America, crime, 205, 208; culture, 65-66; economic reform, 99-101, 103; global-local paradox, 188; income distribution, 140; privatization, 220. *See also specific countries.*

Le Pen, Jean-Marie, 254, 257

Liberalism, synthesis of a new political party, 291-292; values of, 19

Liberalization, 99-103, 146. *See also* Democracy.

Libya, population trends, 36

Living companies, 153, 155, 231

Luntz, Frank, 267, 270

Malaysia, divorce rate, 201; GDP compared to multinationals, 173; and Royal Dutch/Shell, 225

Management, 91, 224-226

Manufacturing, loss of jobs in large companies, 183; media coverage, 265; shift from, 3, 119-121, 131-132

Marx, Karl, 176, 182

Maslow, Abraham, 88, 244-245

May, Rollo, 238, 241, 243

McLuhan, Marshall, 23, 116, 180, 197, 241, 258, 264, 276

Media, and alienation, 257; and crime, 264; and decline of authority, 198; fragmenting effects, 180, 257; and government involvement in world conflict, 152-154, 273-274; and pessimism syndrome, 20, 254, 263-267, 272, 273-274; policy recommendations, 270; and scandal, 263, 264; and sense of place, 252; and socialization spheres, 258

Medical savings accounts, 233, 247

MEMS. *See* Microelectromechanical systems

Mental illness, 256. *See also* Alienation; Depression; Psychology.

Metanarratives, 184-185, 189

Mexico, aging population, 40; alienation, 257; declining authority, 198, 215; disaffection with reform, 188; future challenges, 26; GDP compared to Hispanic-American purchasing power, 178; population trends, 26; and U.S. interests, 69

Meyrowitz, Joshua, 227, 252, 258

Michels, Roberto, 235-236

Microelectromechanical systems, 83

Middle East, and decline of authority, 203; and democracy, 107, 113; instability and energy supply, 32, 56, 60; peace process, 37; population trends, 36, 37; water supply, 53, 55; youth population bulge, 36

Migrations of population, 33. *See also* Immigration.

Militia groups, 151, 182, 253

Minority issues, empowerment of, 108-109, 230; equity, 108-109; investment gaps, 139; new synthesis, 284; pessimism syndrome, 270, 271; technology gaps, 139-140; United States multiculturalism, 178; wealth accumulation, 140

Modernization *vs.* modernity, 213-214

Moore, James, 63, 133-135, 230

Morocco, population trends, 36

Multinational corporations, 173-174

NAFTA. *See* North American Free Trade Agreement

Naisbitt, John, 184, 209

National Center for Health Statistics, 204, 206

National Crime Victimization Survey, 204, 206, 207

Nationalism, and globalization, 166-167; and modernization, 189

Nation-states, relative decline of, 191-192, 195-196, 202-204; virtual state, 219

Natural gas, 61, 64

Natural resources, and human resources economy, 119-120; and price spike economy, 49-64
Neotribalism, 180-182
Networks, 13-14, 133-135, 149, 204
Neuhaus, Richard John, 180, 190, 209
Nevada, school enrollment, 41
New Age, 209-210
New Economy, 118. *See also* Economic trends.
New science, 5. *See also* Complexity theory; Quantum mechanics.
Newsweek, 266
Newtonian science, 4, 5
New York, homicide rate, 206
New York Times, 101, 126, 265
Nietzsche, Friedrich, 241, 244
Nomura Capital Management, 39
Nongovernmental organizations, 220, 221
North America, regionalism, 181
North American Free Trade Agreement, 112, 143, 165
North Carolina, school enrollment, 41
North Korea, world pressure on, 102
Nuclear power, 62
OECD. *See* Organization for Economic Cooperation and Development
Ohmae, Kenichi, 155
Oil, and Persian Gulf instability, 32, 56, 60; price spikes, 64; supply and demand issues, 56-61
On-line trading, 136-137
Optimism, 7-9, 23, 280-281, 295-296
Organization for Economic Cooperation and Development, 56
Organized crime, 208-209
Ortega y Gasset, José, 235, 242, 295
Outsourcing, 144-145
Pakistan, Bhutto on media, 262-263; and U.S. interests, 68
"The Paradigm," 101, 108
Paradox, 10-11
Participation, 5, 218, 247, 259. *See also* Empowerment.
Peacekeeping operations, increasing need for, 34; media effects, 152-154, 273-274; policy recommendations, 68
Pensions, aging populations, 37-42; policy recommendations, 68; and wealth accumulation, 140. *See also* Social Security.
Perceptual reality, and the economy, 136, 265; media role, 136, 254, 263-267, 272; and pessimism syndrome, 20, 261-277; role in knowledge era, 19-20, 118
Persian Gulf, instability, 32, 56, 60; population trends, 36, 37
Pervasive Knowledge Network, 82-83, 84
Pessimism syndrome, and advance in human evolution, 274-277; dangers of, 20, 268-271; and media, 20, 254, 263-267, 272, 273-274; paradox of, 261-263; and per-

sonal satisfaction with life, 267-268; policy recommendations, 275; solutions, 13, 272-274; unfulfilled expectations, 268-271
Peters, Tom, 22, 127
Philippines, GDP compared to multinationals, 173
Pluralism, and business, 182-184; and culture, 177; definition, 175; and knowledge era, 176-182
Policy recommendations, Trend One, 68; Trend Two, 113; Trend Three, 154; Trend Four, 193; Trend Five, 236; Trend Six, 275
Political Order in Changing Societies, 213, 270
Political parties, synthesis of a new party, 291-292; weakening of, 215, 228
Politics, direct democracy, 227-229; and lack of heroes, 259-260; media coverage, 266; rise of demagogues, 254, 270; and values, 289
Population Action International, 54
Population trends, aging in developed world, 37-42; growth in developing world, 31-37; world population growth, 29-31. *See also* Immigration.
Postman, Neil, 250, 258
Postmaterialist values, 100, 103-104, 110
Price spike economy, 49-64
Princeton University, 207, 265
Privatization, and developing countries, 146; and global finance, 203; and government pluralism, 179; law enforcement, 209; and the social sector, 220-222; Social Security, 220, 233
Process *vs.* product, 14-17, 91, 133, 245
Production, globalization of, 173-174
Protectionism, 88, 107, 134, 143, 155, 170, 193
Psychology, alienation, 249-260; anxiety, 240-247; challenges of knowledge era, 237-238, 239-240; existentialism, 241, 243; global mental crisis, 256; human nature and needs, 87-89; "the last man," 241-244; pessimism, 261-277; policy recommendations, 275
Quantum mechanics, 5, 15, 91, 252
Randomness, 95, 223-224. *See also* Chaos theory; Complexity theory.
Raspberry, William, 264, 270, 272, 289
Regionalism, 112, 165, 181
Relationships, 5, 91, 230
Relativism, 184-185, 193, 242
Religion, decline of organized, 209-210; and existentialism, 241; and globalism, 193; and paradox, 11; and Persian Gulf instability, 32; and pessimism syndrome, 270; pluralism of, 177, 180; relativism, 184-185, 193; resurgence of moral values, 190-191
Renewable energy, 78-80
Reorganization of work, 123-132

Responsibility, corporate, 100, 231-232, 293; individual, 21, 193, 196, 238, 275; and knowledge era, 19, 21, 113, 190-191, 193, 275, 281; new agenda of, 233; and virtual corporations, 129, 130
Rifkin, Jeremy, 131, 132
Right-wing opposition groups, 182, 235
The Rise of the Network Society, 13, 133
Royal Dutch/Shell, 59, 153, 173, 225
Russia, AIDS rate, 27; communications, 83; corruption, 214; crime, 205, 208-209; depression rates, 253; environmental issues, 48; lack of confidence in government, 214; natural gas supplies, 61; nuclear energy, 62; and pessimism syndrome, 262; rise of undemocratic leaders, 107
Samuelson, Robert, 177, 263, 267, 270
Saudi Arabia, GNP compared to multinationals, 173; population trends, 37
Savings, inequality in, 140; policy recommendations, 68
School choice, 247, 285, 286
Schroeder, Paul, 101-102
Science and technology, biotechnology, 73-77; global communications, 167-169; information technology, 3-4, 80-84; "new science," 5; renewable energy, 78-80
S-curve, 17-18
Self-actualization, 244-245
Self-correction mechanism, 272-274
"Self-navigators," 234, 276
Self-organization, 5, 94
Sennett, Richard, 199, 211
Sense of place, 240, 252
Service sector, 120-121, 132
Shaw, David, 136, 263-264
Singapore, and corruption, 208; divorce rate, 201; GDP compared to multinationals, 173; "Touch" community service program, 203
Single-parent families, 199-201
Small Business Administration, 183
Social construction, 90-92
"Socialization spheres," 258
Social Security, and aging population, 37, 41; privatization, 220, 233; and wealth accumulation, 140
Socioeconomic modernization, 85-87
Solar power, 78, 79-80, 147
Somalia, 273-274
South Africa, AIDS rate, 27; depression rates, 253; GNP compared to multinationals, 173; U.S. interests, 68
South Korea, alienation, 252, 257; changing family, 203; corruption, 208; democratization, 103; education reform, 285; fertility rate, 33; GDP compared to multinationals, 173; influence of culture, 66, 130; nuclear power, 62; oil imports, 59

Sovereignty, respect for, 110-111, 143, 192
Soviet Union, former, and decline of authority, 202; economic reform, 99-101. *See also* Russia.
Spain, Basque separatist movement, 181; income, 147; influence of culture, 66
Spencer, Herbert, 177, 189
Spirituality, 11, 100, 209-210, 241, 289. *See also* Religion.
Sweden, depression rates, 253
Syria, population trends, 37
Systems, 13-14. *See also* Networks.
Taiwan, democratization, 103; influence of culture, 66, 130; nuclear power, 62
Taoism, 11, 96, 210
Tao Te Ching, 10, 296
Taylor, Jim, 22, 166
Technology, access to, 229; biotechnology, 73-77; and conflict, 152; and crime, 209; and economies of scale, 183; global communications, 167-169; information technology, 80-84; renewable energy, 78-80; transfer, 144
Teen births, 41, 202
Telecommunications. *See* Communications
Telecommuting, 125, 126
Terrorism, 20, 151-152, 155
Thailand, corruption, 208; divorce rate, 201; education reform, 285; fertility rate, 33; influence of culture, 66
Toffler, Alvin, 3, 6, 233
Totalitarian regimes, 88-89, 107, 202, 215
Toynbee, Arnold, 6, 86-87, 290
Toyota, 45-46, 63
Trade, globalization of, 112, 143, 159-165; measuring, 161; multinational corporations, 173-174; and pessimism syndrome, 271; policy recommendations, 154, 193; and regionalism, 181; services *vs.* goods, 144-145; trade wars, 154-155; and U.S. economy, 160; world economy: 1913 *vs.* 1997, 164
Tradition, decline of, 210-211
Tribalism, definition, 175-176; within globalism, 187-194; nature of, 176-182; and relativism, 184-185
Trust, and business, 231; and culture, 66, 119; and globalization, 192-193; and virtual corporations, 129, 130
Tunisia, population trends, 36
Turkey, GNP compared to multinationals, 173; unused cropland, 49; and U.S. interests, 68
Uganda, AIDS rate, 27
Ukraine, nuclear energy, 62; unused cropland, 49
Unemployment, and death of distance, 170; perceptions of, 262; social disparities and implications, 143; surprise scenario: grow-

ing unemployment, 134; Western Europe, 215
Unions, and direct democracy, 228; effects of global capital markets, 136
United Nations, 33, 34, 35, 173, 176
United Nations Environmental Program, 47
United Nations Food and Agriculture Organization, 51
United Nations High Commission on Refugees, 33
United States, aging population, 37-38, 41; cellular phone use, 83; decline of family, 199-201; depression, 253-254; energy use, 56; environmental issues, 43, 47; exports, 147, 160, 163; food production, 49; foreign policy, 271; government decentralization, 179; government employees, 229; government spending, 202; Hispanic population growth, 178; immigration, 33; income distribution, 141-143; international leadership, 109; intrafirm trade, 173; multiculturalism, 178; multinational corporations, 174; nuclear energy, 62; and personal satisfaction with life, 267-268; and pessimism syndrome, 265, 267-268; pivotal states for U.S. interests, 68; political party membership, 215; pollution rates, 43; population trends, 41; rights/responsibilities balance, 196; tariff rates, 164; trade deficit, 58; unemployment, 134
Unwed motherhood, 199, 202
Urbanization, 34-36, 252
U.S. Agency for International Development, 65
U.S. Bureau of Labor Statistics, 121
U.S. Census Department, 138
U.S. Department of Energy, 56, 57, 58, 60, 61, 62, 80
U.S. Department of Justice, 204
U.S. Department of Labor, 132
U.S. Geological Survey, 55
U.S. National Center for Health Statistics, 202, 206, 207
U.S. News & World Report, 177, 266, 272
Values, and anxiety, 240-241; and capitalism, 293-294; civic virtues, 229; and community, 280, 291; decline of, 240-241, 251; education, 275; influence of Disney and comic books, 203; meeting of Western and Eastern values, 290; policy recommendations, 193, 236, 275; postmaterialist, 100, 103-104, 110; primacy of moral values, 19,

288-292; relativism, 184-185, 242; and responsibility, 19; resurgence of, 113, 190-191; and transcendence, 247; and transition, 19, 28, 235
Vietnam, economic opportunities, 33
Violence, growth of small-scale, 151-152; and inequitable income distribution, 137; terrorism, 20, 151-152, 155; and transition, 113. *See also* Crime; War.
Virginia, school enrollment, 41
Virtual corporations, 4, 13-14, 91, 126-127, 129, 130, 178
Voluntarism, 40, 222
Vouchers, 233, 247, 285, 286
Wacker, Watts, 22, 166
Waggoner, Paul, 50-51
Wall Street Journal, 57, 62, 140
War, conflict in the knowledge era, 151-156; decline and lack of heroes, 260; decline of major, 100, 109-113; small-scale, 151-152
Washington, D.C., homicide rate, 206
Washington Post, 198, 262, 265, 270, 288, 289
Water supply, 53-55
Welfare programs, new synthesis, 284; privatization, 220
Wheatley, Margaret, 5, 15, 218
Whitehead, Alfred North, 2, 18, 20
Whitehead, Barbara Dafoe, 199-200
Wind power, 80, 147
Wired, 74, 76, 127, 188
Wireless communications, 83-84, 146-147, 167, 257
Women, empowerment of, 183, 230; equity, 108-110, 142
Work, reorganization of, 123-132
World Bank, 27, 35, 51, 54, 144, 161
World Health Organization, 256
World Resources 1996-1997, 35
World Resources Institute, 35
World Trade Organization, 102, 112
Wriston, Walter, 14, 101, 115
WXRT-FM, Chicago, 198
Xenophobia, 107, 112, 119, 124, 189
Yemen, population trends, 37
Youth, and crime, 205, 207; culture, 87; and decline of authority, 197, 211; population trends, 36, 41
Zambia, AIDS rate, 27
Zen Buddhism, 11, 15, 210
Zhirinovsky, Vladimir, 254
Zimbabwe, AIDS rate, 27